A Tacitus Reader

BC LATIN Readers

Series Editor:
Ronnie Ancona, Hunter College and CUNY Graduate Center

These readers provide well annotated Latin selections written by experts in the field, to be used as authoritative introductions to Latin authors, genres, topics, or themes for intermediate or advanced college Latin study. Their relatively small size (approximately 600 lines) makes them ideal to use in combination. Each volume includes a comprehensive introduction, bibliography for further reading, Latin text with notes at the back, and complete vocabulary. Nineteen volumes are currently scheduled for publication. Check our website for updates: www.BOLCHAZY.com.

A Tacitus Reader

Selections from *Annales, Historiae, Germania, Agricola,* and *Dialogus*

Steven H. Rutledge

Bolchazy-Carducci Publishers, Inc.

Mundelein, Illinois USA

Series Editor: Ronnie Ancona
Volume Editor: Laurie Haight Keenan
Cover Design & Typography: Adam Phillip Velez
Maps: Mapping Specialists, Ltd.

A Tacitus Reader
Selections from *Annales, Historiae, Germania, Agricola,* and *Dialogus*

Steven H. Rutledge

Bolchazy-Carducci Publishers, Inc.
1570 Baskin Road
Mundelein, Illinois 60060
www.bolchazy.com

Printed in the United States of America
2014
by United Graphics

ISBN 978-0-86516-697-4

Library of Congress Cataloging-in-Publication Data

Tacitus, Cornelius, author.
 [Works. Selections]
 A Tacitus reader : selections from Annales, Historiae, Germania, Agricola, and Dialogus /
Steven H. Rutledge.
    pages cm
 ISBN 978-0-86516-697-4 (pbk. : alk. paper)
 I. Rutledge, Steven H., 1963- II. Title.
 PA6705.A4 2013
 937'.07--dc23
                                                                            2013041913

Contents

Appendix A: Maps

Appendix B: Genealogical Charts

Complete Vocabulary

List of Illustrations

Preface

It was my pleasure to undertake this commentary at the invitation of Bolchazy-Carducci and I, hope, to provide a useful guide to students coming to Tacitus for the first time. Tacitus is among the most difficult of Latin authors, particularly for those who may still be struggling to attain a fair level of comfort with the language. That is a rather unfortunate circumstance, since Tacitus parades before us some of the most memorable characters in all of Rome's history. Moreover, while I believe we always should qualify our remarks and avoid hyperbole, simply put, Tacitus is the greatest of the Roman historians and, among Roman authors, perhaps rivaled only by Vergil. His powerful use of language, penetrating insights into human nature, and vivid portrayal of character are all woven into the fabric of several great narratives. Although some might find that the selections in the present volume are excessively slanted at times towards episodes that linger on violence, promiscuity, and death, this needs no apology: James Joyce through Stephen Daedalus famously referred to history as a nightmare from which he was trying to wake. Tacitus, for better or worse, does not allow his readers to avert their eyes from some of history's most hair-raising phantasms.

It would not be easy to thank all who have assisted in this project along the way. First and foremost I would like to thank Ronnie Ancona for the opportunity to work on this volume. For her remarkably helpful assistance along the way I would also like to thank Laurie Haight Keenan who generously gave of her time with my numerous inquiries. Holly Haynes deserves an enormous thanks for looking over and helping to improve the manuscript, as do the anonymous readers provided by Bolchazy-Carducci, who helped substantially in the manuscript's revisions. My special thanks also to Victoria Pagán, who gave input at the start of this project concerning the scope and nature of the selections. My gratitude also goes to my colleague at Maryland, Professor Judith Hallett, for helping me to clarify at several key points a number of questions concerning Tacitus' obscure syntax. I would like to thank Erika Carlson, a former graduate student at the University of Maryland, for assistance on the vocabulary for the *opera minora*, and above all, Charlotte Malerich, a former graduate student, whose assistance has been invaluable, and who has been helpful above and beyond what was asked of her in helping to complete the vocabulary for the present volume.

A special thanks goes to those with whom I first read Tacitus and his fellow ancient historians as a graduate student at Brown, including Professors Adele Scafuro, Kurt Raaflaub, and Charles Fornara, while I owe a very special debt of gratitude to my mentor in many things Tacitean, John Bodel, whose guidance in my initial scholarly endeavors with Tacitus I could scarcely begin to repay.

My thanks also to all the colleagues in my department, who have been most supportive of assisting me while on sabbatical with the completion of this project and to the RASA research board at the University of Maryland, whose generosity and support allowed me to complete this work while on leave. Above all my thanks, as always, to my wife Lori, whose support, encouragement, and patience saw this work through to its end. Finally, I owe a special debt of thanks to my father, Fred M. Rutledge, who passed away in the course of work on this volume; while not a scholar in the professional sense, he instilled in his children and grandchildren both a deep love of reading and learning.

STEVEN H. RUTLEDGE

Introduction

Tacitus' sometimes overly enthusiastic friend, Pliny the Younger, confidently asserted that he believed Tacitus' *Histories* would be immortal (*Ep.* 7.33.1). But antiquity largely passed Tacitus over in silence. By the late third century the emperor Tacitus had to order his namesake's works to be copied and placed in public libraries. Ammianus may briefly break the silence, taking up the role of Tacitus' continuator (see 31.16.9), but Tacitus simply does not appear to have had the same influence as Sallust or Livy over subsequent authors in antiquity. So far as we know, no Quintilian sang his praises, no later historian strove to imitate him; any references to him are late, scattered among commentators and historical summaries. It was left to a later age to vindicate Pliny's opinion. Perhaps tellingly, Tacitus attracted particular attention from Enlightenment authors: for the French essayist Montesquieu, Tacitus was mother's milk; David Hume called him "the greatest and most penetrating genius perhaps of all antiquity"; Thomas Jefferson considered him "the first writer in the world without a single exception"; and Tacitus at last found his great imitator in Edward Gibbon. As after Domitian, Tacitus had broken a long silence yet again; *libertas* and the *conscientia humani generis* had at last rediscovered the voice of one of their most eloquent and passionate advocates.

❧ Tacitus' life and times

Tacitus was born in 55 or 56 CE to a family from Gallia Narbonensis or from Italy's Transpadane region (Syme 1958, 611–24). We know nothing of his childhood, and even his praenomen remains uncertain: a late source (Sidonius Apollonaris, *Ep.* 4.14.1, 4.22.2) indicates it was Gaius, but the *codex Mediceus* gives Publius. His father may have been a procurator of Gallia Belgica and of the equestrian order (Plin. *HN* 7.76). We can glean from the *Dialogus* (1.1–2.1) that he was studying oratory in Rome in 75 CE, when the work is set, and attached either to Marcus Aper or Julius Secundus, the latter of which was a well-known orator and regarded highly by Quintilian (*Inst.* 12.10.11; cf. 10.1.120, 3.12; Suet. *Otho* 9). He married Agricola's daughter in 77 CE (*Agr.* 9.6).

Tacitus was consul suffectus in 97, when he delivered the funeral oration of Verginius Rufus (Plin. *Ep.* 2.1.6). Based on that date, as well as what Tacitus tells us himself and our knowledge of the *cursus honorum*, we can reconstruct his career with some certainty. Tacitus was probably thirty-nine years of age in 97, a conjecture based in part on the appropriateness of that age for a consulship, but also in part on the *Dialogus*, cited above, where Tacitus himself tells us he was present as a young man (*iuvenis admodum*, 1.2). Of his subsequent career Tacitus is quite frank, confessing in the *Historiae* (1.1) that he owed his advancement to Vespasian, Titus, and Domitian. Indeed, he was indebted to Domitian for his consulship; it was also under Domitian that he held his praetorship and was a member of the *quindecemviri sacris faciundis* in 88 CE, whose tasks included consulting the Sybilline Books when occasion demanded (*Ann.* 11.11). A funerary inscription discovered in Rome (*CIL* 6.41106 = 6.1574) has been recently conjectured to be Tacitus' (Alföldy 1995, 251–68; cf. Birley 2000, 230–47). If this is the case, the inscription indicates that he will have held the prestigious office of *quaestor Augusti*, possibly in 81; as Woodman notes (2004, x), a tribuneship of the plebs will have followed in 85. He also worked in service abroad under Domitian, since he was not present in Rome upon Agricola's death in 93 CE, as he himself tells us (*Agr.* 45.5; see Birley 2000, 235–36). After his consulship in 97 he still had an eventful career ahead of him, not merely as a writer, but in the courts and imperial administration too. In 100 CE both he and Pliny took charge of the prosecution against Marius Priscus, a corrupt governor of Africa who was ultimately condemned (Plin. *Ep.* 2.11). By that date Tacitus had embarked on his literary career, since we know from internal dating that he had

already written the *Agricola* between late 97 and early 98 CE, while
the *Germania* followed in 98 (Syme 1958, 46–47). Between 100 and
102 he was at work on the *Dialogus de oratoribus*; the date of 102
is conjectured based on the dedicatee, Fabius Justus, who held the
consulship that year, although the date is still disputed. During this
time we know from Pliny (*Ep.* 4.13) that Tacitus' repute as a great
orator had been established, and that he had taken numerous young
men under his wing in an effort to teach them the ropes of Roman
political life. From Pliny we also learn that he was at work on the
Historiae probably between 101 and 110 CE, after which he turned
to the *Annales*. Tacitus exits history on what, for a Roman senator,
was a very high note, as proconsul of Asia in 112–113 CE (based on
a single inscription, *Orientis Graeci Inscriptiones Selectae* 487), an
office that was among the highest honors for a Roman senator. He
almost certainly lived to finish the *Annales* and likely died sometime
in Hadrian's reign, although the latest historical reference we can
detect in the *Annales* (2.61) possibly refers to Trajan's conquest of
Parthia in 116 CE.

Tacitus lived through a period of transition and danger for the
Empire. In his early life he will have almost certainly been aware of
Nero's suicide and the brutal civil war that followed, and he himself
may have witnessed the violence within the city. He came to political
maturity under the relative stability of the Flavians, though the final
few years of Domitian's repressive regime clearly left their scars. The
Flavian dynasty, as was the case with the Julio-Claudians, came to a
violent end when Domitian was assassinated on September 18, 96 CE.
The succession of the aged Nerva after Domitian's death raised fears
of the same sort of civil strife that followed after Nero, and the situation reached a crisis when the Praetorian Guards humiliated Nerva
and demanded the punishment of Domitian's assassins. Nerva, in
order to prevent further crisis and erosion of his own authority adopted M. Ulpius Traianus (Trajan) as his successor. Nerva's advent
and Trajan's adoption proved favorable for Rome, resulting in a relatively stable government that lasted for nearly eighty years with the
reigns of the so-called five good emperors (Nerva, Trajan, Hadrian,
Antoninus Pius, and Marcus Aurelius).

During much of Tacitus' adult life, throughout both Domitian's and Trajan's reigns, the emperors were occupied with wars on the northern frontiers, and these will be discussed at various points throughout the commentary. Trajan's two Dacian Wars (101–102 and 105–106 CE) and his invasion of Parthian (114–116 CE) were among the most ambitious conquests attempted since Claudius' annexation of Britain in 43 CE, and were undertakings of which Tacitus clearly approved, judging from his criticism of Tiberius as one *proferendi imperii incuriosus* (*Ann.* 4.32). In addition to major operations in the north, Tacitus also witnessed the end of Roman aspirations in Caledonia (modern Scotland, see p. 36), and serious revolts in Judaea and Egypt under Trajan (in 115–116 CE). How much longer he lived after Hadrian's succession in 117 is uncertain.

‹›‹ *Tacitus'* opera minora: *The* Agricola, Germania, *and* Dialogus de oratoribus

Tacitus was first and foremost an orator, and even before he established his reputation as a writer he had also established himself as a well-known speaker according to his friend, Pliny the Younger. It is fitting, then, that the *Agricola* (whose manuscript title is *De vita Iulii Agricolae*) is, as far as we can tell, the first work from his hand, since generically it has close connections to the sort of funerary eulogy Tacitus had been asked to deliver for Verginius Rufus, though in this instance it was written (rather than spoken) and elaborated into the form of a historical biography. The work recounts the career and life of Cn. Julius Agricola, at the center of which was his attempt to complete Britain's conquest under a suspicious emperor. The work starts by deploring the long endurance of Domitian's tyranny but also expresses the hope that Nerva and his designated successor, Trajan, will reconcile "two things once irreconcilable—the Principate and liberty." Agricola's early life is touched upon (he was raised at Massilia in Gallia Narbonensis), before Tacitus turns to a history of the Romans in Britain, which also includes a discussion of the island's geography and ethnography. Only about half of the work is taken up with Agricola's governorship and conquests, which Tacitus contrasts quite favorably in comparison to his predecessors' efforts. His governorship culminates with the battle of Mons Graupius in Caledonia (see p. 36), soon after which he is recalled by Domitian. While Tacitus attributes Agricola's recall to Domitian's fear and envy provoked by the general's success, in reality Rome was facing serious pressures on its northern frontiers, including in Germania and Moesia, and Domitian may have had no choice but to err on the side of caution and redeploy his forces elsewhere. The final portion of the work concerns Agricola's return to Rome and his death, which comes under the shadow of an increasingly repressive emperor (also remarked in Cassius Dio's brief notice of Agricola, 66.20.3), something Tacitus notes in a very moving peroration Agricola was fortunate enough not to live to witness. One may detect a hint of *apologia pro vita sua* in Tacitus' eloquent conclusion, although that would not be surprising, since the work is, on a certain level, a tract on how a senator might maintain his *dignitas* and display his *virtus*, even under a harsh regime.

Tacitus' second work to come down to us is titled the *Germania*, although its full manuscript title is *De origine et situ Germanorum*. The work is primarily of interest because it is the only purely ethnographic monograph in Latin to survive from antiquity. Its central focus is on the tribes north of the Rhine and Danube, and it emphasizes heavily the "noble savage" theme. The most likely date for its publication is 98. Although it has been criticized as relying on "outdated sources" (it appears to draw in no small part on Caesar) and as "structurally incoherent," it was a work that certainly would have appealed to Tacitus' contemporary audience, especially given the military activity that was taking place on Rome's northern frontiers. The work covers a wide range of subjects, from religious customs, to governance, marriage, sexual mores, the cultural diversity among particular tribes, and the history of conflict between Romans and Germans. One can detect in the work mixed feelings on the part of Tacitus for Rome's deadliest foe. On the one hand there is admiration for German *virtus*, for their love of battle, their sense of personal honor and probity, all of which stands in contrast to Roman decadence. On the other hand, there is disdain for their savage barbarity. Such ambiguity was equally at work in the *Agricola*, where, although

Calgacus' love of *libertas* and his *virtus* might be admirable, the barbarian is nonetheless easily corrupted by the Roman enticements to vice—including baths, porticoes, and the study of rhetoric. There is, in addition, a prescient sense of foreboding in the *Germania* concerning the power of the German tribes, particularly were they ever to unite against Rome.

The last of his minor literary productions is also, in a sense, his most un-Tacitean. The *Dialogus de oratoribus* (based on the manuscript title) purports to be a discussion concerning the decline of oratory in Tacitus' day, although he sets the work nearly thirty years in the past, in 75 CE (17.3); the discussion is one where Tacitus tells us he was present, and took place among the foremost orators and literary men of the day (although some scholars dismiss the conversation as a Tacitean fiction). The work is set the day after the dialogue's protagonist, Curiatius Maternus, gave a public reading of his drama entitled *Cato*, a work about Cato the Younger. By this date Cato had become an important symbol for members of the so-called Stoic Opposition, a small group of senators, many related by marriage, who took a stand against the tyranny of the early principate. It is possible, though far from certain, that Maternus met his death shortly after the conversation, given the tendency of the genre to set a dialogue just prior to the death of one of the interlocutors (Bartsch 1994, 105–6, thinks it likely Maternus died soon after, though Mayer 2001, 44–47, is more dubious). If such were the case (and it is conjectural), the convention was one that started with Plato (most famously in the *Phaedo*), and Cicero used it as well (in, e.g., the *De Oratore*). What is certain is that the *Dialogus* shares a unique feature with Plato's *Symposium* as the only other dialogue from antiquity set at the house of a dramatic poet after the presentation of his work.

While a peculiar piece of literature, the *Dialogus* covers a good deal of literary culture and history (see Levene 2004). It purports to be about the decline of oratory, yet one of the primary interlocutors, Maternus, has retired from public life and speaks against the life of the orator altogether. Marcus Aper, on the other hand, contends that oratory is flourishing, even though he bases his claim on morally dubious examples, citing Vibius Crispus and Eprius Marcellus, two notorious prosecutors and time servers under Nero and the Flavians. A well-known public figure, Vipstanus Messalla, later comes on the scene and interrupts the conversation. He then offers his own explanation for the decline of oratory in his day, although his analysis appears trite, blaming careless parents and the enticements of the city (such as circuses) among other causes for decline, in addition to the general decadence in style ushered in by the likes of Cassius Severus, an Augustan writer whose bitter invectives included a harsh rhetoric that landed him in exile. Finally, Maternus at the end of the work offers a historical explanation for the decline of oratory: the Republic offered scope for an orator of Cicero's talent to deliver great orations such as those against Verres. What need now for such rhetoric when Vespasian, *sapientissimus et unus*, governs the state? And who would want great rhetoric if it comes with the price of violent civil strife? Stylistically the *Dialogus* recalls Cicero, since it contains for the most part the sort of regularized classical vocabulary we find in Ciceronean prose, as well as balanced periods and clauses whose sense is generally lucid and full. Nonetheless, the sort of sententious phrases we come to associate with Tacitus do occasionally appear in this work, and it does not want for some memorable barbs.

∾ The civil war of 69 and the HISTORIAE

Tacitus' first major historical work that comes down to us is the *Historiae*. While no manuscript title survives, it is generally surmised, in part due to a reference in a letter of Pliny's (*Ep.* 7.33.1). The work covers the earthshaking events of 69 CE, when Rome saw a succession of four emperors and breaks off all too soon in early 70 CE. We know from Tacitus himself that it continued through the reign of Domitian to 96 CE. The work encompassed twelve books, based on St. Jerome's assertion (in *Comm. Zach.* 3.14) that Tacitus' two major works, the *Annales* and *Historiae*, totaled thirty books, though only the first four and a portion of the fifth survive.

Tacitus' *Historiae* do not cover what set in motion the events of 69, which was the suicide of Nero in June of 68 after the revolt of Galba and his legions in Spain. Relations between Nero and the Senate had been deteriorating ever since 65 (and arguably before) when a plot, known as the Pisonian Conspiracy, was detected; by the spring of 68 matters had reached a breaking point. Nero was declared a public enemy and ended his days by stabbing himself in the throat outside of Rome. Shortly before Nero's death, in the spring of that year, Galba, although seventy-three years of age, was proclaimed emperor in Spain. He then marched to Rome and assumed the purple. With him was L. Salvidienus Otho, who had been a close friend of Nero's and formerly the husband of Poppaea Sabina; Nero appropriated Poppaea from Otho and then sent him off to govern Lusitania (modern Portugal). When Otho returned with Galba he had high hopes of becoming his successor (*Hist.* 1.13).

It is here, in January of 69, that Tacitus begins his work. His narrative of the year's events can be summarized as follows: almost immediately Otho was disappointed in his aspirations when Galba chose a young nobleman, L. Calpurnius Piso Frugi Licinianus, to succeed him. Stung to the quick and fearful of his ultimate fate (1.21), Otho corrupted the Praetorian Guards and brought over to his cause numerous legionaries and auxiliaries still in Rome; with their support, he overthrew Galba, who was assassinated on January 15. Piso, although he hid in the temple of Vesta, was betrayed and executed.

Otho now reigned supreme, though even while Galba was still *princeps* Vitellius, governor of Lower Germany, was raised to the throne by the armies of that province. A confrontation loomed, and in April the forces of Otho and Vitellius clashed at Bedriacum in northern Italy. Otho came very near to success, but in the end, despairing of his situation and not wishing to spill more blood, committed suicide after suffering defeat in battle. He died on April 16, and our two major sources, Tacitus and Suetonius (both of whom most certainly draw on a common source and will also have been able to consult eye-witnesses), give a detailed account of his death and speak admirably of his end (which included the careful burning of correspondence to prevent any incriminations under Vitellius). In the meantime, Vespasian, who had been in command of an army since 67 in an effort to crush a revolt in Judaea, was proclaimed *princeps*.

In his bid for power Vespasian had enlisted the help of L. Mucianus, governor of Syria, and Tiberius Alexander, the Praefect of Egypt. Vespasian's first move was to head for Alexandria, where he was proclaimed emperor on July 1, although his larger strategic reason for going was probably to obtain control of the ample food resources in Egypt, which played a significant role in feeding the people of Rome. Vespasian was a tried-and-true soldier who had participated in Claudius' conquest of Britain; he soon started to win the support not simply of the rich eastern provinces, but of the northern provinces too, and a clash with Vitellius soon became inevitable. In the fall of 69 the Flavian forces defeated the Vitellians at a second battle at Bedriacum. The difference between the two personalities as depicted in our sources (Tacitus, Suetonius, and Cassius Dio) could not be more striking, and Vespasian's *virtus* and *frugalitas* compared favorably to Vitellius, a man from an ancient and corrupt family, whose character was indolent, cruel, and avaricious. The conflict between the two men was fierce, and ended in Vitellius' attempted abdication, his utter desertion by his supporters, and his final lynching in the Forum in December of 69. This takes place against a lurid backdrop of street fighting within the city between the Vitellians and the Flavians (see p. 66), culminating in the conflagration and destruction of the Temple of Jupiter Capitolinus.

After Vespasian's victory Tacitus turns first to the crushing of a revolt in the German provinces led by a man named Civilis, a member of the Treveri tribe (occupying the modern Moselle River Valley in western Germany) and once a Roman loyalist. He then shifts to the siege of Jerusalem and the final stages of the revolt in Judaea, starting with an ethnographic digression on the origin of the Jews. It is here, in the year 70 CE, that his manuscript breaks off, twenty-six chapters into his fifth book. The work established Tacitus, according to Pliny, as a great historian, and we can judge for ourselves the reasons for Pliny's assertion that he believed Tacitus' *Historiae* would be immortal. The work contains hair-raising battle scenes, penetrating analyses of power and human character, sententious wit that can damn within a few syllables, a penchant for the unsparingly lurid, and the ability to evoke empathy through complex character portrayal. It also revisits the question of freedom of expression in the principate, something already explored in the *Agricola*, as well as the nature of the principate in Tacitus' day. At the opening of the work Tacitus also sought to establish his authority as one who was qualified to write a history of the period, since he himself had lived and experienced it. He also contextualizes his work and establishes his own *auctoritas* from the outset, telling his readers precisely why his narrative is of such importance, something we find in the introduction of other Roman historians such as Sallust and Livy, and, for that matter, ancient historians in general, including Herodotus, Thucydides, and Polybius. Yet Tacitus' *Historiae* stands out among these for its emotive force, and its unforgettable and episodic nature. Vitellius' ghoulish battlefield tour, Otho's noble end, and the digression on civil strife throughout Rome's history, all highlight Tacitus' talent as a historian.

∾ *The Julio-Claudians and the* ANNALES

The *Annales* is Tacitus' final work and is considered his masterpiece, which is why it is given so much scope in the present volume. Tacitus starts his work with a brief survey of the reign of Augustus before turning to Tiberius and continuing until the end of the Julio-Claudian dynasty with Nero. One of the mysteries for scholars is why did he not start with Augustus himself, why Tiberius? A possible solution is that Tacitus was attracted to Tiberius, Caligula, Claudius, and Nero precisely for the reasons he tells us. He believed these emperors had not been treated with sufficient objectivity for a variety of reasons and now, given the space of time, such a work could be undertaken. As he explored the institution of the principate, he came to believe the corrupting seeds of the system were inherent in its inception, and promises a work on Augustus in the future (*Ann.* 3.24; see Kraus and Woodman 1997, 91 for discussion). While he never, in the end, fulfilled his promise, we are still left with a brief but vivid and largely negative account of Augustus' regime and his family (concerning which see the stemmata on pp. 153–55).

Augustus, the grand-nephew of Julius Caesar and his heir, came to power after many years of civil strife and put in place a system, known as the principate, that was to last for several centuries. After his defeat of Marc Antony and Cleopatra at Actium in 31 BCE he ruled the Roman state alone from 30 BCE to 14 CE. Tacitus takes a dim view of Augustus (see pp. 75–85). Augustus, however, had a political acumen and sensitivity that his grand-uncle, Julius Caesar, decidedly lacked. He comported himself far more modestly, and put in place a system of governance in which the *princeps* became the patron of the Senate, and the emperor drew upon those most talented and trusted to govern his provinces and command his armies. He also expanded and solidified the boundaries of Rome's *imperium*, particularly in the north (through force) and in the south and east (through a combination of force and diplomacy).

For his successor Augustus chose Tiberius, who was in fact a proven general and a thoroughly capable administrator (Tacitus' hostility notwithstanding). He had served successfully as a general in wars in Germany and Pannonia during Augustus' reign, and competently carried out a number of important administrative functions. He married Augustus' daughter, Julia, after the death of her second husband, M. Vipsanius Agrippa, but the match proved less than felicitous and may have been one of the reasons Tiberius fled into self-exile in Rhodes between 6 BCE and 2 CE. Tiberius found Augustus a tough act to follow. He arguably tried, unsuccessfully, to give the Senate greater autonomy than had Augustus resulting in friction between the Senate and Tiberius, since the habit of servitude now demanded the emperor's constant oversight. Tiberius grew weary of it, to the point that he would leave the Senate muttering in Greek "*O homines ad servitutem paratos!*" (*Ann.* 3.65).

It is with the succession of Tiberius and the death of Augustus in 14 CE that Tacitus' *Annales* commence. The main events in Tacitus' account of Tiberius' reign are as follows: Tiberius' succession itself was an awkward and embarrassing affair, something underscored by the execution of Agrippa Postumus (Augustus' grandson and Tiberius' former stepson) and the mutinies in Germany and Pannonia, successfully put down by Germanicus, Tiberius' nephew, and Drusus,

his son. He was suspected of complicity in the death of his popular
nephew Germanicus in 19 CE, of whom Tiberius was reportedly envi-
ous (see below, p. 89). From 19 CE on he came into increasing conflict
with Germanicus' widow, Agrippina the Elder, who believed her sons,
Nero and Drusus, had a rightful claim to the succession. Throwing
fuel onto this fire was L. Aelius Sejanus, Tiberius' ambitious Praetorian Praefect who is one of Tacitus' greatest villains, seducing and
murdering his way to the top as he first entices Livilla, Tiberius' niece,
into an adulterous affair, poisons her husband (and Tiberius' son)
Drusus, and then turns to the persecution of Agrippina the Elder and
her sons, each of whom is eliminated in their turn through exile or
prison. In the midst of this Sejanus convinces Tiberius, now weary of
family conflict and a servile Senate, to retire to Capri, a pleasant island in the southern part of the Bay of Naples, where Tiberius spends
the last eleven years of his life. In 31 Tiberius discovered that Sejanus
was plotting to overthrow him; regrettably, most of Book 5, which
will have recounted the details of the conspiracy and its discovery, is
missing. We do know from other sources (Cassius Dio and Suetonius)
that Tiberius had Sejanus arrested and executed, and his followers
(as well as a number of Sejanus' family members) suffered the same
fate. Tiberius' last years were not happy, and when he died in 37 the
throne fell to an unfortunate choice, his diabolical nephew Gaius Caligula. Tiberius is one of Tacitus' most complex characters, although
for Tacitus, he can do no right. Even when his actions are ostensibly
"good," for Tacitus these are merely attempts to hide his true nature,
whose hallmarks include cruelty, lust, and envy. Only Germanicus,
Drusus, Livia, and Sejanus kept him in check, and as each perished
his deterioration grew more acute (see p. 104).

   It is regrettable that Tacitus' manuscript breaks off with Tiberius'
death and Caligula's accession, and does not pick up until 47 CE,
six years into Claudius' reign, in Book 11. We consequently have no
record from Tacitus of the mad Caligula's principate, and we can
only imagine how Tacitus would have treated it, although we get a
hint during the grotesquely absurd scene of his "on-off-on-again"
succession and Tiberius' murder at the conclusion of Book 6 (see p.
104). Equally regrettable is the loss of Claudius' succession, the revolt

of Camillus against the new emperor in 42, the conquest of Britain in 43, and the initial antics of Claudius' wife, Messalina, notorious for her prodigious promiscuity. When the *Annales* resume we find Messalina as a powerful player at Claudius' court, though she falls from power after openly marrying the consul, C. Silius, while Claudius is at Ostia, an episode that ends with the freedman, Narcissus, effecting her execution (see p. 125). The only other remarkable event in Claudius' reign as depicted in Tacitus, in addition to the continued conquest of Britain, is the rising power of Agrippina the Younger, whom Claudius married after Messalina's fall. Agrippina was Claudius' niece, daughter of his popular brother Germanicus, who herself had a son, Nero, by the nobleman Cn. Domitius Ahenobarbus. Claudius betrothed Nero to his own daughter, Octavia, while his son with Messalina, Britannicus, was pushed further into the background, an eclipse due to Agrippina's desire to see her own son on the throne. The Claudian books end with Agrippina's murder of Claudius with a poisoned mushroom; that failing, she enlisted Xenephon, the court physician, to finish the job with a poisoned feather posing as an instrument for purging his stomach. Tacitus' Claudius is an unforgettable and ironic portrait of a *princeps* who is incapable of controlling his own house, much less his empire, and as Malloch (2009, 117) has recently observed, he is depicted as so passive "that he is displaced as the focus of his own history."

Nero came to power on October 13, 54 CE. Tacitus' depiction of his reign is a toxic blend of the theatrical, the depraved, and the nightmarish. The youthful Nero was assisted in his governance initially by his mother Agrippina; his tutor, Seneca the Younger; and his Praetorian Praefect, Afranius Burrus. This was perhaps all for the best, since Nero was more interested in indulging his own pleasures rather than in governance. Thus his amorous liaison with Acte, an imperial freedwoman, is followed by his affair with Otho's wife, Poppaea Sabina. In addition, in the evenings he enjoyed roaming the streets with friends and entering into brawls. In 55 he murdered Britannicus, his potential rival to the throne, at a banquet during the Saturnalia, motivated by fear that Agrippina was shifting her allegiances to him since Nero was proving increasingly difficult to control.

From then on, his mother's power diminished, though she was perceived as either sufficiently dangerous, wearisome, or both, so that in 59 he decided to have her murdered (see p. 131). In the midst of all of this, it appears that Seneca and Burrus controlled the daily workings of the Empire. His mistress and soon-to-be wife, Poppaea Sabina, was also an increasingly potent force and instrumental in goading Nero into eliminating his mother (see p. 131), and then procuring first the exile then murder in 62 of Octavia, Nero's former wife. Nero also increasingly devoted himself to the pursuit of the arts, theater, and athletic spectacles.

In 64 a major catastrophe occurred when a massive fire broke out in Rome (see p. 140). Exploiting the destruction, out of the city's ruins Nero built an enormous pleasure palace (which may have been intended for both public and private enjoyment) known as the *Domus Aurea*, or Golden House. Immediately after the conflagration Nero singled out the Christians for punishment (see p. 145). In the next year, 65, a corrupt and ambitious nobleman named C. Calpurnius Piso hatched a conspiracy against Nero with the help of several disgruntled senators and others as well. The plot was betrayed by a suspicious freedman, and the experience, according to our sources, soured Nero against the Senate; in addition, several noted men of letters, including Seneca the Younger, Lucan, and Petronius all met their end as a result of their suspected involvement. In the following year, 66, he had Thrasea Paetus, a member of the so-called Stoic Opposition (see pp. 29–30), put on trial for a variety of offenses, though Thrasea anticipated the verdict with suicide. It is here that Tacitus' manuscript breaks off. We consequently miss Nero's tour of Greece, the revolt of Julius Vindex, and the final overthrow and suicide of Nero himself.

Tacitus' work is not merely a history of the imperial house. It is an annalistic history of the events Tacitus deemed worthy of record. This includes relatively frequent accounts of affairs in Armenia and Parthia (which I have not included in this volume); Parthia was Rome's rival empire in the East, and Armenia served as a buffer kingdom between the two, over which they occasionally quarreled. Tacitus also records periodic campaigns on the northern frontier, such as

Germanicus' expedition beyond the Rhine deep into Germany in 15–16 CE. Insurrections in Gaul and North Africa in the 20s find a place, while Britain, with its dangerous revolt between 59 and 61 CE, also receives its share of attention, particularly in the Neronian books.

Threading its way throughout the entire narrative is the troubled relationship between aristocratic senators and the imperial house. Senators who find themselves on the wrong side of political factions within the emperor's household or guilty of various forms of malfeasance, real or perceived, could hope for little mercy from the *princeps*, according to Tacitus. Ancient aristocratic families such as the Pisones or the Plautii faced peril as a result of confrontation or involvement with members of the imperial court (as the readings on the death of Germanicus and the fall of Messalina illustrate). Conversely, those who served as the willing instruments of imperial malice could expect lucrative rewards, as the reading that introduces Caepio Crispinus and Romanius Hispo shows. It is perhaps not surprising that the fortunes of the families belonging to the imperial Senate were of significant concern to Tacitus, himself a member of that order.

As is the case with the *Historiae*, there are numerous show-stopping scenes scattered throughout the work that are not included in this volume, such as (to name but a few) Germanicus' lurid tour in the Teutoberg Forest, the ridiculous council held by Claudius on choosing a wife after Messalina's execution, and Nero's murder of Britannicus.

Tacitus' work is conjectured to have consisted of eighteen books (see above, p. xix). Of these we have 1–6, though, as noted, most of 5 is missing. Books 7–10 and probably over half of Book 11 are also missing, but Books 12–15 are intact, and much of 16, while the last two books are lost. Structurally the work is divided into hexads, books in groups of six. The first hexad treats the reign of Tiberius, covering twenty-three years (although it also includes the end of Augustus and a brief summary of his principate). Books 7–12 covered the next seventeen years, encompassing the reigns of Caligula and Claudius. Finally, the reign of Nero, a period of fourteen years, took up Books 13–18. Tacitus will use a number of devices to underscore

this structure and its divisions. Hence Tiberius' reign is introduced
with *Primum facinus novi principatus* (1.6), and the opening of Nero's reign echoes this phrase since the third hexad begins with *Prima
novo principatu mors* (13.1). Within hexads themselves, the structure
is occasionally broken down further (see pp. 92–93).

∾ *Tacitus' place in Roman historiography*

Roman writers inherited the genre of history from the Greeks, and
even in our first two surviving Greek historians, Herodotus and
Thucydides, we already see a number of elements that later would be
considered fundamental among both Greek and Roman historians.
Set battles, orations that served to develop characters or that were
used for historical or political analysis, ethnographic digressions,
topographic descriptions, and biographical sketches and obituaries
were all basic to the genre. Fabius Pictor (who wrote a Roman history in Greek) is our first Roman historian, and, as with so many of
his successors, he was active in Roman life and politics; indeed, there
are few exceptions to this rule (though Livy is a notable one). Cato
the Elder (234–149 BCE) was the first to compose a history in Latin.
His work, the *Origines*, was written in seven books and covered Roman history from Aeneas' arrival in Italy up until Cato's day. Cato
frequently used archaic language (using, for example, *siet* for *sit*, or
advorsae for *adversae*), and the work survives only in fragments. Numerous historians intervened between Cato and our next historian,
Sallust, and, like Cato, only fragments of their works remain. These
include Sempronius Asellio, who had served in the campaign at Numantia (134–133 BCE), and wrote a history of his age that included the
revolutionary activities of the Gracchi and the Social War. L. Sisenna,
active in Roman politics in the 70s and 60s BCE, wrote his *Historiae*
in twelve books (possibly continuing Asellio's) and treated events
under Sulla. Other historians include Valerius Antias and Claudius
Quadrigarius, both of whom wrote so-called annalistic histories, i.e.,
lengthy accounts of Rome's history composed year by year rather than
a monograph on a single event, such as Sallust's *Bellum Catilinum*
(so-called because the distinction between *annales* and *historiae* has

now been question by modern scholarship; see Marincola 1999, 288–301, 313–16). Claudius traced Rome's history in twenty-three books from the Gallic sack to 82 BCE, while Antias' history was similar in chronological scope, but in seventy-five books. Both are significant for bringing annalistic history to its peak prior to Livy, and Valerius in particular was noted for his highly rhetorical style.

Some republican grandees worked in what we might consider "sub-genres," such as Aemilius Scaurus and Rutilius Rufus, both of whom wrote their memoirs or *res gestae* (although as Marincola 1999, 281–324 notes, the concept of "sub-genres" is largely a modern construct). L. Lucceius, a friend of Pompey's and active in Rome's political life, wrote a historical monograph of the period from 90 to 81 BCE, and Cicero so admired him that he attempted to solicit a history of his own career from Lucceius' hand (*Fam.* 5.12). Most famously, Caesar wrote his war *commentarii*; Cicero praised the work, but implied in his letter to Lucceius that such *commentarii* were not histories *per se*. They might be read for their own sake but could also be consulted by a historian for integration into a larger narrative. It should be noted however that Caesar's Gallic war commentaries contain many of the elements we would associate with historical writing, including ethnographic digressions, set battles, speeches that respond to one another, and a desire to establish his prestige and *auctoritas* through the narrative of his stunning achievement.

Sallust, who had himself been involved in the raucous politics of the late Republic, is the first Roman historian to have a substantial portion of his works survive: these include a contiguous history (the *Historiae*, only fragments of which now remain) and two war monographs, the *Bellum Catilinum* and the *Bellum Iugurthinum*. His contributions to the formulation of the genre in Roman hands is significant. As near as we can tell (since previous historians are lost or extremely fragmentary), he was the first to write a preface that simultaneously set out the general stance of the historian and his subject, and established the author's authority. That authority rested in no small part on political experience, something that was also the case for Tacitus (see Marincola 1997, 133–48 for discussion). He is also the first Roman historian to give expression to the trauma

Romans had experienced during the major cultural and political up-
heavals that took place in the late Republic, and to try to analyze the
origins of the ostensible decline, as did Livy and Tacitus after him.
While he drew on Cato's style, particularly his archaisms, he also
reveled in lack of balance in his sentence structure, used abstract
language (something illustrative of Thucydides' influence), and was
noted for his *brevitas* (Quint. *Inst.* 10.1.32; see below, p. xxxvi, for
discussion).

The next major Roman historian whose work survives in any
substantial form is Livy, who wrote under Augustus, and whose
training as a rhetorician emerges in his rich and copious style (his
lactea ubertas, "milky richness," as Quintilian called it, *Inst.* 10.1.32).
Livy's work was annalistic in nature, covering year by year the grand
sweep of Roman history from the advent of the Trojans up until 9
BCE, and is prefaced (similarly to Sallust) by a heavily moralizing
formal introduction. Both Sallust and Livy give us some notion of
the expectations of historiography, its purpose, function, and the
demands of the genre, and a number of authors, including Cicero,
Dionysius of Halicarnassus, and Lucian (whose *How to Write History* is the only purely theoretical work devoted to writing history
that survives from antiquity), discussed historical writing in theoretical terms. Cicero's letter to Lucceius, noted above, is the most detailed theoretical discussion among our Latin authors. In it, Cicero
confronts the demands for truth required of history, but at the same
time notes the need for adornment so that it affords pleasure for its
readers, a pleasure based on the vicissitudes of his own fortunes. The
demand for truth in conjunction with the requirement of pleasure
intersected with the expectation that history would cast into relief
virtues to be imitated and vices to be avoided. As has been noted
elsewhere in this series (Pagán 2009, xxvii–xxviii), history was first
and foremost a literary genre, drawing heavily on rhetoric, epic, and
tragedy (see Fornara 1983, 138–41), whose task was both to delight
and instruct. It was intended to cast opprobrium on vice, praise virtue, and celebrate deeds of glory and valor (see, e.g., Tac. *Ann.* 3.65;
see Luce 1991, 2904–27 for discussion of this passage). In addition,
analysis by ancient historians such as Sallust and Tacitus was based

on the probable and the circumstantial, and it would be anachronistic, given the demands of the ancient genre, to expect what we would conceptualize as a modern history, with its use (where possible) of statistics and demographics, its concern to include traditionally disenfranchised groups, or its weighing of evidence in light of contemporary archaeological and social sciences. Hence, while certain facts concerning Tiberius' reign are not in doubt (such as his trust of Sejanus or retirement to Capri), we may doubt certain details of Tacitus' portrayal of Tiberius, particularly when he attributes motives to Tiberius that he cannot have known. His envy of Germanicus, his hatred of various senators, his dissimulation due to natural secretiveness, these contemporary historians may question. Tacitus' portrayal, however, is driven by a set of cultural and political assumptions, as well as the demands of the genre, which intersect and make Tiberius simultaneously loathsome and tragic. Yet Tacitus' Tiberius, perhaps because of these very distortions (examined in detail by Walker 1952, 33–77, 82–157), illustrates a deeper truth for his readers, and that is the potential for power to corrupt and to isolate. From the fascist regimes of Europe in the last century to the contemporary American presidency — how many and who would gainsay that truth?

∾ Tacitus' sources and post-Augustan historians

Tacitus relied on a variety of sources when composing his works. His own memory and eye-witness account no doubt played a part in the *Dialogus* (if we accept his work as reflecting a genuine experience), while the *Agricola* was based in part on conversations with his father-in-law. Both for the *Agricola* and the *Germania* he appears to have relied on Livy and Caesar for some of his geographic and ethnographic information. For his *Historiae* there was a diverse array of sources (see Syme 1958, 176–90, for a detailed discussion). Vipstanus Messalla, whom he probably knew as a young man, left an account of that year. Vespasian wrote war *commentarii*, now lost but available to Tacitus. He also knew men such as Verginius Rufus (and certainly others), who played an important role in events that year, and he may well have drawn on memories of his conversations with them. For the *Historiae* we know that Pliny sent him written accounts of cases tried in the Senate (*Ep.* 7.33) and an eye-witness report of Vesuvius' eruption (*Ep.* 6.16). Because it was a contemporary history, we can imagine that Tacitus relied on the recollection of others beyond Pliny for his information, as well as his own memory of the period.

The *Annales* required a good deal more research; while there was no shortage of sources (now lost), Tacitus tells us these were imperfect at best due to their bias (see Syme 1958, 271–303). Of historians from this period, Aufidius Bassus and Servilius Nonianus were well known. Together their histories covered the period under Augustus and Tiberius, as did the historical works of Cremutius Cordus, whose work resulted in his trial for treason under Tiberius (*Ann.* 4.34–35). Velleius Paterculus, although Tacitus certainly will have disliked his flattering (and still extant) account of Tiberius, was another source he consulted (Woodman and Martin 1989, 85–86). Later on there was also Fabius Rusticus, who had written a history of Nero's reign, as had Cluvius Rufus (for both see *Ann.* 13.20, 14.2), and Pliny the Elder, who wrote a history of the war with the Germans, as well as *Historiae*; extending beyond Nero's reign, they were sources for Tacitus' *Historiae* as well (Syme 1958, 179–80). In addition there were imperial memoirs, such as those by Augustus (his *Res Gestae*, see p. 75), Tiberius (Suet. *Tib.* 61.1), and Agrippina the Younger (*Ann.* 4.53). Moreover, Tacitus occasionally made use of imperial correspondence, such as Tiberius' agonized letter to the Senate after Sejanus' fall (*Ann.* 6.6; concerning the use of Tiberius' letters and his "epistolary persona," see now Morello 2006, 331–54). Tacitus also could refer to extant orations and decrees, as with the inscription that records Claudius' speech on the Gauls (see p. 109), or the punishment of Cn. Calpurnius Piso (see pp. 89–90). Other documents Tacitus used include the *acta senatus*, the official proceedings of the Senate and important for numerous details in Tacitus' work (see Syme 1958, 278–85; Kraus and Woodman 1997, 98). There are other names and sources too, now gone, that Tacitus used in common with Suetonius and Cassius Dio, our other two major surviving sources for the period (along with Plutarch's lives of *Galba* and *Otho* for the year 69). Such use is readily evident, for example, in the *Historiae*, where we have relatively minute details concerning Otho's suicide in Suetonius (*Otho* 11), Plutarch (*Otho* 16–17), and Tacitus (*Hist.* 2.49)—that he drank a little water, tested the daggers, rested for the night, and committed suicide the next day—that seem too specific and similar for them not to have come from a single independent source.

∾ Interpretation and character portrayal in Tacitus

A recent sociological study explored why so many in the United States continue to believe that Saddam Hussein had weapons of mass destruction even after the Bush administration backtracked on its original claim that he in fact did. Perhaps not surprisingly, the research revealed that once something has been made public and repeatedly reported as fact, it remains so fixated in the public mind that it becomes very difficult to refute or even to modify. One of Tacitus' most effective rhetorical techniques is his use of reporting rumors that were prevalent at the time a given historical event took place. By lodging such rumors effectively in his reader's mind, they become a part of the larger, genuinely historic narrative, even when Tacitus takes pains to refute such rumor. They enter, to use a popular post-modernist expression, the realm of "truthiness," perhaps the best example of which is the death of Germanicus. Building up a story of enmity between Germanicus and Piso (*Ann.* 2.43, 2.55–57, 2.69–73), with a dose of Tiberian envy added for good measure, Tacitus reports the use of magic in effecting Germanicus' death, and also reports that there were those who attested to marks indicating that he died by poison. Ask the average reader of Tacitus, Who killed Germanicus? The standard response will be Piso at imperial behest, even though Piso was acquitted of this particular charge by a hostile Senate (*Ann.* 3.14). The best example of such rumor lodging in the readings offered in this volume emerges in the funeral of Augustus. Tacitus spends only a brief amount of time on those at the funeral who were apologists for Augustus. Far greater weight is given to his detractors, and this is the last detailed treatment we are given of Augustus in Tacitus' work. It does not leave a good lasting impression.

Tacitus' muscular *brevitas*, however, frequently leads the reader to a fixed and negative conclusion even more hastily. A few brief strokes of his pen etch in the reader's memory a vivid portrait of a particular character through the literary equivalent of impressionism (see Ryberg 1942, 383–404; Sullivan 1975–76, 312–26). Augustus' wife Livia, for example, is given no detailed treatment until her obituary in Book 5 of the *Annales*. Yet through only a few brief asides and strategically placed reporting of rumors at the opening of the *Annales*, Tacitus creates a powerful sense of her character. For example, at 1.3 discussing the death of Gaius Caesar he simply throws out *vel novercae Liviae dolus abstulit* ("or the treachery of his stepmother Livia got [sc. him] out of the way"). In referring a few lines later to Augustus' preferring of Tiberius over Agrippa Postumus, Tacitus casually mentions that Tiberius entered public life *artibus matris* ("by the wiles of his mother"); again in the same chapter he attributes to her Agrippa Postumus' banishment (with the phrase *Nam senem Augustum* [sc. *Livia*] *devinxerat adeo*, "For she had so subjugated the aged Augustus"). In the next chapter, in the midst of a brief sketch of Tiberius, Tacitus describes Livia as *muliebri inpotentia* ("of womanly imperiousness"), to whom all would soon be in thrall (*serviendum feminae*, "there would need be servitude to a woman"). Thus, through a series of asides and two or three brief remarks within the first four chapters of his work, Livia is firmly established in the reader's imagination as murderous, manipulative, and imperious.

Tacitus will also at times use typology when he sketches his characters (see Walker 1952, 204–34 for discussion of this phenomenon in the *Annales*). Sejanus and Poppaea Sabina are two who come immediately to mind. The first of these was based on Sallust's Catiline (from *Cat.* 5.1–5) and Livy's Hannibal (21.4), the second on Sempronia, again from Sallust (*Cat.* 25). In the course of this commentary two such typological depictions will be offered, the first of a *delator*, Caepio Crispinus (or Romanius Hispo), the second of Sejanus. Tacitus' characters, however, including these, are not simple caricatures. Indeed, Tacitus' *humanitas* emerges from his own engagement with the complexity of the human personality, and individuals such as Germanicus, Agricola, and Otho emerge as very human figures, variously sympathetic, foolish, mediocre, or ill-tempered, but rarely as wholly good or in any sense evil. Therefore while Germanicus might be Tacitus' "golden boy," he is also capable of embarrassing theatrics, such as threatening suicide in front of derisive soldiers (*Ann.* 1.35, see Pelling 1993, 59–85). Otho might be a knave and an assassin, but he was a capable governor of Lusitania and redeemed himself by a suicide that prevents further mass spilling of blood (*Hist.* 2.49). We might think Agricola a good man, and even a great man — but the latter is a reality that is qualified (*Agr.* 44.2). Even Tacitus' monsters are not wholly unsympathetic. The inner torments and the truly tragic nature of Tiberius' reverse trajectory as he devolves from a once competent statesman into an isolated, haunted, albeit perverse character paints an excruciating picture. Very little is unqualified in Tacitus.

Another significant means of character portrayal at Tacitus' disposal was the use of speeches. As was the case for prior historians such as Sallust and Livy, these are entirely Tacitus' own creation; and, again as in other historians, these impart some depth and complexity to his characters. This is certainly the case with Claudius' oration on the Gauls. In this instance the oration Tacitus attributes to the emperor casts him in a more favorable light by altering the original speech from one that, as Syme remarked, was "lumbering and involved," to one that used "a sequence of sharp, alert phrases," eviscerating (and improving) Claudius' original speech to match its theme, "solemn and majestic," of eight centuries of Roman history (1958, 318–19). Galba's speech, on the other hand, which concerns the adoption of Piso, helps to define him as clueless concerning the depth of the political crisis that surrounds him (see pp. 56–57). It bears mentioning that Tacitus' speeches work on a thematic level as well. As Keitel notes (1993, 42–43; cf. Miller 1975, 54–57) different speeches in the course of the same work will explore similar subjects with divers approaches or explore an area of thematic importance to the work in general, thereby contributing to the complexity of the author's presentation and thought. Such complexity is arguably reflected in Tacitus' discussion of *libertas* at the opening of the *Agricola*, which contrasts with Calgacus' different take on *libertas* in the speech Tacitus attributes to him (see p. 36).

∾ *Tacitus' style and language*

Pliny called Tacitus' style of oratory "solemn" (*Ep.* 2.11.16), and he also used this elevated style throughout his surviving works. The various threads that weave together this "solemn" or "dignified" prose are too numerous to recount fully here, and will be noted individually throughout the commentary section. Certain aspects of his prose, however, are outstanding and merit particular attention by any who desire a deeper appreciation of Tacitus as a writer (for a general discussion of Tacitus' style see Oakley 2009, 195–211). The three most essential aspects of his style include his *brevitas*, his use of *variatio*, and his poetic coloring; other elements that make his style particularly distinct include his heavy use of metaphor and his deployment of *sententiae*.

Sallust was a major influence on Tacitus (discussed in detail in Furneaux 1896, 72–73, and Syme 1958, 728–32, both of whom include lists of verbal echoes), and one of the key stylistic elements in which Sallust and Tacitus are similar is *brevitas*. Tacitus achieves his *brevitas* through an elliptical and compressed style, and several elements in Tacitus' language, found in the selections of this commentary, make it extremely compact. These include the frequent omission of verbs and abbreviated expressions (see, e.g., *Hist.* 1.49 and Galba's obituary, where the emperor is described for four lines with a series of adjectives and participial phrases but no verb; six lines if we exclude verbs found in subordinate clauses); frequent use of participular clauses (as in *libertus increpans*, *Ann.* 11.37–38); use of the historical infinitive, which Sallust also used to great effect, (e.g., *Ann.* 15.38, *complere vias, sterni per agros*); and the omission of pronouns (*Hist.* 1.41, *plures obtulisse ultro percussoribus iugulum*). Contributing to this compressed style is his particular fondness for the substantival use of adjectives and participles, as in *Ann.* 15.44, where we find *eius mali, cuncta . . . atrocia aut pudenda, pereuntibus, sontis . . . meritos, unius,* all in the space of twenty-two lines. Tacitus also employs a large number of abstract nouns. Thus in the *Agricola* 3.1 alone we find, in less than half a dozen lines, *res, felicitas, libertas, spes, securitas, fiducia,* and *infirmitas*; these, as Damon has noted (2003, 14), are more common in passages of characterization and analysis rather than narrative. Tacitus' abstract language and obscurity of thought frequently present his readers with compressed language that needs to be unpacked, as in the phrase *recessus ipse ac sinus famae* (*Agr.* 30), or in the phrase *cuius* [antecedent *rem Romanam*] *pari exitio viguit ceciditque* [subject = Sejanus] (*Ann.* 4.1). On the whole, however, while his *brevitas* makes his meaning occasionally elusive, it is also what gives so much power to his prose.

An equally if not more outstanding hallmark of Tacitean style is his *variatio* (see Kraus and Woodman 1997, 110–11), a quality that contributes perhaps first and foremost to the richness of his language. Livy in particular has been noted as influencing this aspect of Tacitus' prose style (see Syme 1958, 733–34; Ogilvie and Richmond 1967, 25–27). There are innumerable ways that *variatio* is expressed in Tacitus, and we here offer just a few examples: in the first selection (*Agr.* 2.2–3.3) as elsewhere we find reversal of the order of names (hence Paetus Thrasea for Thrasea Paetus); throughout the selections we find variation between *dein* and *deinde* or *non modo . . . ac . . . sed* instead of the simple *non modo . . . sed*; there is also the occasional interchange of a preposition for a simple case, as with the phrase *Livia gravis in rem publicam . . . gravis domui Caesarum* (*Ann.* 1.10). He will also vary his use of phrases with a preposition with expressions that use the ablative, creating an imbalanced construction, as in *hic socordia . . . ille per libidines* (*Ann.* 1.9). In addition, he sometimes combines participial constructions with nouns, as in *Ann.* 4.1, *sui obtegens, in alios criminator,* or with the phrase in *Ann.* 15.38, *in edita adsurgens et rursus inferiora populando*; he will even combine clauses that use the subjunctive with participial clauses, as in the alternative indirect question we find at *Ann.* 6.1, *an urbem intraret, seu, . . . speciem venturi simulans.* We also find varied expressions for the same action, such as death, hence *mortalitatem explevisse* and *finivit* (plus an ablative of time when) are both used for Tiberius (*Ann.* 6.50).

As was the case with Sallust, Tacitus eschewed the well-balanced prose that was the hallmark of Cicero's style, with its sentences full of clauses that generally corresponded with one another and whose meaning and syntax were generally complete. The opening of Tacitus' *Agricola*, a portion of which is offered in the first selection, is a prime example of the *inconcinnitas* we find in Tacitus' writing (which also makes it one of the most difficult pieces of Latin prose to comprehend, comparable to Livy's *praefatio*). The passage is noteworthy for its substantive use of adjectives, its heavy use of abstract nouns ending in *-tas*, and its hypotactic structure that employs frequent subordination; indeed, the last sentence continues for more than six lines, using subordinate clauses, apposition, ablative absolutes, jarring use of singular subjects with plural verb forms, parenthetical phrases, and clauses that, taken as a whole, lack balance.

Tacitus also has a fondness for poetic language, and there are some notable echoes of poetic passages among the selections, including *beatissimi saeculi ortu* (*Agr.* 3.1) that recalls Verg. *Ec.* 4.5; *machinator doli* (*Ann.* 1.10), which echo's Verg. *Aen.* 2.264–67; and his description of the *delator* Caepio Crispinus as *egens, ignotus* (*Ann.* 1.74) that recalls Aeneas' self-description at Verg. *Aen.* 1.384. In addition, Furneaux (1896, 64–65) lists a number of words previously found only in poetry that Tacitus used in prose for the first time; examples of such usage in the present selections include *reclinis* (in *Ann.* 14.4 from Ovid *Met.* 10.558), *fusam humi* (in *Ann.* 11.37 from Verg. *Aen.* 6.423), and as already noted *machinator doli*. Contemporary poets, including Statius and Valerius Flaccus, also influenced Tacitus' language (see Woodman 2009, 36–37, for discussion with the relevant citations), as with the adjective *honora* (in *Ann.* 1.10, found in Valerius Flaccus and Statius, see p. 55), used for the first time in prose by Tacitus. The use of poetic constructions is also relatively frequent in Tacitus, including (again, among the current selections) use of the dative to indicate motion towards, *hortor* plus the infinitive (as opposed to the usual iussive noun clause), the use of *in* plus an adjective to indicate duration of time, and the frequent use of poetic forms, such as the abbreviated and archaic form of the third person plural in the perfect. As was the case with Sallust, Tacitus also uses archaisms, although somewhat more sparingly than his predecessor. We therefore find the archaic form *deum* for *deorum* (*Germ.* 2.1; *Ann.* 4.1), archaic words such as *mercimonium*, (*Ann.* 15.38, found, e.g., in Plaut. *Cur.* 564), and *apiscor* for *adpiscor* (*Ann.* 4.1). In addition there is the general poetic "feel" or atmosphere Tacitus can create. Thus when Nero murders his mother, the peaceful night with the treacherous device of the collapsible boat reminds one of the capture of Troy in Vergil's *Aeneid*; Galba's assassination and obituary recall Priam's death in the same work; and Messalina's fall, as Dickison (1977) has noted, reads like a Roman farce.

Tacitus wraps all of these rhetorical devices around a vocabulary designed to reinforce some of the key themes and interests we find in his works, especially in his construction of the tyrannical personality, the workings of power, and its corrupting influence. Words such as *libertas, servitium, saevitia, potestas, potentia, dominatio, inlecebrae, libido, cupido, simulo, dolus, obtentus, stuprum*, and their cognates arise frequently. Tacitus is particularly fond of negative words formed with the prefix *in-*, such as *incuriosus, informis, inevitabile, intestabilis*, and also uses nouns ending in *-tor*, not infrequently with negative associations (see Walker 1952, 60), as in *criminator* in *Ann.* 4.1 (a word, along with a number of others, that occurs for the first time in Tacitus). The occasional use of intensifiers such as *at*, unique turns of a phrase such as *mortalitatem explevisse* (*Ann.* 6.50), the use of paradox in phrases such as *inhumana securitas*, understatement (e.g., *magis extra vitia quam cum virtutibus*), the effective use of comparative clauses (e.g., *sic ingenia studiaque oppresseris facilius quam revocaveris*), or the careful use of a powerful word (as *polluere* at *Ann.* 6.1), are all deployed to great effect. Tacitus' Latin also derives its power from the diverse imagery on which he draws in order to reinforce the violence of his subject. Such imagery found throughout the selections in the present work includes disease (*contactu, remedia*), burning and fire (*incensus, exarserat*), verbs of bursting (*prorupit*), and verbs of creeping (*occultis libellis saevitiae principis adrepit*). Indeed, Tacitus' use of both metaphor and simile is quite powerful. Thus the mob views battle as though a game (*Hist.* 3.83) or Tiberius' lust is directed against noble youths as though against captives (*velut in captos*, *Ann.* 6.1).

Finally, Tacitus is perhaps best known for his use of the sententious or pointed style (equivalent to the contemporary "sound bite"). The style was one that he himself discussed in the *Dialogus* as coming into vogue with Cassius Severus (under Augustus), and that Seneca the Younger was himself known to have employed, in which succinct, sometimes quite barbed rhetorical points aimed straight for the jugular. It was a style that was suited to the law courts of the day, and Tacitus, himself a noted barrister and sometime prosecutor, knew how to use them with devastating acumen, often placing them in the strategically deadly position at the end of a sentence. Some of his more famous *sententiae* among the current selections include *solitudinem faciunt, pacem appellant* (directed by Calgacus against the Romans themselves); *omnium consensu capax imperii nisi imperasset* (summarizing Galba's career as *princeps*); *proximis temporibus triumphati magis quam victi sunt* (implicitly deriding Domitian's false triumph over the Germans). This particular aspect of Tacitus' style has received extensive attention, with perhaps the most interesting and nuanced account in Sinclair's book-length study (1995), and, more recently, in Keitel (2006); also see in general Plass (1988).

∾ *Rhetorical devices*

The following is a set of rhetorical devices that Tacitus uses more than once in this commentary's selections and are listed here as a convenient reference for students. These include:

alliteration: repetition of sound, as in *Vibidiam, virginum Vestalium vetustissimam*, (*Ann.* 11.32, 20)

anaphora: the repetition of words at the beginning of successive phrases or clauses, as in *non Cinnae, non Sullae longa dominatio* (*Ann.* 1.1, 4–5)

antithesis: the juxtaposition of two opposites, as in *palam compositus pudor, intus summa apiscendi libido* (*Ann.* 4.1, 17)

asyndeton: the omission of coordinating conjunctions, and an aspect of Tacitean *brevitas*, as in *Marsos Gambrivios Suebos Vandalios* (*Germ.* 2.4, 20–21)

brachylogy: the omission of a main finite verb from one of two clauses, a means by which Tacitus achieved his *brevitas* and compression, as in *sicut vetus aetas vidit quid ultimum in libertate esset, ita nos quid in servitute* (*Agr.* 2.1–3.3, 10–12)

chiasmus: in which nouns and adjectives are arranged in an ABBA construction, as in *ad coniungii spem . . . et necem mariti* (*Ann.* 4.3, 40–41)

ellipse: the suppression of a word or several words of importance for the full expression of thought but necessary to complete the construction, as in *aliam fore laetae rei faciem*, introduced by an implied verb of thinking (*Ann.* 14.8, 6–7)

hendiadys: the use of two elements to form a singularity of expression and a way in which Tacitus achieves his compression, as in *recessus ipse ac sinus famae* (*Agr.* 30, 13)

litotes: an affirmative statement made with a negative, a way to achieve understatement, as in *magis extra vitia quam cum virtutibus* (*Hist.* 1.49, 21–22)

pleonasm: use of two elements, one of which is often redundant, as in *singuli viritim* (*Ann.* 11.24, 9)

tricolon: a series of three element (words, phrases, or clauses), sometimes balanced, sometimes deliberately lacking balance, as in *auferre, trucidare, rapere* (*Agr.* 30, 21)

✑ *Suggested reading*

The following bibliography includes works beyond those cited in this commentary (indicated by an asterisk at the end of the entry) and are intended to point students to further resources on the historical, cultural, and literary background of Tacitus' works. In addition students may wish to consult H. Benario's bibliographies of Tacitean scholarship, published each decade since 1964 in special editions of *Classical World* (vols. 58, 63, 71, 80, 89, 98), which also offer brief summaries of virtually every publication.

Alföldy, G. *Mitteilung des deutschen archaeologische Instituts: Römische Abteilung* 102 (1995): 251–68.

Ash, R. *Ordering Anarchy: Armies and Leaders in Tacitus' Histories*. London, 1999.*

———. "Fission and fusion: shifting Roman identities in the *Histories*." In *The Cambridge Companion to Tacitus*, edited by A. J. Woodman, 85–99. Cambridge, 2009.

Bartsch, S. *Actors in the Audience. Theatricality and Doublespeak from Nero to Hadrian*. Cambridge, MA, 1994.

Bernario, H. *Tacitus. Germania*. Warminster, 1999.

Birley, A. R. "The Life and Death of Cornelius Tacitus." *Historia* 49 (2000): 230–47.

Brunt, P. A. "Stoicism and the Principate." *Papers of the British School in Rome* 43 (1975): 7–35.

Champlin, E. *Nero*. Cambridge, MA, 2003.

Clarke, K. "An Island Nation: Re-Reading Tacitus' *Agricola*." *Journal of Roman Studies* 91 (2001): 94–112.

Damon, C. "The Trial of Cn. Piso in Tacitus' *Annales* and the *Senatus Consultum de Cn. Pisone Patre*: New Light on Narrative Technique." *American Journal of Philology* 120 (1999): 143–62.

———. *Tacitus. Histories, Book I*. Cambridge, 2003.

Damon, C. and S. Takács. (eds). "The *Senatus Consultum de Cn. Pisone Patre*." *American Journal of Philology* (1999): 1–162.

Dickison, S. K. "Claudius: *Saturnalicius Princeps*." *Latomus* 36 (1977): 634–47.

Dunkle, J. R. "The Rhetorical Tyrant in Roman Historiography: Sallust, Livy and Tacitus." *Classical World* 65 (1971): 12–20.

Fagan, G. G. "Messalina's Folly." *Classical Quarterly* 52 (2002): 566–79.

Fornara, C. W. *The Nature of History in Ancient Greece and Rome.* Berkeley, 1983.

Furneaux, H. *The Annals of Tacitus. Vols. 1–2.* 2nd edition. Oxford, 1896, 1907.

Goodyear, F. R. D. *The Annals of Tacitus. Vols. 1–2.* Cambridge, 1972, 1981.

Griffin, M. T. "The Lyons tablet and Tacitean hindsight." *Classical Quarterly* 32 (1982): 404–18.

———. "Tacitus as a Historian." In *The Cambridge Companion to Tacitus*, edited by A. J. Woodman, 168–83. Cambridge, 2009.

Hammond, M. "*Res olim dissociabiles: Principatus ac Libertas*: Liberty under the early Roman Empire." *Harvard Studies in Classical Philology* 67 (1963): 93–113.

Haverfield, F. "Four Notes on Tacitus." *Journal of Roman Studies* 2 (1912): 195–200.

Haynes, H. *The History of Make-Believe. Tacitus' Histories.* Berkeley, 2003.

———. "Tacitus' Dangerous World." *Classical Antiquity* 23 (2004): 33–61.

———. "Survival and Memory in the *Agricola*." In *Ingens Eloquentiae Materia: Rhetoric and Empire in Tacitus*, edited by R. Ash and M. Malamud, 149–70. *Arethusa* 39.2 (2006).

Horsfall, N. "Illusion and Reality in Latin Topographical Writing." *Greece and Rome* 32 (1985): 197–208.

Houston, G. "Tiberius on Capri." *Greece and Rome* 32 (1985): 179–96.

Jones, B. *The Emperor Domitian.* London, 1992.*

Keitel, E. "Principate and Civil War in the *Annals* of Tacitus." *American Journal of Philology* 105 (1984): 306–25.

———. "Otho's Exhortation in Tacitus' *Historiae*." *Greece and Rome* 34 (1987): 73–82.

———. "*Sententia* and Structure in Tacitus *Histories* 1.12–49." In *Ingens Eloquentiae Materia: Rhetoric and Empire in Tacitus*, edited by R. Ash and M. Malamud, 219–44. *Arethusa* 39.2 (2006).

Kraus, C. S. "The Tiberian hexad." In *The Cambridge Companion to Tacitus*, edited by A. J. Woodman, 100–115. Cambridge, 2009.

Kraus, C. S., and A. J. Woodman. *Latin Historians*. Oxford, 1997.

Levene, D. S. "Tacitus' *Dialogus* as Literary History." *Transactions of the American Philology Association* 134 (2004): 157–200.

Levick, B. *Claudius*. New Haven, 1990.*

———. *Tiberius the Politician*. 2nd edition. London, 1999.*

Luce, T. J. "Ancient Views on the Causes of Bias in Historical Writing." *Classical Philology* 84 (1989): 16–31.

———. "Tacitus on 'History's Highest Function': *praecipuum munus annalium* (*Ann*. 3.65)." *Aufstieg und Niedergang des römischen Welt* 2.33.4 (1991): 2904–27.

Malloch, S. V. "Hamlet without the Prince? The Claudian *Annales*." In *The Cambridge Companion to Tacitus*, edited by A. J. Woodman, 116–26. Cambridge, 2009.

Marincola, J. *Authority and Tradition in Ancient Historiography*. Cambridge, 1997.

———. "Genre, Convention, and Innovation in Greco-Roman Historiography." In *The Limits of Historiography. Genre and Narrative in Ancient Historical Texts*, edited by C. S. Kraus, 281–324. Leiden, 1999.

Martin, R. *Tacitus*. London, 1981.

———. *Tacitus Annals V and VI*. Warminster, 2001.

———. "From manuscript to print." In *The Cambridge Companion to Tacitus*, edited by A. J. Woodman, 241–52. Cambridge, 2009.

Martin, R., and A. J. Woodman. *Tacitus: Annals Book IV*. Cambridge, 1989.

Mayer, R. (ed). *Tacitus, The Dialogus*. Cambridge, 2001.

Mellor, R. *Tacitus*. London, 1993.

Miller, N. P. "Dramatic Speech in the Roman Historians." *Greece and Rome* 22 (1975): 45–57.

Morello, R. "A Correspondence Course in Tyranny: The *Cruentae Litterae* of Tiberius." In *Ingens Eloquentiae Materia: Rhetoric and Empire in Tacitus*, edited by R. Ash and M. Malamud, 331–54. *Arethusa* 39.2 (2006).

Morford, M. "How Tacitus Defined Liberty." *Aufstieg und Niedergang der römischen Welt* 2.33.4 (1991): 3420–49.

Morgan, G. *69 A.D. The Year of Four Emperors*. Oxford, 2006.*

Oakley, S. P. "Style and language." In *The Cambridge Companion to Tacitus*, edited by A. J. Woodman, 195–211. Cambridge, 2009.

Ogilvie, R. M., and I. Richmond. *Cornelii Taciti, De Vita Agricolae*. Oxford, 1967.

O'Gorman, E. "No Place like Rome: Identity and Difference in the *Germania* of Tacitus." *Ramus* 22 (1993): 135–54.

———. *Irony and Misreading in the Annals of Tacitus*. Cambridge, 2000.

Pagán, V. E. *A Sallust Reader: Selections from Bellum Catilinae, Bellum Iugurthinum, and Historiae*. Mundelein, IL, 2009.

Pelling, C. B. R. "Tacitus and Germanicus." In *Tacitus and the Tacitean Tradition*, edited by T. J. Luce and A. J. Woodman, 59–85. Princeton, 1993.

Plass, P. *Wit and the Writing of History: The Rhetoric of Historiography in Imperial Rome*. Madison, 1988.

Pomeroy, A. "Theatricality in Tacitus's *Histories*." In *Ingens Eloquentiae Materia: Rhetoric and Empire in Tacitus*, edited by R. Ash and M. Malamud, 171–91. *Arethusa* 39.2 (2006).

Putnam, M. C. J. "Virgil and Tacitus *Ann.* 1.10." *Classical Quarterly* 39 (1989): 563–64.

Raaflaub, K. "Between Myth and History: Rome's Rise from Village to Empire (the Eighth Century to 264)." In *A Companion to the Roman Republic*, edited by N. Rosenstein and R. Morstein-Marx, 125–46. Blackwell, 2006.

Rutledge, S. "Tacitus in Tartan: Textual Colonization and Expansionist Discourse in Tacitus' *Agricola*." *Helios* 27 (2000): 75–95.

———. *Imperial Inquisitions. Prosecutors and Informants from Tiberius to Domitian*. London, 2001.

Ryberg, I. S. "Tacitus' Art of Innuendo." *Transactions of the American Philological Association* 73 (1942): 383–404.

Sailor, D. *Writing and Empire in Tacitus*. Cambridge, 2008.

Santoro L'Hoir, F. *Tragedy, Rhetoric, and the Historiography of Tacitus' Annales*. Ann Arbor, 2006.

Scott, R. D. *Religion and Philosophy in the Histories of Tacitus*. Papers and Monographs of the American Academy in Rome 22. Rome, 1968.

Sinclair, P. *Tacitus the Sententious Historian. A Sociology of Rhetoric in Tacitus' Annals 1–6*. University Park, PA, 1995.

Sullivan, D. "Innuendo and the 'Weighted Alternative' in Tacitus." *Classical Journal* 71 (1975–76): 312–26.

Syme, R. *Tacitus*. Oxford, 1958.

———. *Ten Studies in Tacitus*. Oxford, 1970.

Thomas, R. "The *Germania* as Literary Text." In *The Cambridge Companion to Tacitus*, edited by A. J. Woodman, 59–72. Cambridge, 2009.

Walker, B. *The Annals of Tacitus. A Study in the Writing of History*. Manchester, 1952.

Wellesley, K. *Tacitus. The Histories III*. Sydney, 1972.

———. *The Year of the Four Emperors*. 3rd edition. London, 2000.*

Wirszubski, C. H. *Libertas as a Political Idea at Rome during the late Republic and early Principate*. Cambridge, 1950.

Wiseman, T. P., "Lying Historians: Seven Types of Mendacity." In *Lies and Fiction in the Ancient World*, edited by C. Gill and T. P. Wiseman, 122–46. Austin, 1993.

Woodcock, E. C. *The Annals of Tacitus, Book XIV*. London, 1939.

Woodman, A. J. "Tacitus' Obituary of Tiberius." *Classical Quarterly* 39 (1989): 197–205.

———. "Amateur Dramatics at the Court of Nero: *Annales* 15.48–74." In *Tacitus and the Tacitean Tradition*, edited by T. J. Luce and A. J. Woodman, 104–28. Princeton, 1993.

———. *Tacitus. The Annals*. Indianapolis, 2004.

———. "Tacitus and the contemporary scene." In *The Cambridge Companion to Tacitus*, edited by A. J. Woodman, 31–43. Cambridge, 2009.

Latin Text

At several points in this commentary readers will find references to *M*. This refers to either the so-called *Mediceus primus* or *Mediceus secundus*. The *Mediceus primus* is a ninth-century manuscript brought to Rome in the early sixteenth century from which derives all subsequent copies of Tacitus' *Annales* 1–6. The *Mediceus secundus* dates to the eleventh century and is the sole text for the rest of the *Annales* and also the sole text from which subsequent copies of the *Historiae* derive as well. Tacitus' masterworks thus survived by the slimmest of threads. The stemmata of the *opera minora* discovered in Hersfeld in 1425, and derived from a single manuscript, is considerably more complicated; though we are unclear on the details, by 1455 Pier Candido Decembrio reports seeing a single manuscript in Rome containing all three works. By the end of the fifteenth century there were a number of manuscripts with one or more of the works made from two or three manuscripts, possibly descended from the original Decembrio saw in Rome. Complicating the question of the *opera minora* is the *codex Aesinas* (the so-called Jesi Manuscript), which contains the *Agricola* and *Germania* and may actually be a part of the original Hersfeld manuscript dated to the ninth century. For an excellent and lucid discussion about the complicated matter of the manuscripts of Tacitus' works see Martin (2009, 241–52; cf. 1981, 236–39).

The Latin text in this commentary follows the editions of R. M. Ogilvie and M. Winterbottom for the *Opera Minora* and C. D. Fisher's of the *Historiae* and *Annales*. Divergences from these texts include:

Agr. 3.2 (line 28): **ut dixerim** for **ut <sic> dixerim**

Hist. 3.83 (line 16): **ante** instead of **et ante**

Ann. 1.10 (line 37): **que tedii et** has been omitted

Ann. 1.74 (line 3): **Romanio** for **Romano**

Ann. 15.38 (line 15): **[aetas]** has been omitted

NOTE: Throughout the text I have also remained faithful to Fisher's and Ogilvie's use of *-is* for the accusative plural.

⟶ *AGRICOLA 2.1–3.2*
The tyranny of Domitian and the advent of Nerva and Trajan

Legimus, cum Auruleno Rustico Paetus Thrasea, Herennio   2.1
Senecioni Priscus Helvidius laudati essent, capitale fuisse,
neque in ipsos modo auctores, sed in libros quoque eorum
saevitum, delegato triumviris ministerio ut monumenta
5 clarissimorum ingeniorum in comitio ac foro urerentur.
scilicet illo igne vocem populi Romani et libertatem senatus   2
et conscientiam generis humani aboleri arbitrabantur,
expulsis insuper sapientiae professoribus atque omni bona
arte in exilium acta, ne quid usquam honestum occurreret.
10 dedimus profecto grande patientiae documentum; et sicut   3
vetus aetas vidit quid ultimum in libertate esset, ita nos
quid in servitute, adempto per inquisitiones etiam loquendi
audiendique commercio. memoriam quoque ipsam cum
voce perdidissemus, si tam in nostra potestate esset oblivisci
15 quam tacere.

Nunc demum redit animus; et quamquam primo statim   3.1
beatissimi saeculi ortu Nerva Caesar res olim dissociabiles
miscuerit, principatum ac libertatem, augeatque cotidie
felicitatem temporum Nerva Traianus, nec spem modo ac

20 votum securitas publica, sed ipsius voti fiduciam ac robur

adsumpserit, natura tamen infirmitatis humanae tardiora

sunt remedia quam mala; et ut corpora nostra lente

augescunt, cito extinguuntur, sic ingenia studiaque oppres-

seris facilius quam revocaveris: subit quippe etiam ipsius

25 inertiae dulcedo, et invisa primo desidia postremo amatur.

quid, si per quindecim annos, grande mortalis aevi spatium,　2

multi fortuitis casibus, promptissimus quisque saevitia

principis interciderunt, pauci et, ut dixerim, non modo

aliorum sed etiam nostri superstites sumus, exemptis e

30 media vita tot annis, quibus iuvenes ad senectutem, senes

prope ad ipsos exactae aetatis terminos per silentium

venimus?

∾ AGRICOLA 30.1–5
The speech of Calgacus at the battle of Mons Graupius

'Quotiens causas belli et necessitatem nostram intueor,　30.1

magnus mihi animus est hodiernum diem consensumque

vestrum initium libertatis toti Britanniae fore: nam et uni-

versi coistis et servitutis expertes, et nullae ultra terrae ac

5 ne mare quidem securum inminente nobis classe Romana.

ita proelium atque arma, quae fortibus honesta, eadem etiam

ignavis tutissima sunt. priores pugnae, quibus adversus　2

Romanos varia fortuna certatum est, spem ac subsidium

in nostris manibus habebant, quia nobilissimi totius Britan-

10 niae eoque in ipsis penetralibus siti nec ulla servientium

litora aspicientes, oculos quoque a contactu dominationis

inviolatos habebamus. nos terrarum ac libertatis extremos　3

recessus ipse ac sinus famae in hunc diem defendit: nunc
terminus Britanniae patet, atque omne ignotum pro magni-
15 fico est; sed nulla iam ultra gens, nihil nisi fluctus ac saxa,
et infestiores Romani, quorum superbiam frustra per obsequium ac modestiam effugias. raptores orbis, postquam   4
cuncta vastantibus defuere terrae, mare scrutantur: si
locuples hostis est, avari, si pauper, ambitiosi, quos non
20 Oriens, non Occidens satiaverit: soli omnium opes atque
inopiam pari adfectu concupiscunt. auferre trucidare rapere   5
falsis nominibus imperium, atque ubi solitudinem faciunt
pacem appellant.

✨ *GERMANIA 1.1, 2.1–2*
A description of Germany and the origins of the Germans

Germania omnis a Gallis Raetisque et Pannoniis Rheno   1.1
et Danuvio fluminibus, a Sarmatis Dacisque mutuo metu
aut montibus separatur; cetera Oceanus ambit, latos sinus
et insularum inmensa spatia complectens, nuper cognitis
5 quibusdam gentibus ac regibus, quos bellum aperuit.

    *   *   *

Ipsos Germanos indigenas crediderim minimeque aliarum   2.1
gentium adventibus et hospitiis mixtos, quia nec terra olim
sed classibus advehebantur qui mutare sedes quaerebant, et
inmensus ultra utque sic dixerim adversus Oceanus raris ab
10 orbe nostro navibus aditur. quis porro, praeter periculum
horridi et ignoti maris, Asia aut Africa aut Italia relicta

Germaniam peteret, informem terris, asperam caelo, tristem
cultu aspectuque nisi si patria sit?

Celebrant carminibus antiquis, quod unum apud illos   2
15 memoriae et annalium genus est, Tuistonem deum terra
editum. ei filium Mannum, originem gentis conditoremque,
Manno tris filios adsignant, e quorum nominibus proximi
Oceano Ingaevones, medii Hermiones, ceteri Istaevones
vocentur. quidam, ut in licentia vetustatis, pluris deo ortos
20 pluresque gentis appellationes, Marsos Gambrivios Suebos
Vandalios, adfirmant, eaque vera et antiqua nomina.

❧ *GERMANIA 37.2–5*
A history of the wars with the Germans

sescentesimum et quadra-   37.2
gesimum annum urbs nostra agebat cum primum Cimbro-
rum audita sunt arma Caecilio Metello ac Papirio Carbone
consulibus. ex quo si ad alterum imperatoris Traiani con-
5 sulatum computemus, ducenti ferme et decem anni col-
liguntur: tam diu Germania vincitur. medio tam longi aevi   3
spatio multa in vicem damna. non Samnis, non Poeni, non
Hispaniae Galliaeve, ne Parthi quidem saepius admonuere:
quippe regno Arsacis acrior est Germanorum libertas. quid
10 enim aliud nobis quam caedem Crassi, amisso et ipse
Pacoro, infra Ventidium deiectus Oriens obiecerit? at   4
Germani Carbone et Cassio et Scauro Aurelio et Servilio
Caepione Maximoque Mallio fusis vel captis quinque simul
consularis exercitus populo Romano, Varum trisque cum eo

15 legiones etiam Caesari abstulerunt; nec inpune C. Marius
in Italia, divus Iulius in Gallia, Drusus ac Nero et
Germanicus in suis eos sedibus perculerunt. mox ingentes
C. Caesaris minae in ludibrium versae. inde otium, donec   5
occasione discordiae nostrae et civilium armorum expugna-
20 tis legionum hibernis etiam Gallias adfectavere ac rursus
pulsi. nam proximis temporibus triumphati magis quam
victi sunt.

∾ DIALOGUS 1.1–3
Introduction and address to Fabius Iustus

Saepe ex me requiris, Iuste Fabi, cur, cum priora saecula   1.1
tot eminentium oratorum ingeniis gloriaque floruerint,
nostra potissimum aetas deserta et laude eloquentiae orbata
vix nomen ipsum oratoris retineat; neque enim ita appel-
5 lamus nisi antiquos, horum autem temporum diserti causidici et advocati et patroni et quidvis potius quam oratores
vocantur. cui percontationi tuae respondere, et tam magnae   2
quaestionis pondus excipere ut aut de ingeniis nostris male
existimandum <sit> si idem adsequi non possumus aut
10 de iudiciis si nolumus, vix hercule auderem si mihi mea
sententia proferenda ac non disertissimorum, ut nostris
temporibus, hominum sermo repetendus esset, quos
eandem hanc quaestionem pertractantes iuvenis admodum
audivi. ita non ingenio sed memoria et recordatione opus   3
15 est, ut quae a praestantissimis viris et excogitata subtiliter
et dicta graviter accepi, cum singuli diversas †vel easdem†

sed probabiles causas adferrent, dum formam sui quisque
et animi et ingenii redderent, isdem nunc numeris isdemque
rationibus persequar, servato ordine disputationis.

∾ *DIALOGUS 2.1–2*
Setting the scene

Nam postero die quam Curiatius Maternus Catonem   2.1
recitaverat, cum offendisse potentium animos diceretur,
tamquam in eo tragoediae argumento sui oblitus tantum
Catonem cogitasset, eaque de re per urbem frequens sermo
5 haberetur, venerunt ad eum M. Aper et Iulius Secundus,
celeberrima tum ingenia fori nostri, quos ego utrosque non
modo in iudiciis studiose audiebam, sed domi quoque et in
publico adsectabar mira studiorum cupiditate et quodam
ardore iuvenili, ut fabulas quoque eorum et disputationes
10 et arcana semotae dictionis penitus exciperem: quamvis
maligne plerique opinarentur nec Secundo promptum esse
sermonem et Aprum ingenio potius et vi naturae quam
institutione et litteris famam eloquentiae consecutum; nam   2
et Secundo purus et pressus et, in quantum satis erat,
15 profluens sermo non defuit, et Aper omni eruditione in-
butus contemnebat potius litteras quam nesciebat, tamquam maiorem industriae et laboris gloriam habiturus
si ingenium eius nullis alienarum artium adminiculis inniti
videretur.

∾ *HISTORIAE 1.15, 1.16*
Galba's adoption of Piso

'si te privatus lege curiata apud pontifi-   1.15
ces, ut moris est, adoptarem, et mihi egregium erat Cn.
Pompei et M. Crassi subolem in penatis meos adsciscere, et
tibi insigne Sulpiciae ac Lutatiae decora nobilitati tuae adie-
5 cisse: nunc me deorum hominumque consensu ad imperium
vocatum praeclara indoles tua et amor patriae impulit ut
principatum, de quo maiores nostri armis certabant, bello
adeptus quiescenti offeram, exemplo divi Augusti qui sororis filium Marcellum, dein generum Agrippam, mox nepotes
10 suos, postremo Tiberium Neronem privignum in proximo
sibi fastigio conlocavit. sed Augustus in domo successorem
quaesivit, ego in re publica, non quia propinquos aut socios
belli non habeam, sed neque ipse imperium ambitione accepi,
et iudicii mei documentum sit non meae tantum necessitudi-
15 nes, quas tibi postposui, sed et tuae.'

        *   *   *

'Si immensum imperii corpus stare ac librari sine re-   16
ctore posset, dignus eram a quo res publica inciperet: nunc
eo necessitatis iam pridem ventum est ut nec mea senectus
conferre plus populo Romano possit quam bonum successo-
20 rem, nec tua plus iuventa quam bonum principem. sub Tiberio et Gaio et Claudio unius familiae quasi hereditas fui-
mus: loco libertatis erit quod eligi coepimus; et finita Iuliorum
Claudiorumque domo optimum quemque adoptio inveniet.
nam generari et nasci a principibus fortuitum, nec ultra ae-

25 stimatur: adoptandi iudicium integrum et, si velis eligere,

consensu monstratur.'

ᴗᴥ *HISTORIAE 1.41, 1.49*
Galba's assassination and obituary

Viso comminus armatorum agmine vexillarius comi-   1.41

tatae Galbam cohortis (Atilium Vergilionem fuisse tradunt)

dereptam Galbae imaginem solo adflixit: eo signo manifesta

in Othonem omnium militum studia, desertum fuga populi

5 forum, destricta adversus dubitantis tela. iuxta Curtii la-

cum trepidatione ferentium Galba proiectus e sella ac pro-

volutus est. extremam eius vocem, ut cuique odium aut ad-

miratio fuit, varie prodidere. alii suppliciter interogasse

quid mali meruisset, paucos dies exolvendo donativo depre-

10 catum:plures obtulisse ultro percussoribus iugulum: age-

rent ac ferirent, si ita e re publica videretur. non interfuit

occidentium quid diceret. de percussore non satis constat:

quidam Terentium evocatum, alii Laecanium; crebrior fama

tradidit Camurium quintae decimae legionis militem impresso

15 gladio iugulum eius hausisse. ceteri crura brachiaque (nam

pectus tegebatur) foede laniavere; pleraque vulnera feritate

et saevitia trunco iam corpori adiecta.

*   *   *

hunc exitum habuit Servius Galba, tribus et septua-   49

ginta annis quinque principes prospera fortuna emensus et

20 alieno imperio felicior quam suo. vetus in familia nobilitas,

magnae opes: ipsi medium ingenium, magis extra vitia quam

cum virtutibus. famae nec incuriosus nec venditator; pecuniae alienae non adpetens, suae parcus, publicae avarus;
amicorum libertorumque, ubi in bonos incidisset, sine re-
25 prehensione patiens, si mali forent, usque ad culpam igna-
rus. sed claritas natalium et metus temporum obtentui, ut,
quod segnitia erat, sapientia vocaretur. dum vigebat aetas
militari laude apud Germanias floruit. pro consule Africam
moderate, iam senior citeriorem Hispaniam pari iustitia con-
30 tinuit, maior privato visus dum privatus fuit, et omnium consensu capax imperii nisi imperasset.

❧ *Historiae* 3.82–83

Street fighting between Vitellians and Flavians and the degradation of the city

concurrere et in campo   3.82
Martio infestae acies. pro Flavianis fortuna et parta totiens
victoria: Vitelliani desperatione sola ruebant, et quamquam
pulsi, rursus in urbe congregabantur.

5 Aderat pugnantibus spectator populus, utque in lu-   83
dicro certamine, hos, rursus illos clamore et plausu fovebat.
quotiens pars altera inclinasset, abditos in tabernis aut si
quam in domum perfugerant, erui iugularique expostulantes
parte maiore praedae potiebantur: nam milite ad sanguinem
10 et caedis obverso spolia in vulgus cedebant. saeva ac de-
formis urbe tota facies: alibi proelia et vulnera, alibi bali-
neae popinaeque; simul cruor et strues corporum, iuxta
scorta et scortis similes; quantum in luxurioso otio libidinum, quidquid in acerbissima captivitate scelerum, prorsus

15 ut eandem civitatem et furere crederes et lascivere. conflixe-
rant ante armati exercitus in urbe, bis Lucio Sulla, semel
Cinna victoribus, nec tunc minus crudelitas: nunc inhumana securitas et ne minimo quidem temporis voluptates
intermissae: velut festis diebus id quoque gaudium accede-
20 ret, exultabant, fruebantur, nulla partium cura, malis publicis laeti.

ꙮ *ANNALES 1.1*
Tacitus' introduction and qualifications as a historian

Urbem Romam a principio reges habuere; libertatem   1.1
et consulatum L. Brutus instituit. dictaturae ad tempus su-
mebantur; neque decemviralis potestas ultra biennium, neque
tribunorum militum consulare ius diu valuit. non Cinnae,
5 non Sullae longa dominatio; et Pompei Crassique potentia
cito in Caesarem, Lepidi atque Antonii arma in Augustum
cessere, qui cuncta discordiis civilibus fessa nomine principis
sub imperium accepit. sed veteris populi Romani prospera
vel adversa claris scriptoribus memorata sunt; temporibus-
10 que Augusti dicendis non defuere decora ingenia, donec
gliscente adulatione deterrerentur. Tiberii Gaique et
Claudii ac Neronis res florentibus ipsis ob metum falsae,
postquam occiderant recentibus odiis compositae sunt.
inde consilium mihi pauca de Augusto et extrema tradere,
15 mox Tiberii principatum et cetera, sine ira et studio, quorum
causas procul habeo.

◌ *ANNALES* 1.9–10

The funeral of Augustus and two views of his principate

at   1.9

apud prudentis vita eius varie extollebatur arguebaturve.

hi pietate erga parentem et necessitudine rei publicae, in

qua nullus tunc legibus locus, ad arma civilia actum quae

5   neque parari possent neque haberi per bonas artis. multa

Antonio, dum interfectores patris ulcisceretur, multa Lepido

concessisse. postquam hic socordia senuerit, ille per libi-

dines pessum datus sit, non aliud discordantis patriae reme-

dium fuisse quam ut ab uno regeretur. non regno tamen

10   neque dictatura sed principis nomine constitutam rem pu-

blicam; mari Oceano aut amnibus longinquis saeptum im-

perium; legiones, provincias, classis, cuncta inter se conexa;

ius apud civis, modestiam apud socios; urbem ipsam ma-

gnifico ornatu; pauca admodum vi tractata quo ceteris

15   quies esset.

Speaking against duty towards parents & times

Dicebatur contra: pietatem erga parentem et tem-   10

public things takes pretext moreover enthusiasm

pora rei publicae obtentui sumpta: ceterum cupidine domi-

provokes tyranny by bribing veterans.

nandi concitos per largitionem veteranos, paratum ab

adulescente privato exercitum, corruptas consulis legiones,

20   simulatam Pompeianarum gratiam partium; mox ubi decreto

patrum fascis et ius praetoris invaserit, caesis Hirtio et

Pansa, sive hostis illos, seu Pansam venenum vulneri ad-

fusum, sui milites Hirtium et machinator doli Caesar abstu-

lerat, utriusque copias occupavisse; extortum invito senatu

25   consulatum, armaque quae in Antonium acceperit contra

rem publicam versa; proscriptionem civium, divisiones
agrorum ne ipsis quidem qui fecere laudatas. sane Cassii
et Brutorum exitus paternis inimicitiis datos, quamquam
fas sit privata odia publicis utilitatibus remittere: sed Pom-
30 peium imagine pacis, sed Lepidum specie amicitiae deceptos;
post Antonium, Tarentino Brundisinoque foedere et nuptiis
sororis inlectum, subdolae adfinitatis poenas morte exsolvisse. pacem sine dubio post haec, verum cruentam:
Lollianas Varianasque cladis, interfectos Romae Varrones,
35 Egnatios, Iullos. nec domesticis abstinebatur: abducta
Neroni uxor et consulti per ludibrium pontifices an concepto necdum edito partu rite nuberet;
Vedii Pollionis luxus; postremo Livia gravis in rem publicam mater, gravis domui Caesarum noverca. nihil deorum
40 honoribus relictum cum se templis et effigie numinum per
flamines et sacerdotes coli vellet. ne Tiberium quidem
caritate aut rei publicae cura successorem adscitum, sed
quoniam adrogantiam saevitiamque eius introspexerit, comparatione deterrima sibi gloriam quaesivisse. etenim Augu-
45 stus paucis ante annis, cum Tiberio tribuniciam potestatem
a patribus rursum postularet, quamquam honora oratione,
quaedam de habitu cultuque et institutis eius iecerat quae
velut excusando exprobraret.

∾ *ANNALES 1.74*

Romanius Hispo's prosecution of Granius Marcellus and the rise of the DELATORES

Nec multo post Granium Marcellum praetorem Bi-   1.74
thyniae quaestor ipsius Caepio Crispinus maiestatis postulavit, subscribente Romanio Hispone: qui formam vitae
iniit, quam postea celebrem miseriae temporum et audaciae
5   hominum fecerunt. nam egens, ignotus, inquies, dum occultis libellis saevitiae principis adrepit, mox clarissimo
cuique periculum facessit, potentiam apud unum, odium
apud omnis adeptus dedit exemplum, quod secuti ex pau-
peribus divites, ex contemptis metuendi perniciem aliis ac
10 postremum sibi invenere. sed Marcellum insimulabat
sinistros de Tiberio sermones habuisse, inevitabile crimen,
cum ex moribus principis foedissima quaeque deligeret accusator obiectaretque reo. nam quia vera erant, etiam dicta
credebantur. addidit Hispo statuam Marcelli altius quam
15 Caesarum sitam, et alia in statua amputato capite Augusti
effigiem Tiberii inditam.

∾ *ANNALES 2.69*

Witchcraft, poison, and magic spells used against Germanicus

At Germanicus Aegypto remeans cuncta quae apud   2.69
legiones aut urbes iusserat abolita vel in contrarium versa
cognoscit. hinc graves in Pisonem contumeliae, nec minus
acerba quae ab illo in Caesarem intentabantur. dein Piso
5   abire Syria statuit. mox adversa Germanici valetudine

detentus, ubi recreatum accepit votaque pro incolumitate
solvebantur, admotas hostias, sacrificalem apparatum, festam
Antiochensium plebem per lictores proturbat. tum Seleu-
ciam degreditur, opperiens aegritudinem, quae rursum Ger-
10   manico acciderat. saevam vim morbi augebat persuasio
veneni a Pisone accepti; et reperiebantur solo ac parietibus
erutae humanorum corporum reliquiae, carmina et devotiones et nomen Germanici plumbeis tabulis insculptum,
semusti cineres ac tabo obliti aliaque malefica quis creditur
15   animas numinibus infernis sacrari. simul missi a Pisone
incusabantur ut valetudinis adversa rimantes.

∿ *ANNALES 4.1–2, 4.3*
The rise of Sejanus

C. Asinio C. Antistio consulibus nonus Tiberio annus   4.1
erat compositae rei publicae, florentis domus (nam Germanici mortem inter prospera ducebat), cum repente turbare
fortuna coepit, saevire ipse aut saevientibus viris praebere.
5   initium et causa penes Aelium Seianum cohortibus praetoriis praefectum cuius de potentia supra memoravi: nunc
originem, mores, et quo facinore dominationem raptum
ierit expediam. genitus Vulsiniis patre Seio Strabone equite
Romano, et prima iuventa Gaium Caesarem divi Augusti
10   nepotem sectatus, non sine rumore Apicio diviti et prodigo
stuprum veno dedisse, mox Tiberium variis artibus devinxit
adeo ut obscurum adversum alios sibi uni incautum inte-
ctumque efficeret, non tam sollertia (quippe isdem artibus
victus est) quam deum ira in rem Romanam, cuius pari

15 exitio viguit ceciditque. corpus illi laborum tolerans, animus
    audax; sui obtegens, in alios criminator; iuxta adulatio et
    superbia; palam compositus pudor, intus summa apiscendi
    libido, eiusque causa modo largitio et luxus, saepius in-
    dustria ac vigilantia, haud minus noxiae, quotiens parando
20 regno finguntur.

     Vim praefecturae modicam antea intendit, dispersas   2
    per urbem cohortis una in castra conducendo, ut simul
    imperia acciperent numeroque et robore et visu inter se
    fiducia ipsis, in ceteros metus oreretur. praetendebat lasci-
25 vire militem didictum; si quid subitum ingruat, maiore
    auxilio pariter subveniri; et severius acturos si vallum
    statuatur procul urbis inlecebris. ut perfecta sunt castra,
    inrepere paulatim militaris animos adeundo, appellando;
    simul centuriones ac tribunos ipse deligere. neque senato-
30 rio ambitu abstinebat clientes suos honoribus aut provinciis
    ornandi, facili Tiberio atque ita prono ut socium laborum
    non modo in sermonibus, sed apud patres et populum cele-
    braret colique per theatra et fora effigies eius interque
    principia legionum sineret.

         *   *   *

35   igitur cuncta temptanti promptis-   3
    simum visum ad uxorem eius Liviam convertere, quae soror
    Germanici, formae initio aetatis indecorae, mox pulchritu-
    dine praecellebat. hanc ut amore incensus adulterio pellexit,
    et postquam primi flagitii potitus est (neque femina amissa
40 pudicitia alia abnuerit), ad coniungii spem, consortium regni
    et necem mariti impulit. atque illa, cui avunculus Augustus,

socer Tiberius, ex Druso liberi, seque ac maiores et posteros
municipali adultero foedebat ut pro honestis et praesentibus
flagitiosa et incerta expectaret. sumitur in conscientiam
45 Eudemus, amicus ac medicus Liviae, specie artis frequens
secretis.

◌ *ANNALES 6.1*
Tiberius' debauchery on Capri

Cn. Domitius et Camillus Scribonianus consula-   6.1
tum inierant, cum Caesar tramisso quod Capreas et Surrentum interluit freto Campaniam praelegebat, ambiguus
an urbem intraret, seu, quia contra destinaverat, speciem
5 venturi simulans. et saepe in propinqua degressus, aditis
iuxta Tiberim hortis, saxa rursum et solitudinem maris
repetiit pudore scelerum et libidinum quibus adeo indomitis exarserat ut more regio pubem ingenuam stupris pollueret. nec formam tantum et decora corpora set in his
10 modestam pueritiam, in aliis imagines maiorum incitamentum cupidinis habebat. tuncque primum ignota antea
vocabula reperta sunt sellariorum et spintriarum ex foeditate loci ac multiplici patientia; praepositique servi qui conquirerent pertraherent, dona in promptos, minas adversum
15 abnuentis, et si retinerent propinquus aut parens, vim
raptus suaque ipsi libita velut in captos exercebant.

❧ *ANNALES 6.50–51*

Tiberius' death and obituary, and the succession of Caligula

septimum   6.50

decimum kal. Aprilis interclusa anima creditus est mortalitatem explevisse; et multo gratantum concursu ad capienda
imperii primordia G. Caesar egrediebatur, cum repente
5   adfertur redire Tiberio vocem ac visus vocarique qui recreandae defectioni cibum adferrent. pavor hinc in omnis,
et ceteri passim dispergi, se quisque maestum aut nescium
fingere; Caesar in silentium fixus a summa spe novissima
expectabat. Macro intrepidus opprimi senem iniectu multae
10   vestis iubet discedique ab limine. sic Tiberius finivit octavo
et septuagesimo aetatis anno.

Pater ei Nero et utrimque origo gentis Claudiae,   51
quamquam mater in Liviam et mox Iuliam familiam adoptionibus transierit. casus prima ab infantia ancipites; nam
15   proscriptum patrem exul secutus, ubi domum Augusti pri-
vignus introiit, multis aemulis conflictatus est, dum Marcellus
et Agrippa, mox Gaius Luciusque Caesares viguere; etiam
frater eius Drusus prosperiore civium amore erat. sed
maxime in lubrico egit accepta in matrimonium Iulia, impu-
20   dicitiam uxoris tolerans aut declinans. dein Rhodo regressus
vacuos principis penatis duodecim annis, mox rei Romanae
arbitrium tribus ferme et viginti obtinuit. morum quoque
tempora illi diversa: egregium vita famaque quoad privatus
vel in imperiis sub Augusto fuit; occultum ac subdolum
25   fingendis virtutibus donec Germanicus ac Drusus super-

fuere; idem inter bona malaque mixtus incolumni matre;

intestabilis saevitia sed obtectis libidinibus dum Seianum

dilexit timuitve: postremo in scelera simul ac dedecora prorupit

postquam remoto pudore et metu suo tantum ingenio

30   utebatur.

◌ *ANNALES 11.24*
Claudius' speech on allowing Gauls into the Senate

'maiores   11.24

mei, quorum antiquissimus Clausus origine Sabina simul in

civitatem Romanam et in familias patriciorum adscitus est,

hortantur uti paribus consiliis in re publica capessenda,

5   transferendo huc quod usquam egregium fuerit. neque enim

ignoro Iulios Alba, Coruncanios Camerio, Porcios Tusculo,

et ne vetera scrutemur, Etruria Lucaniaque et omni Italia

in senatum accitos, postremo ipsam ad Alpis promotam ut

non modo singuli viritim, sed terrae, gentes in nomen

10   nostrum coalescerent. tunc solida domi quies et adversus

externa floruimus, cum Transpadani in civitatem recepti,

cum specie deductarum per orbem terrae legionum additis

provincialium validissimis fesso imperio subventum est. num

paenitet Balbos ex Hispania nec minus insignis viros e Gallia

15   Narbonensi transivisse? manent posteri eorum nec amore in

hanc patriam nobis concedunt. quid aliud exitio Lacedae-

moniis et Atheniensibus fuit, quamquam armis pollerent,

nisi quod victos pro alienigenis arcebant? at conditor nostri

Romulus tantum sapientia valuit ut plerosque populos eodem

20   die hostis, dein civis habuerit. advenae in nos regnaverunt:

libertinorum filiis magistratus mandare non, ut plerique

falluntur, repens, sed priori populo factitatum est. at cum

Senonibus pugnavimus: scilicet Vulsci et Aequi numquam

adversam nobis aciem instruxere. capti a Gallis sumus:

25 sed et Tuscis obsides dedimus et Samnitium iugum subiimus.

ac tamen, si cuncta bella recenseas, nullum breviore spatio

quam adversus Gallos confectum: continua inde ac fida pax.

iam moribus artibus adfinitatibus nostris mixti aurum et opes

suas inferant potius quam separati habeant. omnia, patres

30 conscripti, quae nunc vetustissima creduntur, nova fuere:

plebeii magistratus post patricios, Latini post plebeios,

ceterarum Italiae gentium post Latinos. inveterascet hoc

quoque, et quod hodie exemplis tuemur, inter exempla

erit.'

∾ *ANNALES 11.29–30*
Messalina's fall, Part I: Her adulteries and conspiracy revealed

ipse ad   11.29

occasiones intentus, longa apud Ostiam Caesaris mora, duas

paelices, quarum is corpori maxime insueverat, largitione ac

promissis et uxore deiecta plus potentiae ostentando perpulit

5 delationem subire.

Exim Calpurnia (id paelici nomen), ubi datum   30

secretum, genibus Caesaris provoluta nupsisse Messalinam

Silio exclamat; simul Cleopatram, quae id opperiens

adstabat, an comperisset interrogat, atque illa adnuente cieri

10 Narcissum postulat. is veniam in praeteritum petens quod

ei Vettios, Plautios dissimulavisset, nec nunc adulteria
obiecturum ait, ne domum servitia et ceteros fortunae
paratus reposceret. frueretur immo his set redderet uxorem
rumperetque tabulas nuptialis. 'an discidium' inquit 'tuum
15 nosti? nam matrimonium Silii vidit populus et senatus et
miles; ac ni propere agis, tenet urbem maritus.'

∾ ANNALES 11.31–32
Messalina's fall, Part II: Her nuptial celebrations with Silius

at Messalina non alias solutior luxu, adulto autumno   11.31
simulacrum vindemiae per domum celebrabat. urgeri prela,
fluere lacus; et feminae pellibus accinctae adsultabant ut
sacrificantes vel insanientes Bacchae; ipsa crine fluxo
5   thyrsum quatiens, iuxtaque Silius hedera vinctus, gerere
cothurnos, iacere caput, strepente circum procaci choro.
ferunt Vettium Valentem lascivia in praealtam arborem
conisum, interrogantibus quid aspiceret, respondisse tempestatem ab Ostia atrocem, sive coeperat ea species, seu forte
10 lapsa vox in praesagium vertit.

Non rumor interea, sed undique nuntii incedunt, qui   32
gnara Claudio cuncta et venire promptum ultioni adferrent.
igitur Messalina Lucullianos in hortos, Silius dissimulando
metu ad munia fori digrediuntur. ceteris passim dilabentibus
15 adfuere centuriones, inditaque sunt vincla, ut quis reperie-
batur in publico aut per latebras. Messalina tamen, quamquam res adversae consilium eximerent, ire obviam et aspici a
marito, quod saepe subsidium habuerat, haud segniter intendit

misitque ut Britannicus et Octavia in complexum patris
20 pergerent. et Vibidiam, virginum Vestalium vetustissimam,
oravit pontificis maximi auris adire, clementiam expetere.
atque interim, tribus omnino comitantibus — id repente
solitudinis erat — spatium urbis pedibus emensa, vehiculo,
quo purgamenta hortorum eripiuntur, Ostiensem viam intrat
25 nulla cuiusquam misericordia quia flagitiorum deformitas
praevalebat.

ᐁ *ANNALES 11.37–38*
Messalina's fall, Part III: Her execution

Interim Messalina Lucullianis in hortis prolatare   11.37
vitam, componere preces, non nulla spe et aliquando ira:
tantum inter extrema superbiae gerebat. ac ni caedem eius
Narcissus properavisset, verterat pernicies in accusatorem.
5 nam Claudius domum regressus et tempestivis epulis dele-
nitus, ubi vino incaluit, iri iubet nuntiarique miserae (hoc
enim verbo usum ferunt) dicendam ad causam postera die
adesset. quod ubi auditum et languescere ira, redire amor
ac, si cunctarentur, propinqua nox et uxorii cubiculi memoria
10 timebantur, prorumpit Narcissus denuntiatque centurionibus
et tribuno, qui aderat, exequi caedem: ita imperatorem
iubere. custos et exactor e libertis Euodus datur; isque
raptim in hortos praegressus repperit fusam humi, adsidente
matre Lepida, quae florenti filiae haud concors supremis
15 eius necessitatibus ad miserationem evicta erat suadebatque
ne percurssorem opperiretur: transisse vitam neque aliud
quam morti decus quaerendum. sed animo per libidines

corrupto nihil honestum inerat; lacrimaeque et questus inriti

ducebantur, cum impetu venientium pulsae fores adstititque

20 tribunus per silentium, at libertus increpans multis et

servilibus probris.

Tunc primum fortunam suam introspexit ferrumque   38

accepit, quod frustra iugulo aut pectori per trepidationem

admovens ictu tribuni transigitur. corpus matri concessum.

25 nuntiatumque Claudio epulanti perisse Messalinam, non

distincto sua an aliena manu. nec ille quaesivit, poposcitque

poculum et solita convivio celebravit. ne secutis quidem

diebus odii gaudii, irae tristiae, ullius denique humani

adfectus signa dedit, non cum laetantis accusatores aspiceret,

30 non cum filios maerentis.

❧ *ANNALES 14.4–6*

Nero's matricide, Part I: The collapsible boat

iam pluribus sermonibus modo   14.4

familiaritate iuvenili Nero et rursus adductus, quasi seria

consociaret, tracto in longum convictu, prosequitur abeun-

tem, artius oculis et pectori haerens, sive explenda simu-

5 latione, seu periturae matris supremus aspectus quamvis

ferum animum retinebat.

Noctem sideribus inlustrem et placido mari quietam   5

quasi convincendum ad scelus dii praebuere. nec multum

erat progressa navis, duobus e numero familiarium Agrip-

10 pinam comitantibus, ex quis Crepereius Gallus haud procul

gubernaculis adstabat, Acerronia super pedes cubitantis

reclinis paenitentiam filii et reciperatam matris gratiam per

gaudium memorabat, cum dato signo ruere tectum loci
multo plumbo grave, pressusque Crepereius et statim exani-
15 matus est: Agrippina et Acerronia eminentibus lecti parietibus ac forte validioribus quam ut oneri cederent protectae
sunt. nec dissolutio navigii sequebatur, turbatis omnibus
et quod plerique ignari etiam conscios impediebant. visum
dehinc remigibus unum in latus inclinare atque ita navem
20 submergere: sed neque ipsis promptus in rem subitam consensus, et alii contra nitentes dedere facultatem lenioris in
mare iactus. verum Acerronia, imprudentia dum se Agrippinam esse utque subveniretur matri principis clamitat,
contis et remis et quae fors obtulerat navalibus telis con-
25 ficitur: Agrippina silens eoque minus adgnita (unum tamen
vulnus umero excepit) nando, deinde occursu lenunculorum
Lucrinum in lacum vecta villae suae infertur.

Illic reputans ideo se fallacibus litteris accitam et   6
honore praecipuo habitam, quodque litus iuxta non ventis
30 acta, non saxis impulsa navis summa sui parte veluti terrestre
machinamentum concidisset; observans etiam Acerroniae
necem, simul suum vulnus aspiciens, solum insidiarum
remedium esse, si non intellegerentur; misitque libertum
Agerinum qui nuntiaret filio benignitate deum et fortuna
35 eius evasisse gravem casum; orare ut quamvis periculo
matris exterritus visendi curam differret; sibi ad praesens
quiete opus.

∾ *ANNALES 14.8*
Nero's matricide, Part II: Agrippina's murder

Anicetus villam statione cir-   14.8
cumdat refractaque ianua obvios servorum abripit, donec ad
foris cubiculi veniret; cui pauci adstabant, ceteris terrore
inrumpentium exterritis. cubiculo modicum lumen inerat
5   et ancillarum una, magis ac magis anxia Agrippina quod
nemo a filio ac ne Agerinus quidem: aliam fore laetae rei
faciem; nunc solitudinem ac repetinos strepitus et extremi
mali indicia. abeunte dehinc ancilla 'tu quoque me deseris'
prolocuta respicit Anicetum trierarcho Herculeio et Obarito
10 centurione classiario comitatum: ac, si ad visendum venisset,
refotam nuntiaret, sin facinus patraturus, nihil se de filio
credere; non imperatum parricidium. circumsistunt lectum
percurssores et prior trierarchus fusti caput eius adflixit. iam
in mortem centurioni ferrum destringenti protendens uterum
15 'ventrem feri' exclamavit multisque vulneribus confecta est.

*

∾ *ANNALES 15.38*
The great fire of 64 CE

Sequitur clades, forte an dolo principis incertum   15.38
(nam utrumque auctores prodidere), sed omnibus quae huic
urbi per violentiam ignium acciderunt gravior atque atrocior.
initium in ea parte circi ortum quae Palatino Caelioque
5   montibus contigua est, ubi per tabernas, quibus id mercimonium inerat quo flamma alitur, simul coeptus ignis et
statim validus ac vento citus longitudinem circi corripuit.

neque enim domus munimentis saeptae vel templa muris
cincta aut quid aliud morae interiacebat. impetu perva-
10 gatum incendium plana primum, deinde in edita adsurgens
et rursus inferiora populando, antiit remedia velocitate mali
et obnoxia urbe artis itineribus hucque et illuc flexis atque
enormibus vicis, qualis vetus Roma fuit. ad hoc lamenta
paventium feminarum, fessa aetate aut rudis pueritiae,
15 quique sibi quique aliis consulebant, dum trahunt
invalidos aut opperiuntur, pars mora, pars festinans, cuncta
impediebant. et saepe dum in tergum respectant lateribus
aut fronte circumveniebantur, vel si in proxima evaserant,
illis quoque igni correptis, etiam quae longinqua crediderant
20 in eodem casu reperiebant. postremo, quid vitarent quid
peterent ambigui, complere vias, sterni per agros; quidam
amissis omnibus fortunis, diurni quoque victus, alii caritate
suorum, quos eripere nequiverant, quamvis patente effugio
interiere. nec quisquam defendere audebat, crebris multorum
25 minis restinguere prohibentium, et quia alii palam faces
iaciebant atque esse sibi auctorem vociferabantur, sive ut
raptus licentius exercerent seu iussu.

✆ ANNALES 15.44
The persecution of the Christians after the fire

      sed non ope humana,   15.44
non largitionibus principis aut deum placamentis decedebat
infamia quin iussum incendium crederetur. ergo abolendo
rumori Nero subdidit reos et quaesitissimis poenis adfecit
5 quos per flagitia invisos vulgus Christianos appellabat.

auctor nominis eius Christus Tiberio imperitante per
procuratorem Pontium Pilatum supplicio adfectus erat;
repressaque in praesens exitiabilis superstitio rursum
erumpebat, non modo per Iudaeam, originem eius mali,

10   sed per urbem etiam quo cuncta undique atrocia aut
pudenda confluunt celebranturque. igitur primum correpti
qui fatebantur, deinde indicio eorum multitudo ingens
haud proinde in crimine incendii quam odio humani
generis convicti sunt. et pereuntibus addita ludibria, ut

15   ferarum tergis contecti laniatu canum interirent, aut cruci-
bus adfixi aut flammandi, atque ubi defecisset dies in
usum nocturni luminis urerentur. hortos suos ei spectaculo
Nero obtulerat et circense ludicrum edebat, habitu aurigae
permixtus plebi vel curriculo insistens. unde quamquam

20   adversus sontis et novissima exempla meritos miseratio
oriebatur, tamquam non utilitate publica sed in saevitiam
unius absumerentur.

Commentary

∾ AGRICOLA 2.1–3.2

The tyranny of Domitian and the advent of Nerva and Trajan

The *Agricola*, Tacitus' biography of his father-in-law Cn. Julius Agricola, is his earliest work to survive, written in 97–98 (based on 3.1 where it appears Nerva is still alive, and 44.5, where Trajan is referred to as *princeps*; Ogilvie and Richmond 1967, 10–11). While its central focus is Agricola and his campaigns in Britain between 78 and 84, Tacitus uses its preface to extol the more open and free environment under Nerva and his designated successor, Trajan, and to lament poignantly the long period of tyranny and enforced silence under Domitian (81–96 CE). The nature of freedom—*libertas*—under the rule of the emperors is a central issue Tacitus explores throughout his writings, and looks forward to the *libertas* that he notes was established with the Republic (*Ann.* 1.1), but ceased with the Principate (*Hist.* 1.1). This first work consequently establishes an important concern for Tacitus, and its significance is one much discussed by scholars (see Wirszubski 1950, 123–43; Hammond 1963, 93–113; Morford 1991, 3420–449; and most recently Sailor's outstanding discussion of the work's preface, 2008, 51–72). As the passage makes clear, Tacitus believes that both senatorial and human dignity in general can be reconciled to the rule of the *princeps*, provided that the emperor shows respect for senatorial freedom.

1   **Auruleno Rustico** Q. Aurulenus Junius Rusticus was a member of the so-called Stoic Opposition (see Tac. *Ann.* 16.24; Cass. Dio 67.13; Plin. *Ep.* 1.5.2; Brunt 1975, 7–35), a small group of senators related through family connections; they took a

stand, based on Stoic principles, against the more tyrannical emperors starting with Nero. For his execution in 93 and his work on Thrasea see Suet. *Dom.* 10.3. Aurulenus, along with Thrasea Paetus, Herennius Senecio, and Helvidius Priscus, had family ties with one another, as well as their opposition to the *princeps* in common. There is an orthoghraphical variant on his name, which is given as Arulenus at *Ann.* 16.26.

Paetus Thrasea His actual name was Thrasea Paetus. Tacitus frequently reverses the position of names for the sake of *variatio* (see p. xxxvii), placing the cognomen first and the nomen second. Thrasea was a senator who had incurred the enmity of Nero and his minister Cossutianus Capito by, among other things, protesting Agrippina's murder by walking out of the Senate (*Ann.* 14.12); he was prosecuted and committed suicide in 66 (*Ann.* 16.21–22, 16.24–29, 16.33–35).

1–2 **Herennio Senecioni** Originally from Baetica in Hispania, Herennius Senecio was a member of the Stoic Opposition. An up-and-coming senator, he had prosecuted Baebius Massa (later an instrument of Domitian, *Agr.* 45.1) for corruption in Baetica (Plin. *Ep.* 7.33.4–8). Mettius Carus later prosecuted Herennius for writing a life of Helvidius Priscus based on *commentarii* supplied to him by Helvidius' widow Fannia (Plin. *Ep.* 7.19.5).

2 **Priscus Helvidius** Again the name is reversed. He was Thrasea Paetus' son-in-law and forced into exile by Nero at the same time Thrasea was condemned. Outspoken against Nero, his ministers (Tac. *Hist.* 4.4–6, 43), and Vespasian as well (Dio 66.12), his fierce independence ultimately resulted in his execution. His own son, Helvidius Priscus the Younger, went on to hold a suffect consulship in 92 under Domitian, though he too was executed under mysterious circumstances, possibly due to his composition of a parody against Domitian (Suet. *Dom.* 10.4).

laudati essent plpf. subjunctive in a subordinate clause in indirect discourse

Fig. 1. Domitian was the son of the emperor Vespasian and Tacitus' great nemesis. It was the tyranny late in Domitian's reign that influenced Tacitus' sometimes grim view of power and the Principate. Capitoline Museums, Rome. Wikimedia Commons.

3–4   **in . . . saevitum** sometimes used impersonally in Tacitus with the prep. *in* + the acc.; e.g., *Ann.* 4.20, *saevitum tamen in bona* (with *esse* omitted)

4   **delegato . . . ministerio** abl. absolute, with *ministerio* translated here "duty"

       triumviris dat. pl.; a commission of three men in charge of imposing capital sentences

monumenta for a literary work as a *monumentum* cf. Hor. *Carm.* 3.33.1; for history as a public *monumentum* see Marincola (1997, 57–62)

5   **clarissimorum ingeniorum** "of most illustrious talents"; reflects the opening of the work that starts *clarorum virorum facta*, which borrows from the opening of Cato's *Origines*.

urerentur impf. subjunctive in a purpose clause

6   **illo igne** abl. of means

6–7   **vocem . . . libertatem . . . conscientiam . . . aboleri arbitrabantur** All are subject acc. in indirect discourse with *aboleri*, a pres. pass. infinitive, as the main verb in indirect discourse after *arbitrabantur*. For a similar expression see *Ann.* 4.35 and the burning of Cremutius Cordus' works, *credunt extingui posse etiam sequentis aevi memoriam.*

8   **expulsis insuper sapientiae professoribus** *expulsis . . . professoribus* is an abl. absolute; *insuper* is adverbial here, "besides." Domitian expelled and persecuted philosophers, particularly those who had Stoic sympathies; see Plin. *Ep.* 3.11.2; Suet. *Dom.* 10.3–4; Cass. Dio 67.13.3.

8–9   **atque omni bona arte in exilium acta** a continuation of the abl. absolute in line 8; *bona arte* here refers not to technical skill, but to the quality of one's character and intellect; cf., e.g., *Ann.* 5.1, (Livia) *uxor facilis et cum artibus mariti.* Ogilvie and Richmond (1967, 135) note that Tacitus' usage of *bonae artes* draws on Sallust *Cat.* 10.4 and *Iug.* 1.3.

9   **in exilium** acc. of motion towards with the prep. *in*

quid usquam honestum *quid* after *ne* in a result clause is translated as an indef. pron. modified by *honestum*, "honorable," "of good repute"

occurreret impf. subjunctive in a purpose clause, "be found"; cf. *Ann.* 14.53 *una defensio occurrit quod muneribus tuis obniti debui*

11   **vetus aetas vidit quid ultimum in libertate esset** *vetus aetas* is an abstract personification here (cf. *Agr.* 1.1, *incuriosa*

suorum aetas), "former age." *ultimum* arguably has a double meaning in this passage, referring both to the last period of the Republic when *libertas* still flourished and the ultimate extremes of violence in its waning days. For the chronological meaning of *ultimum* see, e.g., *Hist.* 1.11, *Galba iterum Vinius consules incohavere annum sibi ultimum*; for the sense of extremity see, e.g., *Ann.* 12.67, (Agrippina) *quando ultima timebantur, Xenophontis medici conscientiam adhibet.*

quid . . . esset impf. subjunctive in an indirect question

ita nos a brachylogy; understand *vidimus.*

12   **quid in servitute** The indirect question is here continued with the verb *esset* omitted.

12–13   **adempto . . . commercio** abl. absolute

loquendi audiendique Both are gerunds.

12   **per inquisitiones** *per* + the acc. here indicates means or instrumentality.

13   **memoriam** Concerning the role of memory and survival in the *Agricola*'s preface, see Hayne's (2006) excellent discussion.

14   **perdidissemus** plpf. subjunctive in the apodosis of a mixed condition, the apodosis having the sense of past contrary to fact

14–15   **si tam . . . quam tacere** "if it were so much in our power to forget as to remain silent"

oblivisci quam tacere Both infinitives constitute the subject of *esset.*

16   **nunc demum redit animus** *animus* here could convey two meanings: "spirit" in the sense of courage, but also "opinion" in the sense of one's freedom now to express it.

16–18   **quamquam . . . miscuerit** a long concessive clause

16   **primo statim** *statim* is here to be taken closely with *beatissimi saeculi ortu. primo* and *statim* are together for emphasis (cf. *Hist.* 1.31); lit. "Although at first Nerva, immediately at the birth of a most happy period."

17   **beatissimi saeculi ortu** recalls Verg. *Ecl.* 4.5 (*saeclorum nas-
        citur ordo*); the phrase refers here to the advent of a new order
        under Nerva and Trajan. *ortu* is an abl. of time. For the reign
        of a *princeps* as a *saeculum* cf. Plin. *Ep.* 10.1.2; 10.97.2; cf. Tac.
        Agr. 44.5, <*non licuit*> *durare in hanc beatissimi saeculi lucem
        ac principem Traianum videre.*

        res olim dissociabiles The phrase is explained in the next
        line; *dissociabiles* is found only here in Tacitus.

18   **miscuerit** pf. subjunctive in a concessive clause

        augeatque pres. subjunctive conjoined by the enclitic *-que* to
        the previous concessive clause

19   **felicitatem temporum** "the happiness of the times"; cf. *Hist.*
        1.1; Pliny *Ep.* 10.58.7

        Nerva Traianus M. Ulpius Traianus took Nerva's name upon
        adoption (see p. xv)

19–21   **nec spem modo ac votum securitas publica, sed ipsius voti
        fiduciam ac robur adsumpserit** an example of Tacitean ob-
        scurity; take *spem . . . votum . . . fiduciam ac robur* as the direct
        objects of *adsumpserit*, with *securitas publica* as the subject.

21   **adsumpserit** pf. subjunctive as a part of the concessive clause
        with *quamquam* in line 16, which is completed in its sense in
        this line with *tamen*

        natura tamen infirmitatis humanae "nevertheless, due to
        the nature of human weakness"; *natura* is abl. of means with a
        causal sense (as is often the case in Tacitus).

22   **remedia** an example of the medical imagery found throughout
        Tacitus; cf. below ***Agr.* 30.2.11**, *a contactu dominationis*; also
        see, e.g., *Hist.* 1.2 (*infecti caedibus scopuli*); *Ann.* 11.6 where he
        refers to the *vis morborum* and *fori tabes* concerning *delatores*

        ut "as"

23   **ingenia studiaque** "talents and their pursuits"

23–24   **oppresseris . . . revocaveris** both fut. pf.

24   **facilius quam** indicating a compar. clause

24-25 **subit quippe etiam ipsius inertiae dulcedo** Here *subit* translates "comes over" ("us," understood) with *dulcedo*, "pleasantness," as the subject.

25 **invisa . . . desidia** nom. sing., subject of *amatur*

26-32 The structure of this long sentence begins with a rhetorical
interr., *quid*. The main structure is picked up first in the *si*
clause and runs as follows: *si (multi . . . promptissimus quisque)
interciderunt . . . pauci et (superstites) sumus . . . (exemptis) tot
annis quibus . . . (ad ipsos terminos) venimus.*

26 **quid** introduces a rhetorical question, "What, if etc."

per quindecim annos refers to the reign of Domitian and the
silence his tyranny imposed.

grande mortalis aevi spatium in apposition to *quindecim
annos*

27-28 **multi . . . promptissimus quisque . . . interciderunt** Take
both *multi* and *promptissimus quisque* as the subject of
interciderunt.

27 **fortuitis casibus** abl. of cause

promptissimus quisque "each who was most resolute"; refers
to those such as Aurulenus and Herennius mentioned above

saevitia abl. of means with a causal sense

28-29 **pauci . . . sumus** *pauci* is the subject of *sumus*.

28 **ut dixerim** "as I have said"; for the more standard *ut ita dicam*
see, e.g., *Germ.* 2.1; the pf. instead of the pres. subjunctive is
used here.

29 **aliorum . . . nostri superstites sumus** "we are survivors not
only of others but even of ourselves"; *aliorum* and *nostri* =
gen. with *superstites*; *nostri* here is the reflex. pron. referring
back to the subject of *sumus*.

29-30 **exemptis . . . annis** abl. absolute; translate *exemptis* "removed."

e media vita "from the midst of life"; abl. of separation. Tacitus was in his mid to late twenties when Domitian came to
power.

30-31 **ad senectutem . . . ad ipsos . . . terminos** acc. of motion to-
       wards with the prep. *ad*

30   **quibus** abl. of time when

31   **exactae aetatis**, "of life that has been finished," cf. Hor. *Carm.*
       3.33.1

❧ *AGRICOLA 30.1–5*
The speech of Calgacus at the battle of Mons Graupius

The battle of Mons Graupius (84 CE) was the climax of Agricola's
conquests. Here his barbarian opponent, Calgacus, whom Tacitus
portrays as the last defender of the Britons' freedom before the Romans' final and complete conquest of the island, exhorts his troops
prior to the battle. Tacitus, by having Calgacus speak frankly about
the oppressive nature of Roman domination and rapaciousness, uses
this opportunity to explore the nature of Rome's *imperium*. The oration, Tacitus' own creation, is one of several in Roman historians
giving the "barbarian" perspective, with echoes of those attributed
by Sallust to Micipsa and Adherbal (*Iug.* 10, 14), by Caesar to Crito-
gnatus (*BG* 7.77), and subsequently by Tacitus to Civilis (*Hist.* 4.32).
There are now several interesting discussions that consider the in-
teraction of Roman and "barbarian" identity in this speech; see Rutledge (2000, 86–92), Clarke (2001, 103–6), and Haynes (2004, 44–
45). As Clarke succinctly notes, Tacitus makes Calgacus' speech "a
masterpiece of Roman oratory: full of sententiae . . . [and] balanced
antithesis," which concludes with a "grand rhetorical crescendo"; in
other words, thoroughly Roman and thoroughly Tacitean.

2   **animus est** governs the accusatives that follow since *animus
       est* implies indirect discourse; here *animus = spes.*

2-3   **hodiernum diem consensumque vestrum** subject acc. in in-
       direct discourse; connects the events of the day to the single-
       mindedness of Rome's opponents that will mark the *initium
       libertatis*, with Calgacus optimistically asserting that the

outcome of the battle will favor the Britons, and mark the beginning of the ebb of Roman power on the island.

2   **consensumque** "combined action"; cf. *Germ.* 31.1

3   **fore** the fut. infinitive of *sum* in indirect discourse

3–5   **nam . . . Romana** Note the striking juxtaposition of language emphasizing simultaneously their current freedom from servitude followed by the *ac* that points to their imminent danger.

4   **coistis** = *coivistis*

    servitutis gen. governed by *expertes*

    nullae ultra terrae Supply *sunt*; the phrase illustrates the scope of Agricola's, hence Rome's, conquest to the very edges of civilization; the remoteness of the Britons is emphasized several times in the speech (see lines 12–15).

    ultra an adv. here

5   **inminente nobis classe Romana** *nobis* is dat. after *inminente* in an abl. absolute. Both here and in line 16 what remains beyond (*ultra*) for the Britons is not merely sea and/or rock, but the menace of Rome.

6–7   **ita . . . sunt** an example of the sort of jarring and surprising contrast Tacitus uses to form an unexpected relationship between two opposing qualities (*fortibus . . . ignavis*)

    fortibus . . . ignavis m. pl. dat. substantives creating an antithesis and depending on *honesta* and *tutissima*

7   **priores pugnae** here a personification

    quibus abl. of means referring to *pugnae*

8   **varia fortuna** Take as an abl. of manner. The *varia fortuna* of the *priores pugnae* refers to those battles fought against Agricola after he took up his command in 78. Tacitus gives a year-by-year description of his campaigns in chapters 18–27.

    certatum est a pf. pass.; the verb is used as an impersonal several times in Tacitus; see, e.g., *Hist.* 1.70, *ubicumque certatum foret*; cf. *Agr.* 36.1.

10   **eoque** an abl. of cause connecting the fact that they are *nobil-
      issimi* by virtue of their keeping even their eyes averted from
      tyranny (*a contactu dominationis*)

      penetralibus here used metaphorically; cf. Tac. *Dial.* 12.1
      (*haec eloquentiae primordia, haec penetralia*)

      servientium "the servile"; a substantive referring to the Gauls

11   **a contactu dominationis** another instance of medical imag-
      ery; cf. above, p. 34, note to line 22

      dominationis The word in Tacitus has the sense of absolute
      tyrannical power; see, e.g., *Ann.* 1.1 and p. 72 below.

12   **nos terrarum ac libertatis extremos** Note the connection be-
      tween the political, the geographic, and the ethnographic; the
      Britons are not only the last people on earth, but the last to
      enjoy freedom from Roman domination.

      extremos "situated at the edge"; the adj. governs the gen. *ter-
      rarum ac libertatis*

13   **recessus ipse ac sinus famae** Take together as hendiadys, "the
      very refuge and tract of rumor"; the phrase is an obscure one,
      an example of Tacitean compression

14   **terminus** Tacitus again emphasizes the remote and distant
      nature of Agricola's conquest at the very end of Britain.

      omne ignotum pro magnifico a brief *sententia*; *ignotum* and
      magnifico are both adjectives used as substantives.

      pro magnifico "as something magnificent"

15   **nulla iam ultra gens** a rhetorical echo of *nullae ultra terrae* in
      line 4

16–17 **obsequium ac modestiam** The phrase is repeated almost ver-
      batim at *Agr.* 42.4, where Tacitus notes that there can be great
      men under bad emperors who can earn their share of praise if
      obsequiumque ac modestiam are present in conjunction with
      industria ac vigor.

17   **effugias** potential subjunctive

18   **cuncta vastantibus defuere terrae** *defuere* = *defuerunt*; *terrae* is the subject.

 cuncta the direct object of *vastantibus*

 vastantibus substantive dat., the direct object of *defuere*

19   **locuples . . . pauper** the first in a close grouping here of antitheses in the next two lines

19–20   **non Oriens, non Occidens** an antithesis in anaphora

20   **satiaverit** a fut. pf.

 omnium gen. pl.; take with *soli*.

20–21   **opes atque inopiam** the last of three antitheses within as many lines

21   **auferre trucidare rapere** Note the tricolon in asyndeton of which Tacitus is fond (cf. *Ann.* 4.49, *pollui cuncta sanie, odore, contactu*). Here the three verbs function as substantives, as though the actions are being quoted ("to steal, to butcher, to pillage, they call empire"). It constitutes one of the most famous lines from the Tacitean corpus, is emblematic of his sententious or pointed style, and arguably the speech's climax.

 pari adfectu abl. of manner

22   **falsis nominibus** abl. of manner with both *imperium* and *pacem*; cf. Tac. *Hist.* 1.37

∾ GERMANIA *1.1, 2.1–2*

A description of Germany and the origins of the Germans

The *Germani* was the collective name the Romans gave to the tribes of the two provinces of Upper and Lower Germany, the provinces of Raetia and Noricum, and to those who lived beyond Rome's borders in north, central, and eastern Europe. The Germans made up a series of tribes that went by various names in Tacitus' time; of these among the most renowned were the Teutones, Cimbri, Suebi, Cherusci, Chauci, Quadi, and Marcomanni. Tacitus' choice for an ethnographic treatise on the diverse tribes of this region will have been appropriate in his day. Domitian had waged a series of wars in a region known as the Agri Decumates (in the modern Neckar Valley). Throughout the treatise, which draws in part on some of Caesar's ethnographic digression on the *Germani* in his *Bellum Gallicum* (6.21–28), Tacitus remarks at various points the probity of the German character, their virtuous way of life, and love of freedom, to contrast it with the decadent Rome of his day (for the significance of this contrast see O'Gorman 1993, 135–54). The following selections are from the work's introduction, which includes a geographic description of the country and a discussion of the origins of the Germans; for a good discussion of some of the problems we face in Roman topographical writing such as this, see Horsfall (1985, 197–208).

1   **Germania omnis** a direct echo of Caesar's famous *Gallia est omnis divisa, GBell.* 1.1

     a Gallis Raetisque et Pannoniis All are abl. of separation.

1–2   **Rheno et Danuvio** in apposition to *fluminibus*; both are abl. of means; the first is the Rhine, the second the Danube river.

2   **a Sarmatis Dacisque** Both are abl. of separation. The Sarmatians (an Iranian-speaking nomadic people) and the Dacians were of current interest for Tacitus and his audience: Domitian had waged campaigns and forged alliances with both, while Trajan was to campaign against the Dacians in 101–102 and 105–106.

2–3   **mutuo metu aut montibus** an alliteration and an example of Tacitean inconcinnity, where the psychological reasons for separation abruptly shift to physical ones

4   **insularum inmensa spatia** refers possibly to the islands of northern Germany, Denmark, and the Rhine delta in modern Holland.

     complectens modifies *Oceanus* in line 3.

4–5   **cognitis quibusdam gentibus ac regibus** abl. absolute; the reference is vague due to the imprecise *nuper*, but given the reference to those places mentioned in line 4, may well refer to the campaigns of Drusus and Tiberius nearly a century before.

5-6   The rest of *Germania* 1 (1.2) is omitted. Tacitus there discuss-
        es the origins and course of the Rhine and Danube rivers. He
        then turns to the origins of the Germans themselves, where
        our text resumes at 2.1.

6   **ipsos Germanos indigenas** i.e., the Germans are believed to
        be native to the land. His discussion of the Britons' origins
        (*Agr.* 11.1) reflects the language used here, *indigenae an ad-
        vecti . . . parum compertum*. For use of the verb *advehebantur*
        see line 8 of the text.

        crediderim a pf. subjunctive indicating potential or suppo-
        sition; for a similar use of this verb see *Agr.* 12.6 (used in a
        pointed aside).

        minimeque"and by no means"; here an adv.

7   **adventibus et hospitiis mixtos** *adventibus . . . hospitiis* are
        abl. after *mixtos*, which modifies *Germanos*; for *misceo* + the
        abl. cf., e.g., Sal. *Iug.* 57.5

7-8   **quia . . . quaerebant** The structure of this clause is as follows:
        quia olim (sc. *illi*) *qui quaerebant mutare sedes advehebantur
        nec terra sed classibus.*

        terra . . . classibus Both are abl. of means.

9   **inmensus ultra . . . adversus Oceanus** "the ocean beyond vast
        and unfavorable"; the reference is to the North Sea.

        utque sic dixerim cf. above, p. 35 line 28

9-10   **raris . . . navibus aditur** "is rarely approached by ships"; the
        verb is here used impersonally with an abl. of means, while
        raris here is adverbial; use of the adj. as an adv. is a common
        usage throughout Latin literature.

11   **horridi et ignoti maris** The Romans were well aware that the
        north Atlantic was vast and contained more perils than the
        Mediterranean; cf. Caes. *BGall.* 3.8 in his discussion of the
        Veneti, a seafaring people on the Atlantic coast of Gaul, *in
        magno impetu maris atque aperto.*

        Asia aut Africa aut Italia relicta an abl. absolute with *relicta*
        attracted into the singular due to its final position next to *Italia*

12   **peteret** The subjunctive here indicates potential; translate "who would seek."

12–13 **informem terris, asperam caelo, tristem cultu aspectuque** a tricolon construction; all the nouns are abl. of specification or respect; translate *caelo* "climate."

13   **nisi si patria sit** "unless it were [his] homeland"; the protasis of a future less vivid condition

14   **carminibus antiquis** abl. of means; cf. Tac. *Ann.* 2.88 where he notes Arminius is still celebrated in song, *caniturque adhuc barbaras apud gentes.* Cicero relates a similar phenomenon for the Romans in their early history, see *Brut.* 75.

15   **memoriae et annalium** "of their history and annals"; for *memoria* as "history" see, e.g., *Ann.* 3.51 *haec aliaque ex vetere memoria petita . . . memorabimus.*

15–16 **Tuistonem deum terra editum** *Tuistonem deum* is the subject acc. in indirect discourse after *celebrant* with *editum* as the main verb (with *esse* omitted); *terra* is an abl. of origin. Tacitus gives a more detailed discussion of the German deities, as well as religious lore and custom at *Germ.* 3 and 8–10.

16   **ei** dat. indirect object after *adsignant* referring to *Tuistonem* in the previous line

17   **Manno** dat. of indirect object with *adsignant*

17–19 **proximi Oceano Ingaevones, medii Hermiones, ceteri Istaevones vocentur** All the adjectives here are substantives in apposition to the individual tribes; *vocentur* functions as a copulative verb; all the adjectives are therefore nom. as are the tribes they modify.

18   **Oceano** dat. with *proximi*

19   **vocentur** Here the subjunctive has the sense of result stemming from the phrase *e quorum nominibus.*

       quidam This could refer to the *Germani* themselves, though Tacitus could possibly have in mind Roman historians who wrote about the *Germani* including Caesar, Pliny the Elder, and Aufidius Bassus.

ut in licentia vetustatis lit. "as in the license of antiquity"; translate freely "as is the case due to the license that is granted to deep antiquity."

19–21 **pluris . . . ortos pluresque . . . appellationes . . . adfirmant** *pluris . . . ortos* and *pluresque . . . appellationes* are acc. pl. in indirect discourse after *adfirmant* with an orthographical variation on *pluris*; translate "certain men affirm that more [i.e., German tribes] have arisen from the god and that there are more names of the race, the Marsi, etc."

19 **deo** abl. of origin, refers to Tuisto, who is referred to above as *deum* as opposed to Mannus, who is the offspring of Tuisto, according to Benario (1999, 65).

20–21 **Marsos Gambrivios Suebos Vandalios** in apposition to *appellationes*, and all in asyndeton

20 **Marsos** The Marsi inhabited the area of the Ruhr and Lippe.

Gambrivios Little is known of the Gambrivii.

Suebos a large tribe that dwelled between the Elbe and Oder, discussed in detail at *Germ.* 38

21 **Vandalios** The Vandali would be a name applied to a series of major tribes that lived as far as the Vistula and subsequently invaded the late Empire, establishing kingdoms in Spain and North Africa.

eaque vera et antiqua nomina Understand the verb *esse*; all are acc. pl. in indirect discourse.

⌖ *GERMANIA 37.2–5*

A history of the wars with the Germans

Tacitus goes on to discuss the Germans' public institutions (6–15), and their private life (16–27), before turning in the remainder of the work to a description of the individual tribes of the west and north-west along the Rhine, and of those west to east along the Danube, before finally turning to the quasi-mythical tribes of the far north. In chapter 37 he interrupts his narrative and gives a brief history of

Roman conflict with the Germans: the Romans first fought a series of wars against the Germans between 113 and 101 BCE, during which, in northern Italy and southern Gaul, the Romans and their allies suffered a series of spectacular and traumatic defeats at the hands of the Cimbri and Teutones, who were eventually defeated at Aquae Sextae (in southern France) in 102 BCE and at Vercellae (in northern Italy) in 101 BCE by Gaius Marius and Lutatius Catulus. Caesar later led a series of campaigns (58–50 BCE) against a number of German tribes famously described in the Gallic War commentaries (see above, p. xxix); Caesar's campaigns were fierce, and included several instances of what we would now consider genocide and ethnic cleansing (such as his slaughtering of the Usipetes and Tencteri in 55 BCE, during which he boasted of 430,000 enemy dead, *BGall.* 4.15). During the reign of Augustus, by virtue of his attempt to establish a permanent physical boundary for the Empire along the Elbe and Danube, the Romans were in constant conflict with the Germans, culminating in the loss of three legions in the Teutoberg forest under Quinctilius Varus in 9 CE (which forced Augustus to settle for a boundary on the Rhine). As noted above, war with the Germans was still pertinent in Tacitus' own day. It is likely that Tacitus drew upon Pliny the Elder, who had written a history of Rome's wars with the Germans, for his summary account (Plin. *Ep.* 3.5.4). Extant sources for these wars, in addition to Caesar himself, include Cassius Dio, Velleius Paterculus, and Plutarch's life of C. Marius. As Thomas has noted (2009, 63–66), the passage constitutes an inversion of the norm, whereby instead of an ethnographic digression in a historical work, we here have a historical digression in an ethnographical treatise.

1–2   **sescentesimum et quadragesimum annum urbs nostra age-bat** "Our city was six hundred and forty years old"; the verb *ago* + a numerical value + *annum* is an idiomatic time expression (similar to *decem annos natus* = ten years old). Tacitus will have been dating the city from 753 BCE (*ab urbe condita*), putting his readers in the year 113 BCE.

3   **audita sunt** indicative in a *cum* temporal clause

3–4   **Caecilio Metello ac Papirio Carbone consulibus** Both prop-
er names are abl. in an abl. absolute with *consulibus* in apposition to both. Caecilius Metellus was from an ancient and
noble family and had no role in the fighting against the Germans. Papirius Carbo, on he other hand, was defeated in that
year (113 BCE) by the Cimbri at Noreia, the capital of what
later was the province of Noricum.

4   **ex quo** Supply *tempore*.

       ad alterum imperatoris Traiani consulatum i.e., to the sec-
ond consulship of the emperor Trajan in 98 CE

5   **computemus** "if we should count"; a pres. act. subjunctive in
the protasis of a mixed condition

       ducenti ferme et decem anni Tacitus is considering the pe-
riod from 113 BCE to 98 CE.

6   **tam diu Germania vincitur** lit. "so long a time is Germany
being conquered"; translate freely, "for so long a time has the
conquest of Germany taken"

6–7   **medio tam longi aevi spatio** "in the interval of so long an
age" (referring to the two hundred and ten years in line 5);
medio . . . spatio is abl. of time.

7   **multa in vicem damna** i.e., the successes and failures on both
sides that Tacitus expands on below; translate *damna*, "losses."

       Samnis refers to the Samnites, an Italic people who lived in
the Appenines and southern portions of Italy, with whom the
Romans had a series of fierce wars between the fourth and
early third century BCE. The Samnites inflicted a notorious
humiliation on the Romans at the Battle of the Caudine Forks
in 321 BCE where the Romans surrendered and were forced to
pass under the yoke. Livy is our main source for the episode
at 9.1–6; cf. p. 115 line 25.

       Poeni refers to the Carthaginians, against whom the Romans
fought three wars in 264–241, 218–201, and 149–146 BCE. Of these
the first two were the most hard fought, and during the second
one the Romans were forced to fight Hannibal in Italy itself.

8   **Hispaniae Galliaeve** For variation Tacitus now changes from
     naming peoples to provinces. The Romans fought nearly two
     hundred years to subdue the peoples of the Iberian peninsula,
     most famously in the Numantine War that lasted from 154 to
     133 BCE. As for *Galliae*, the Romans were traumatized by the
     capture of their city in 390 BCE by Brennus, a Gallic chieftain,
     and fought a series of wars against the Galli of northern Italy
     in the 220s BCE. For a more detailed discussion see the selec-
     tion concerning Claudius' speech on the entrance of the Gauls
     into the Senate, below p. 109.

     Parthi The Parthians started to emerge as a power in their
     own right in the third century BCE. By Caesar's day their
     empire stretched from Mesopotamia to the Indus River. The
     Romans had no natural boundaries with the Parthians, and
     hostilities between the two empires erupted periodically, as
     Tacitus will note below.

     admonuere = *admonuerunt*; take closely with *saepius* and
     translate "have urged us to action more frequently."

9   **quippe** "for in fact"; an adv.

     regno an abl. of comparison with *acrior*

     Arsacis gen. sing. m., refers to the first king of the Parthians,
     Arsaces; here used to refer collectively to the Parthian king-
     dom as a whole

9–11 **quid enim aliud nobis quam . . . Oriens obiecerit** "For what
     else has the East cast against us than . . ."; the verb here takes
     an acc. of the charge, *quid . . . aliud*, while the subject of the
     charge, *nobis*, is in the dat.; the verb itself is a pf. subjunctive
     in a rhetorical question and expects a negative response.

10   **caedem Crassi** Tacitus here refers to the death of M. Crassus,
     one of the members of the first triumvirate, killed (along with
     his son) at the battle of Carrhae in Parthia (in modern Iraq) in
     53 BCE. The defeat entailed the loss of the legions' standards,
     which were not recovered until Augustus successfully negoti-
     ated their return in 20 BCE.

10–11 **amisso et ipse Pacoro, infra Ventidium deiectus Oriens**
amisso . . . Pacoro is an abl absolute; *et ipse* refers to the *Oriens*
that has here been *deiectus infra Ventidium*, i.e., "laid under
the heel of Ventidius"

11 **Pacoro** son of the Parthian king who was killed in 39 BCE in
battle against the Romans

Ventidium P. Ventidius served in Gaul with Caesar, was consul in 43 BCE, and defeated the Parthians in battle at Mount
Gindarus in 38 BCE. He was the only Roman to lead a triumph
over the Parthians. Trajan, under whom Tacitus was writing,
eventually had only limited success in his attempt at conquer-
ing the Parthians between 115 and 117 CE.

at The conjunction here expresses contrast between two different elements, in this instance the difficulty Rome faced in
confronting Germans as compared to other enemies.

12–13 **Carbone et Cassio et Scauro Aurelio et Servilio Caepione
Maximoque Mallio fusis vel captis** a long abl. absolute with
fusis and *captis* modifying the list of Roman names

12 **Cassio** L. Cassius Longinus was defeated and killed by the Tig-
urini at Tolosa (modern Toulouse) in southern Gaul in 107 BCE.

Scauro Aurelio M. Aurelius Scaurus (whose name Tacitus
here reverses) was consul in 108 and was executed by the Cimbri in 105 BCE after being taken prisoner.

12–13 **Servilio Caepione** Q. Servilius Caepio was consul in 106 BCE
and proconsul in 105; he refused to cooperate with the commander Mallius, contributing to the Romans' catastrophic defeat at Aurasio (L'Orange), in which the Romans and their allies
lost, according to our ancient sources, upwards of 80,000 men,
and was one of the most crushing defeats Rome ever suffered.
He was later prosecuted and exiled for *repetundae* (misconduct
while in office) for stealing Gallic treasures from Tolosa.

13 **Maximoque Mallio** The name is inverted; Cn. Mallius Maximus was consul in 105 BCE and commander of a consular
army at Aurasio.

13–15 **quinque ... abstulerunt** Tacitus now shifts from his long abl. absolute to a construction using the indicative.

14 **consularis exercitus** acc. pl. direct object of the main verb; refers to the five consular armies lost under Carbo, Cassius, Caepio, Scaurus, and Mallius

populo Romano dat. of separation with the main verb

14–15 **Varum trisque cum eo legiones** direct object of the main verb. P. Quinctilius Varus lost three legions in the Teutoberg Forest in 9 CE; the Germans attacked him under the command of the famous German leader Arminius, chief of the Cherusci. The battle site at Kalkriese in northwestern Germany has recently been discovered and excavated.

15 **Caesari** dat. of separation, referring to Augustus

inpune i.e., without loss to the Romans

C. Marius See above for his victories over the Germans; victorious over Jugurtha, he was consul every year from 104 to 100 BCE in order to handle the crisis. Marius' ultimate success against the Germans is attributable to three major factors: a barbarian respite from fighting for several years (and a diversion by the barbarians to other provinces); Marius' reforms of the army during this period; and the division by the Germans of their forces once fighting was resumed.

16 **divus Iulius** refers to Caesar's campaigns against Ariovistus and the Germans in 58 BCE and the periodic campaigns he waged against German tribes in the course of his conquests (58–50 BCE).

Drusus ac Nero the two stepsons of Augustus. Drusus died in 9 BCE while on campaign in Germany after a fall from his horse. Between 12 and 9 BCE he campaigned to and reached the Elbe; his brother Nero, (subsequently the emperor Tiberius), succeeded to Drusus' command and campaigned in Germany from 9 to 7 BCE, and 4 to 6 CE, then 10 to 12 in order to restore Roman prestige after the loss of the legions under Varus.

17   **Germanicus** See introduction, p. xxiv; also see below, p. 89; his activities in Germany are related in detail in *Annales* 1–2.

17–18 **ingentes ... minae ... versae** *ingentes ... minae* is the subject, *versae* the main verb with the *sunt* dropped.

18   **C. Caesaris** Caligula had made similar threats to invade Britain in 39 CE; see Suet. *Calig.* 19.3.

      in ludibrium "were turned into a mockery"; for the construction cf. *Ann.* 6.46, *ne memoria Augusti, ne nomen Caesarum in ludibria et contumelias verterent, metuebat*

      inde otium Supply *erat*.

19   **occasione discordiae nostrae** The reference is to the civil strife in 69 CE, see pp. xix–xxii. Civilis, a Batavian noble, led a revolt of the Treveri and other tribes (both Gallic and Germanic), exploiting Roman discord. The rebellion was crushed in 70 CE after Vespasian became emperor.

      occasione an abl. of means or cause

19–20 **expugnatis ... hibernis** an abl. absolute

20   **adfectavere** = *adfectaverunt*; translate "aimed at" (with the intent to attack).

21   **pulsi** 3rd pl. pf. pass. with *sunt* omitted

      proximis temporibus abl. of time when

21–22 **triumphati magis quam victi sunt** triumphed over as opposed to actually defeated because Domitian was rumored to have falsified the reports of his conquest and subsequently led hired captives in blond wigs in a pseudo triumph; see *Agr.* 39.1, Cass. Dio 67.4.1; Pliny *Pan.* 16.3; Ogilvie and Richmond (1967, 285)

✎ *DIALOGUS 1.1–3*

Introduction and address to Fabius Iustus

As one of Rome's most noted orators, the subject of this work, the state of oratory in contemporary Rome, will have been of great interest to Tacitus. The *Dialogus*, as Tacitus here tells us, is a conversation he reports to have heard as a young man; its subject is the decline of oratory, which Tacitus assumes here in the introduction. Tacitus states that in his youth he was under tutelage of M. Aper and Julius Secundus, both renowned orators, when he sat in on the conversation. As was the case with Cicero before him, such secondhand reporting allowed the author to distance himself from the opinions of the interlocutors, and Tacitus is eager to emphasize that these are not his opinions, but rather those of the three major discussants: M. Aper (who argues that oratory has not, in fact, declined), Vipstanus Messalla (who gives a highly moralistic reason for its decline), and Curiatius Maternus (who gives an historical explanation). While Messalla (whose name is sometimes spelled Messala) does not appear in the introduction, Secundus and Aper receive brief but memorable character sketches in the following chapter (2.2). The *Dialogus'* introduction follows the convention as established by Cicero and Aristotle, who began their dialogues with a brief prologue that sets the scene, sometimes addressing a friend or acquaintance (Cic. *Att.* 4.16.3).

1   **ex me requiris** "you ask of me"; *requiris* takes the prep. *ex* + abl.

       Iuste Fabi The name is reversed. Fabius Justus, a mutual friend of Tacitus and Pliny, was consul suffectus in 102 CE. If he were expected to deliver an oration of thanks for the bestowal of his office to the *princeps* then he would prove an appropriate addressee for Tacitus on the subject of rhetoric.

2   **ingeniis gloriaque** Both are abl. of means or cause.

       floruerint pf. subjunctive in a *cum* clause

3   **laude** abl. of separation with *deserta* and *orbata*

deserta a metaphorical antithesis to *floruerint*

4   **retineat** pres. act. subjunctive in an indirect question

appellamus The object of the verb is *oratores* understood and modified by *antiquos* in line 5.

5   **diserti** "skilled speakers"; take closely with *horum . . . temporum*.

5–7 **causidici . . . vocantur** *causidici, advocati, patroni,* and *quidvis* are predicatives of *diserti*. The structure is *diserti vocantur causidici*, etc. As Mayer (2001, 89) notes, the names recall those whose role is strictly in the law courts, not political life.

6   **et quidvis potius quam oratores** "and anything rather than orators"

7–14 **cui . . . audivi** The structure of this long sentence is as follows: *vix hercule auderem respondere cui percontationi tuae, et excipere pondus tam magnae quaestionis si mea sententia proferenda mihi (ut aut de ingeniis nostris existimandum <sit> male si non possumus adsequi idem aut si nolumus de iudiciis) ac non sermo hominum disertissimorum, ut nostris temporibus, repetendus esset, quos audivi, admodum iuvenis, pertractantes hanc eandem quaestionem.* Note the use of pleonasm in this sentence (hence the doubling of *respondere et . . . excipere*), the use of coordinating conjunctions for balanced clauses (e.g., *aut de ingeniis . . . aut de iudiciis*), a rhythmic balance to the individual clauses in the sentence, and a completeness to the syntax.

7   **cui percontationi tuae** The rel. here functions as a demonstrative pron. at the start of the sentence and is dat., along with the noun and adj., after the verb.

7–8 **respondere . . . excipere** Both are complementary infinitive with *auderem*.

9   **existimandum <sit>** pass. periphrastic with the verb *<sit>* in the subjunctive in a result clause (the *<sit>* is a conjectural reading of Lipsius that I have kept)

adsequi complementary infinitive after *possumus*

10   **vix hercule auderem** impf. subjunctive; an apodosis of a pres.
      contrary to fact condition that is picked up by *esset* in line
      12 below. The phrase is intended to distance Tacitus from his
      subject; see above, p. 50.

11   **proferenda** pass. periphrastic with the verb *esset* omitted

11–12 **ut nostris temporibus** "such as there are in our times"; a paren-
      thetical aside similar to *ut ita dicerim* (cf. above, p. 35 line 28)

12   **repetendus esset** not a pass. periphrastic but a pure use of the
      fut. pass. pple.; translate "were not about to be repeated."

13   **iuvenis** modifies the implied subject of the verb.

14–19 The structure of this long sentence is as follows: *est non ita*
      opus ingenio, sed memoria et recordatione, ut persequar nunc
      isdem numeris isdemque rationibus, ordine disputationis ser-
      vata, quae accepi et subtiliter excogitata et graviter dicta a prae-
      stantissimis viris cum singuli adferrent diversas †vel easdem†
      sed probabiles causas dum quisque redderent formam et sui
      animi et ingenii.

14   **audivi** Mayer (2001, 90) argues that this establishes the work
      as fiction, citing Cic. *Fam.* 9.8.1.

14–15 **ingenio . . . memoria . . . recordatione opus est** *ingenio, me-*
      moria, and *recordatione* are all abl. after *opus est*, an idiom
      meaning "there is need" or "it is necessary" + the abl. Taci-
      tus follows the well-established generic form of the dialogue
      whereby the dramatic milieu was often set well in the past
      in order to further distance the author from close association
      with the opinions expressed in it. Cicero, for example, sets the
      De Oratore in 91 BCE, although the work itself dates to around
      55 BCE.

15   **praestantissimis** To give *auctoritas* to a given subject Plato
      and Cicero would frequently have the foremost statesmen and
      intellects of the day as interlocutors. In Cicero's *De Oratore*,
      for example, M. Licinius Crassus and C. Antonius, two of the
      most famous orators of the period, discuss what contributes to
      creating a good orator. While the characters in a dialogue are

almost always historically based and the setting is grounded in the historical circumstances of the period, the opinions expressed and the conversation itself are likely the author's own creation.

16   **†vel easdem†** The text here is corrupt and the reading uncertain.

17   **adferrent** impf. subjunctive in a *cum* (temporal) clause; the verb has the sense of "bringing forward" (by way of explanation).

       dum "while," "and in so doing" (so Mayer 2001, 90–91)

       formam "nature"

       quisque a sing. for the pl.

17–18   **sui . . . et animi et ingenii** i.e., his own mind and talent; for *forma animi* see *Agr.* 46.3.

18   **redderent** impf. subjunctive; Mayer (2001, 91) argues that the subjunctive here is explained through assimilation to *adferrent*.

       numeris abl. of means, "points in their discourse," see the *OLD numerus* 12.

19   **rationibus** "methods of reasoning"; abl. of means

       persequar subjunctive in a purpose clause

❧ *DIALOGUS 2.1–2*

Setting the scene

Three lines of text where Tacitus notes that one of the interlocutors (M. Aper) preferred modern oratory to the more old-fashioned variety are here omitted. Tacitus then proceeds to set the scene and to introduce the dialogue's interlocutors. The conversation is occasioned by the public reading of Curiatius Maternus' tragedy *Cato* (see p. xviii). The subject of the tragedy was controversial, and following this passage Aper and Secundus urge Maternus to be wary of undertaking such controversial subjects in the future. Maternus refuses, and his confrontational stance against the court has been the source of much scholarly controversy, since it contradicts Maternus' professed desire to retire to the "woods and groves" (*nemora vero et luci*, 12.1). Bartsch's discussion (1994, 98–147) offers among the most interesting solutions, arguing that Maternus' contradictions constitute an instance of double-speak, and illustrate how deeply internalized the imperial tyranny had become. The short descriptions of Aper and Secundus look forward to Tacitus' masterful use of rapid, brief rhetorical strokes in sketching the personalities that parade through his historical works.

1   **nam** The previous sentence which the *nam* picks up, introducing the formal setting and characters in the dialogue, is omitted here.

postero die abl. of time when

quam with expressions of time = "after"

Curiatius Maternus Nothing is known of Maternus outside of this dialogue. He has been identified, unconvincingly, with the Maternus who was executed under Domitian (Cass. Dio, 67.12.5).

Catonem a drama about Cato the Younger; for his significance see p. xviii.

2   **recitaverat** for recitation of literary works, often as a preliminary to publication, see *OCD recitatio*

offendisse pf. act. infinitive in indirect discourse; the subject is Maternus.

potentium presumably members of the imperial court and those associated with it

diceretur impf. subjunctive in a *cum* temporal clause

3   **eo** here used as a pronominal adj. with *argumento*

argumento i.e., the subject plot of the play

sui oblitus *sui* here is a reflex. pron. in the gen. sing. referring back to Maternus; *oblitus* is from *obliviscor* and takes the gen.

tantum, "only"; here an adv.

4   **cogitasset** = *cogitavisset*, plpf. subjunctive with *tamquam*

5   **haberetur** impf. pass. subjunctive, still as a part of the *cum* clause

M. Aper nothing else is known of him outside of the *Dialogus*. His name means "boar" in Latin, and reflects his speaking style, which some felt was violent (Tacitus refers to it with the phrase *vi naturae*). Tacitus' characterization of Aper as slightly abrasive is an homage to those personalities in Ciceronian and Platonic dialogue who take up morally dubious arguments. As is the case with Aper, they often have significant names reflecting their opinion and character, such as Thrasymachus ("he who is mighty in battle") in Plato's *Republic*, who argues that might makes right.

Iulius Secundus a man of noted rhetorical ability and remarked as such by Quintilian (*Inst.* 12.10.11); but for a few brief remarks he is, like Tacitus, a silent bystander.

6   **quos . . . utrosque**, "both of whom"

7   **domi** locative; Tacitus may be referring to the custom whereby a young man of good standing would "apprentice" closely with an orator by living at his house and attending him in the Forum and Senate in order to become a practiced orator and statesman; see, e.g., Plin. *Ep.* 2.14.10.

8   **mira . . . cupiditate** abl. of manner

8–9   **quodam ardore iuvenili** abl. of manner

9   **fabulas** "accounts," "conversations" (a common definition in post-Augustan literature)

10   **semotae dictionis** "intimate conversation"

     exciperem impf. subjunctive in a purpose clause

11   **opinarentur** impf. subjunctive in a concessive clause

     Secundo dat. of possession with *esse*, an infinitive in indirect discourse

11–12   **promptum . . . sermonem** *sermonem* can mean "oratorical" or "rhetorical style" while *promptum* here means "ready" or "quick"; translate the phrase "a style of oratory that was quick to the draw."

12   **ingenio . . . vi** Both are abl. of means.

13 **institutione et litteris** Both are abl. of means constituting hendiadys ("academic training in literature," Mayer 2001, 94).

famam eloquentiae *eloquentiae* is dat.; translate "a reputation for eloquence."

14–15 **Secundo . . . non defuit** dat. or abl. with *defuit*, i.e., "Secundus did not lack"

14 **purus et pressus** in reference to oratorical style, "unadorned and concise"

in quantum satis erat an idiomatic phrase, "to a degree that was sufficient," qualifying the adj. *profluens* that follows

15 **profluens** "flowing"; Tacitus also used the adjectives *promptus* and *profluens* to describe Augustus' oratory; see *Ann.* 13.3.

omni eruditione abl. of means

17 **habiturus** part of a periphrastic construction by which the subjunctive used in a concessive clause with *tamquam* indicates potential; supply *esset.*

18 **nullis . . . adminiculis** abl. or dat. with the verb *inniti*

alienarum "superfluous"; Mayer (2001, 95) explains this to mean "his talent was sufficiently practiced to need no further accomplishments."

19 **videretur** impf. subjunctive indicating potential, "if he should seem"

❧ *HISTORIAE 1.15, 1.16*
Galba's adoption of Piso

By 68 CE the rule of Nero had grown intolerable, and the Senate and provincial armies increasingly restive. In the spring of that year the armies of Spain declared Galba emperor, and Nero committed suicide in June. Galba however was an old man for his day, and he had to choose a successor quickly. Unfortunately the aged *princeps* had made a series of bad moves: violence attended his entrance into Rome; he reneged on his promised donative to the troops; and he had passed over Otho for the succession (see p. xx). In this speech Galba

gives his reasons for adopting as his successor L. Calpurnius Piso
(see p. xx), a senator from an old and noble family; the use of adoption as a hereditary system in the Empire was an extremely important one in determining imperial succession. Here Tacitus has Galba
depict the system of adoption that looks beyond the emperor's own
family as preferable to adoption exclusively within the ruling house,
as under the Julio-Claudians, although Mucianus' speech to Vespasian (*Hist.* 2.77) subsequently presents a different view in which
Mucianus urges Vespasian to seize power on the grounds that there
was a worthy heir in his house (constituting a deliberate response to
Galba here, see Keitel 1987, 73). Galba's oration is consequently the
first of several examinations in the *Historiae* (and *Annales*) over the
nature of the succession in the Principate. Suetonius (*Galb.* 17), Plutarch (*Galb.* 23), and Cassius Dio (68.5) all relate the episode, but un-
like Tacitus, do not report Galba's speech. As Damon (2003, 136–37)
notes, the speech is used to highlight how poorly Galba grasps the
nature of the crisis that surrounds him.

1   **te** i.e., Piso.

        privatus i.e., as a private citizen; modifies Galba, the under-
        stood subject

        lege curiata abl. of means. Adoption took place normally be-
        fore the Roman people through the curiate assembly in the
        presence of the Pontifex Maximus (a position Galba *de facto*
        held as emperor).

2   **ut moris est** "as is our custom"; *moris est* = a gen. of quality

        adoptarem impf. subjunctive in the protasis of a pres. con-
        trary to fact condition

        mihi egregium erat "it were outstanding for me"; the impf.
        erat creates a mixed condition.

3   **Pompei . . . Crassi subolem** Galba here refers to the illustrious
        lineage of L. Calpurnius Piso Frugi Licinianus, who traced
        his ancestry back to two noble families of the Republic, but
        whose family had also been active in affairs of state under the
        early *principes* (although Piso, who was thirty at the time of

adoption, had held only a minor office and had not set out on the standard *cursus honorum*). Galba was childless and Suetonius (*Galb.* 17) states that Piso was his chosen heir well before January 69 when this adoption takes place, though Plutarch (*Galb.* 23.1) says it was a sudden choice.

in penatis meos adsciscere *in penatis meos* is an acc. of motion towards and a metonym for "into my family" (referring to the Penates or household gods); cf. *Germ.* 25.1, *suam quisque sedem, suos penates regit*; also see *Ann.* 6.51, line 21 below; *adsciscere* is a complementary infinitive with the phrase *egregium erat*.

4   **tibi insigne** corresponds to *mihi egregium* above; i.e., "distinguished for you."

Sulpiciae ac Lutatiae refers here to Galba's own lineage, which came from two ancient noble families from the Republic; he was the great-grandson of Q. Lutatius Catulus who died in 61 BCE; for his family connections see Suet. *Galb.* 2.3; Plut. *Galb.* 3.1.

adiecisse pf. act. infinitive, complementary with *insigne* (*erat* understood)

5   **consensu** abl. of means; the irony of Galba's use of the phrase *consensu ad imperium* will become clear in his obituary below. As Damon notes too (2003, 137), Tacitus emphasizes with this phrase that Galba has fundamentally misread how deeply dissatisfied some of the provinces and much of the soldiery were with him. Galba has also misread the will of the gods (*deorum*); at *Hist.* 1.27 Galba obtains ill omens (*tristia exta*) from the haruspex, which constitutes the signal for Otho to start his coup.

6   **praeclara indoles tua** Since Piso had done nothing yet to really distinguish himself, the reference to *praeclara indoles* ("illustrious character") probably refers to his ancestry; for *indoles* in reference strictly to moral character see, e.g., *Ann.* 11.23, *adhuc memorari exempla, quae priscis moribus ad virtutem et gloriam Romana indoles prodiderit.*

7   **maiores nostri** The reference is to the civil wars between Pompey and Caesar, and later between Augustus and Antony.

armis abl. of means

7–8 **bello adeptus** *bello* is an abl. of means.

8 **quiescenti** i.e., to Piso; from what follows, Galba clearly means that he is attempting a peaceful succession rather than one marked by conflict.

offeram pres. act. subjunctive in a iussive noun clause after *impulit* in line 6

exemplo abl. of means

sororis i.e., Octavia, whose son Marcellus (Augustus' nephew) was the son of C. Claudius Marcellus (consul of 49 BCE) to whom Octavia was married prior to Antony. A potential successor, Marcellus was married to Augustus' daughter Julia in 25, but died in 23 BCE.

9 **generum Agrippam** M. Vipsanius Agrippa, Augustus' trusted friend and advisor, married Augustus' daughter Julia after the death of Marcellus in 23 BCE, but died in 12 BCE.

nepotes i.e., Gaius and Lucius Caesar, the sons of M. Agrippa and Julia; see p. 84.

10 **privignum** Tiberius was the son of M. Claudius Marcellus, from an ancient noble family, and of Livia Drusilla, whom Augustus married in 38 BCE.

10–11 **in proximo sibi fastigio** "in the next degree of eminence to himself"

12–13 **propinquos aut socios belli** Galba is thinking here probably of M. Agrippa or of Augustus' stepsons, Drusus and Tiberius; all had served Augustus well in his military affairs.

13 **habeam** pres. act. subjunctive in a causal clause; note the variation with the following *sed* clause with *accepi* in the indicative; see Damon (2003, 138) for discussion.

ambitione abl. of means; here a negative trait referring to excessive desire for honor; translate "by courting favor"; cf., e.g., *Agr.* 1.2, *celeberrimus quisque ingenio ad prodendam virtutis memoriam sine gratia aut ambitione.*

14   **sit** a potential subjunctive in the sing. by attraction to *documentum*

14–15   **non . . . tantum . . . sed** "not only . . . but"

14   **necessitudines** "close family connections"

15   **quas tibi postposui** "whom I have put after you"; *postposui* takes an acc. + dat. 15–16 In what follows in the remaining 13 lines of chapter 15 Galba states that he could have chosen Piso's older brother as successor, but deemed Piso more worthy; he further notes Piso's virtue and states that his character has been tested by adversity, adding some moralizing observations about the nature of the Principate before turning once again to a justification of his decision. The selection resumes at *Hist.* 1.16.

16   **librari** "to keep its balance"

17   **posset** impf. subjunctive in the protasis of a pres. contrary to fact condition

dignus eram a quo res publica inciperet lit. "I were a worthy man by whom a republic would be started"; translate freely, "it would be worthy that the republic start with me." He means that if the Empire could withstand a republican form of government he would have restored it to such, but (as the succession of Claudius revealed) it could not. For the construction cf. line 2 above.

18   **eo necessitatis . . . ventum est** "it has come to the point of necessity"; *eo* is an adv. used in close conjunction with the gen. while *ventum est* is a verb of motion used impersonally.

19   **plus** a substantive, the direct object of *conferre*

possit pres. act. subjunctive in a result clause

20   **bonum principem** i.e., Piso himself

21   **unius familiae . . . hereditas** that is to say, of the Julio-Claudian dynasty

22   **loco libertatis erit quod eligi coepimus** "In the place of liberty will be that we have begun to be chosen"; *quod* here is a conj. meaning "that" or "the fact that"; for a good discussion of the significance of *libertas* in Galba's speech see Haynes (2003, 50–53).

22–23   **finita . . . domo** an abl. absolute. The dynasty ended with Nero's suicide.

24   **generari et nasci** "to be bred and born"

        a principibus abl. of origin

        fortuitum sc. *est*

25   **adoptandi** the gerund of *adoptare*

        integrum "free" or "open"; supply *est*.

        velis pres. act. subjunctive indicating potential

26   **consensu** abl. of means; again, Galba is wrong concerning "consensus," since the decision rested with Galba who was possibly influenced by his courtier, Cornelius Laco according to Damon (2003, 134–35).

∾ HISTORIAE 1.41, 1.49
Galba's assassination and obituary

The following passages relate Galba's murder and obituary (also see p. xx). The first of the passages is a vivid account of Galba's assassination, and Tacitus lingers on some of the more lurid details, a tendency not untypical of the literature of the age. The confused alternative accounts of Galba's last words, of his murderer, and his postmortem mutilation all are reflective of the chaos and violence that enveloped Rome in 69 CE. The overall impression gives Galba's death a rather Vergilian feel, reflecting Priam's end (*Aen.* 2.526–58) with a final utterance, his lurid death at a sacred location, and his body abandoned and headless. Galba's obituary is illustrative of Tacitus' literary talents at their best, painting in a series of short elliptical phrases a portrait that is both comprehensive and complex before dismissing Galba with a terse and damning summation.

1   **Viso . . . agmine** an abl. absolute; the reference is to the Praetorian Guards who now actively support Otho and are running riot in the city, determined to cut down Galba.

3   **Galbae imaginem** Images of the emperors were attached to
the praetorian and legionary standards.

solo dat. of motion towards; this particular use of the dat., associated with poetry (frequently found, for example, in Vergil,
e.g., *Aen.* 1.6, 377, 616), is one Tacitus occasionally employs;
the construction is generally, as here, associated with compound verbs.

eo signo abl. of means

manifesta Supply *erant*.

4   **in Othonem** *in* = "towards"

studia "inclinations"

desertum Supply *est*.

fuga abl. of means

5   **destricta** Supply *sunt*.

dubitantis pres. act. pple. in the acc. after *adversus*, functioning as a substantive

iuxta Curtii lacum a small sacred site on the Via Nova directly across the street from the Basilica Julia on the north-
west side of the Forum; cf. Suet. *Galb.* 20.2; Plut. *Galb.* 27.1.
The story is that in the very early Republic there was a chasm
in the earth that could only be closed by an act of *devotio*,
an action in which an individual offered his or her life will-
ingly as a service to the state or army; a certain M. Curtius
rode his horse into the chasm and sacrificed himself. The
tale is told in detail in Livy 7.6. As Damon points out (2003,
184), Galba's death here is a bit of Tacitean irony since it was
where annual vows were given for the emperor's safety (Suet.
Aug. 57.1).

6   **trepidatione** abl. of means or cause

ferentium pres. act. pple. in the gen.; here a substantive

proiectus sc. *est*

e sella i.e., from the sedan chair on which he was being
carried

7   **vocem** "utterance"; for other reports of his last words see Suet. *Galb.* 20.1; Cass. Dio 64.7.4; Plut. *Galb.* 27.1–2.

8   **prodidere** = *prodiderunt*, referring to the collective pl. encompassed by the sing. *cuique* in line 7, who felt hatred or admiration towards Galba

      alii Supply *prodiderunt eum.*

      interogasse = *interogavisse*, a pf. act. infinitive in indirect discourse

9   **quid mali** "what harm"; a partitive gen.

      meruisset a plpf. subjunctive in an indirect question

      paucos dies direct object of *deprecatum*

      exolvendo donativo the gerundive in the dat. case, here indicating purpose

      deprecatum an acc. pf. deponent pple. in indirect discourse, modifying the understood subject of the clause (*Galbam*)

10   **plures obtulisse ultro percussoribus iugulum** Understand again *prodiderunt* with *plures*; *obtulisse* is a pf. act. infinitive in indirect discourse. The detail of offering his neck to the assassins recalls Cicero's demise.

10–11 **agerent ac ferirent** Both are in the impf. subjunctive in indirect statement and function as imperatives; translate "have done with it and strike."

11   **si ita e re publica videretur** The reading of *e* is problematic; translate lit. "if it thus seemed best from the state"; or freely, "if it seemed the best thing for the state"; *e* is omitted in *M*. Scott (1968, 57) suggests Galba's action is intended to mirror the *devotio* of M. Curtius at the Lacus Curtius (see above, line 5).

11–12 **interfuit occidentium** "it was not a concern of those doing the killing"; *occidentium* is a gen. pl. substantive with *interfuit*.

12   **diceret** impf. act. subjunctive in an indirect question

      non satis constat "it is not sufficiently agreed"

13   **quidam ... alii** sc. *prodiderunt*

evocatum An *evocatus* could be a veteran of the Praetorian Guard or urban cohort, but it could also refer to a member of the *princeps'* own elite bodyguard.

14–15 **impresso gladio** an abl. absolute

15 **iugulum eius hausisse** "to have gouged his neck"; *hausisse* is a pf. act. infinitive in indirect discourse.

16 **laniavere** = *laniaverunt*

16–17 **feritate et saevitia** Both are abl. of means with a causal sense.

17 **trunco … corpori** *trunco* here is an adj.; translate "mutilated."

adiecta sc. *sunt*

17–18 In *Hist.* 1.42–48 Tacitus relates the brutal assassination of Piso and the fierce punishment of various members of Galba's court, including the consul T. Vinius, Cornelius Laco the Praetorian Praefect, and the powerful freedman Marcianus Icelus, before finally presenting Galba's obituary at 1.49.

18–19 **tribus et septuaginta annis** abl. of time when

19 **quinque principes** Born in the reign of Augustus, he flourished under Tiberius, Caligula, Claudius, and Nero. He was first consul under Tiberius in 33 CE with L. Sulla (Tac. *Ann.* 6.15) when Tiberius predicted Galba's brief tenure as *princeps* (Tac. *Ann.* 6.20).

prospera fortuna abl. of manner

20 **alieno imperio … suo** "with the Empire another's than his own"; an abl. absolute with a compar. abl.

vetus in familia nobilitas Supply *erat*; for Galba as a member of the *vetus nobilitas* see above, p. 58 line 4.

21 **magnae opes** Supply *erant*; Galba was one of the wealthiest of private citizens at the time; see Plut. *Galb.* 3.1.

ipsi dat. of possession; supply *erat*.

extra vitia with the acc. *extra* = "free from" and is litotes; supply *erat*. Tacitus here damns with slight praise. Galba is credited both by Tacitus (through Otho, *Hist.* 1.37) and Suetonius (*Galba* 12.1) with *saevitia* and *avaritia*. For the set of antitheses we find in this obituary see Plass (1988, 40–42).

22   **famae nec incuriosus nec venditator** "he was neither indif-
        ferent of his reputation nor was he a braggart"; for *incuriosus*
        + the gen. in Tacitus cf. *Agr.* 1.1, *incuriosa suorum aetas*; *Ann.*
        4.32, *princeps proferendi imperii incuriosus erat. venditator* is
        found only here in Tacitus.

22–23   **pecuniae alienae** gen. with *adpetens*; cf. *Hist.* 4.84 *voluptatum*
        quam religionum appetens; supply *erat*.

        pecuniae alienae . . . suae parcus a phrase from Sallust *Cat.*
        5.4 describing Catiline that Tacitus has here reworked

23   **publicae avarus** *avarus* takes the gen.; *publicae* modifies *pe-*
        cuniae in the previous line.

24–25   **amicorum libertorumque . . . patiens** *amicorum liberto-*
        rumque are gen. with *patiens*; supply *erat*; cf. Suet. *Galb.* 15.2
        for his indulgence towards friends; also Tac. *Hist.* 1.12.

24   **ubi in bonos incidisset** "when he had happened on good
        ones," the *bonos* referring to his *amici* and *liberti*; *incidisset* is
        plpf. subjunctive in an indirect question.

25   **forent** an alternative form of the impf. subjunctive of *essent* in
        a present contrary to fact protasis

        ad culpam ignarus "he was ignorant to a fault," supply *erat*.

26   **natalium** in the m. pl. = "birth"

        sed . . . obtentui *obtentui* is dat. of purpose, supply *erat* and
        translate "served as a disguise/a screen." According to Tacitus,
        dissimulation of this sort was a survival strategy for Roman
        senators; for emperors it was just another aspect of imperial
        hypocrisy.

27   **quod segnitia erat** cf. *Agr.* 6.3, where Tacitus describes Agricola
        as *gnarus sub Nerone temporum, quibus inertia pro sapientia fuit*

        vocaretur impf. subjunctive in a result clause

28   **militari laude** abl. of means; for his provincial commands see
        Suet. *Galb.* 6–8; Plut. *Galb.* 3.2–3. He was legate of Upper Ger-
        many under Caligula, governed Africa under Claudius, and
        Spain under Nero.

28–29   **pro consule Africam moderate** *pro consule* is indeclinable; the clause is an example of brachylogy; to complete its sense supply *continuit.*

29   **pari iustitia** an abl. of manner describing how he governed Spain; cf. Suet. *Galb.* 9.1 who says his rule was inconsistent

30   **privato** a compar. abl.; *privatus* refers to his status as a private citizen.

30–31   **et omnium . . . nisi imperasset** This final judgment on Galba's principate is perhaps one of the most perfect and biting examples of the sententious style in all of Tacitus.

31   **imperasset** = *imperavisset*, an abbreviated form of the plpf. subjunctive in the protasis of a mixed condition indicating past contrary to fact that lends a succinctness to this already brief, barbed statement

ꙮ *Historiae 3.82–83*

Street fighting between Vitellians and Flavians and the degradation of the city

Galba's successor, Otho, was immediately confronted with the revolt of the legions of Germany, who had thrown in their lot with Vitellius, a man of ancient, noble lineage, but a cruel and indolent Sybarite. In April of 69 at Bedriacum, in northern Italy, Vitellius' legions defeated Otho, who committed suicide; later that year the forces of Vespasian (i.e., the Flavians), defeated Vitellius in northern Italy (see p. xxi for discussion). The following passage describes the violent conflict between the troops of the emperor, Vitellius, and his challenger, Vespasian, within the city itself. The battle is viewed by the dregs of the city as a theatrical spectacle to be enjoyed and cheered on as they mindlessly pursue their pleasures in the course of the Saturnalia, which was taking place that very month (for the element of theater here, see Pomeroy 2006, 186–89). The passage, as Ash has noted (2009, 94–95), is an example of how Tacitus shows that civil war inverts Roman identity, turning Romans into a foreign enemy fighting against their own country.

| 1 | **concurrere** a historical infinitive used for vividness |

2–3   **fortuna et parta totiens victoria** i.e., the Flavians had good fortune and victory both

2   **parta** The *est* is omitted here.

3   **desperatione sola** abl. of means or cause

    ruebant in a hostile sense of rushing to the attack; cf. *Ann.* 4.25, *ille . . . ruendo in tela captivitatem haud inulta morte effugit*

4   **congregabantur** "were regrouping"

5   **pugnantibus** pres. pple. as a substantive in the dat. with *aderat*

    spectator populus The two nouns here are in apposition.

    utque "and as," a bitter parenthetical aside

6   **hos . . . illos** i.e., the Flavians and Vitellians

    plausu abl. of means

7   **quotiens . . . inclinasset** *inclinasset* = *inclinavisset*, the subjunctive here indicates indefinite frequency; the verb is often used in military terminology; cf. *Ann.* 1.64, *inclinantes iam legiones.*

7–8   **abditos . . . expostulantes** *abditos* here is a substantive pple., the subject of the clause in indirect discourse after *expostulantes.*

    si quam in domum *quam* functions as an indef. adj. after *si* modifying *domum*; both are acc. of motion towards.

8   **perfugerant** The indicative is here used for added vividness to an already harrowing account of the participation of the mob in the butchery and mayhem.

    erui iugularique Both are infinitive after *expostulantes.*

9   **parte maiore . . . potiebantur** *parte maiore* is an abl. after *potiebantur.*

9–10   **milite . . . obverso** an abl. absolute; *milite* here is a sing. for a collective pl. = "soldiery."

10   **caedis** acc. pl.

in vulgus cedebant Tacitus varies his case usage with *cedere*, alternately using the dat. (as in *Ann.* 13.39, *reliqua praeda victoribus cessit*) and the acc. + *in* (as in *Ann.* 6.43, *omnes in unum cedebant*).

10–11 **saeva . . . facies** Supply *erat*.

11 **urbe tota** "throughout the entire city"; an abl. used as the locative

alibi . . . alibi "in one place . . . in another"; here used as a co-ordinating conj.

11–12 **alibi . . . popinaeque** Supply *erant. popinae*, "eating houses," were places that in the Roman historical record did not have the most savory of reputations; cf. Sall. *Cat.* 13.3 for his disparagement of *ganeae* (which had an even more dubious repute than *popinae* since they supposedly were frequented by prostitutes).

12–13 **simul . . . similes** Supply *erant*.

13 **scortis similes** *scortis* is dat. with *similes*, here used as a substantive; Wellesley *ad loc.* takes it to mean male prostitutes.

quantum . . . libidinum *libidinum* is a partitive gen.; supply *erant*.

14 **quiquid . . . scelerum** *scelerum* is a partitive gen. with *erant* understood.

prorsus "absolutely"; it is to be taken closely with *crederes* in the next line.

15 **ut . . . crederes** an impf. subjunctive in a result clause

16 **ante armati exercitus** Translate *ante* as an adv., "before," following the reading of *M*; Tacitus' phrase conveys some indignation at the violation of the city itself, into which no army or commander with *imperium* could enter except in the ceremony of a triumph. The presence of *armati exercitus* constitutes a religious transgression of the city's sacred boundary, the *pomerium*.

bis Lucio Sulla Sulla was the warlord of the late Republic who first marched an army against the city, and did so twice. The first time was in 88 BCE when Sulpicius Severus, a close ally of Sulla's rival, C. Marius, abrogated his Asian command against

Mithridates. Sulla marched on the city, drove Marius away in flight, murdered Sulpicius, massacred Marius' supporters, and set up a puppet government. The second time was in 82 BCE, upon his return from Asia, when he killed numerous political opponents through (amongst other means) proscriptions, and thereby earned a reputation for great cruelty.

17   **Cinna** was left in charge when Sulla left for Asia but subsequently went over to the Marian faction, helped Marius to retake the city by force, and established a despotism that lasted from 87 to 84 BCE until Cinna was murdered in a mutiny by his own men. For the *dominatio* of Cinna and Sulla see Tac. *Ann.* 1.1 and p. 72.

   victoribus here in apposition to both Cinna and Sulla, hence the pl. in an abl. absolute

   crudelitas Sulla's cruelty was almost proverbial; see, e.g., Cic. *Att.* 9.14.2; Val. Max. 6.8.2, 9.2.1; Sen. *Contr.* 9.2.19; Sen. *Suas.* 6.3; Sen. *Clem.* 1.12.1–2; cf. Tac. *Hist.* 2.38; *Ann.* 6.46; also see Plut. *Sull.* 31; Livy *Per.* 87; App. *BCiv.* 1.95

17–18   **inhumana securitas** a very striking phrase, lit. "a savage sense of well-being," (the *erat* understood) with a violence that exceeded the boundaries of humanity due to the sense of anarchic liberation felt by those who pursued their pleasures amidst such horror

18   **et ne minimo quidem temporis** "and at no time even in the least"; an adverbial expression with a partitive gen.

18–19   **voluptates intermissae** Supply *sunt*.

19   **festis diebus** abl. after *fruebantur*

   id quoque *id* refers back to the entire previous clause, i.e., the fact that the pursuit of pleasures were not halted despite the fighting within the city, and contributed to the luridly festive atmosphere.

   accederet impf. subjunctive after *velut*, introduced by *exultant*; translate the whole clause "They were running riot as if they were celebrating a holiday and this was an added enjoyment."

20   **nulla partium cura** either an abl. absolute or an abl. of description referring back to the *vulgus* of line 10; *partium* refers to the two fighting factions.

       malis publicis either an abl. of means with *laeti* that functions causally or an abl. of specification

∾ *ANNALES 1.1*

Tacitus' introduction and qualifications as a historian

Tacitus here introduces his *magnum opus*, the *Annales*. At the outset Tacitus masterfully links several key themes that he will follow throughout his work. He begins with a very rapid narrative of Rome's history from the monarchy to the advent of the Principate. From the start *libertas*, which Tacitus sees as contemporaneous with the establishment of the Republic, intrudes as a central theme to his work. Tacitus then proceeds to give an analysis of power and how it was variously deployed and abused in the course of Rome's history, until it was concentrated entirely in the hands of Augustus. As noted in the introduction, the dynamics of power are of great interest to Tacitus, and he puts his readers on notice here that this will be the central subject of his work. He accomplishes all of this in the very compressed space of three sentences before stating his own reasons for undertaking the work and asserting his own qualifications for writing a history of the Julio-Claudians: their history has yet to be written by one who was not fearful, malicious, or fawning; he explicitly emphasizes his objectivity as a historian and the distance from his subject. For a good discussion of this passage in the larger context of Tacitus' work see Kraus (2009, 100–115).

1   **urbem . . . habuere** The phrase recalls Sall. *Cat.* 6.1, *Urbem Romam, sicut ego accepi, condidere atque habuere initio Troiani*; as Kraus notes (2009, 104), Tacitus' use of Sallust here "suggests that the *Annals* will participate in the Sallustian analysis of socio-political debasement reflected by and concentrated in a single, poisonous citizen whose own corruption exploits that of the state."

principio The word is echoed in *principis* and *principatum* in lines 7 and 15; for discussion see Kraus (2009, 103), who argues that this passage subtly connects the Principate to monarchy, and deconstructs the Augustan façade; it simultaneously also announces Tacitus as Livy's continuator, picking up, in a sense, where Livy left off.

habuere = *habuerunt*

libertatem as noted above, p. 29, a central theme already encountered in Tac. *Agr.* 2.1, by which Tacitus refers to the political freedom enjoyed by the Senate and established with the Republic (traditionally) in 509. For a discussion of the significance of *libertas* in this passage see Kraus and Woodman (1997, 94–96).

2   **L. Brutus** The story is told at the end of Livy's first book (1.57–60) of how L. Junius Brutus, also know as the *Liberator*, was instrumental in expelling the last of the kings, which allowed for the establishment of republican institutions.

ad tempus "for the moment," "in times of crisis"; Tacitus refers here to the institution of the dictatorship; the office was established not long after the monarchy was abolished as a temporary extraordinary magistracy within the army in times of crisis.

3   **decemviralis potestas** In 451 BCE the constitution was suspended and ten patricians were put in charge of preparing a law code. They were headed by App. Claudius and disbanded less than two years later when Verginia was famously murdered by her father to save her from Claudius' lust. The constitution was restored, and in 449 BCE the consuls published the Twelve Tables. For the episode see Livy 3.32–54. The term *potestas* refers generally to the official power of a magistrate, particularly as regards the tribunate; cf., e.g., *Ann.* 1.3, 1.7.

ultra biennium Supply *valuit*.

4   **tribunorum militum consulare ius** See Livy 4.6–8 through 6.42; from 444 to 367 BCE military tribunes held consular power, substituting for consuls themselves. The institution, as Tacitus states, did not last.

Cinnae See above, p. 69.

4–7   **non . . . cessere** Tacitus uses a series of brief phrases in these
lines, employing anaphora, asyndeton, and ellipse to underscore the brevity of previous breaches of the constitution as
opposed to the permanent establishment of the Principate.

4–5   **non . . . non** anaphora in asyndeton with the verb understood

5   **Sullae** See above, p. 68. Sulla was made dictator in 82 but ab-
dicated in 79 BCE, and died the next year.

longa dominatio The *dominatio* of Cinna and Sulla each lasted three years or less but were markedly more violent than
previous official dictatorships, hence the use of this strong
word; to complete the sense of the phrase, supply *erat*.

Pompei Crassique Tacitus refers to two members of the so-
called first triumvirate. Pompey was assassinated in Egypt in
48 BCE after Caesar defeated him at Pharsalus; for Crassus see
above, p. 46.

potentia In Tacitus this word frequently implies influence
and is sometimes coupled with *potestas*; see, e.g., *Dial.* 5.5,
6.3, 13.4; *potentia* here indicates influence, and underscores
the informal alliance of the first triumvirate, as opposed to
the official *potestas* of the *decemviri* above.

6–7   **cito . . . cessere** *cessere = cesserunt*; + *in* and the acc., translate
"fell to."

6   **cito in Caesarem** due to the deaths of the two other members
of the triumvirate; *cito* is a debatable point, since the alliance
survived intact between the three from 60 to 53 BCE. However, Caesar's successful conquest of Gaul, starting in 58 BCE,
would certainly mean that his *potentia* loomed large over that
of his political partners.

Lepidi M. Lepidus was the third member of the second triumvirate who made an alliance with Antony after the latter's
defeat at Mutina in 43 BCE. He was stripped of his power by
Augustus in 36 BCE and forced into retirement.

Antonii M. Antony, whose relationship with Augustus would gradually sour and who was defeated with Cleopatra at Actium in 31 BCE, but whose descendants, including Caligula, Claudius, and Nero, are the central characters of Tacitus' work.

7   **qui** the antecedent is *Augustum*

cuncta ... fessa *cuncta* is a substantive modified by *fessa* and the direct object of *accepit*.

nomine principis *nomine* is an abl. of means; *principis* comes from a term used during the Republic, the *princeps senatus*, or foremost man of the Senate, whose *auctoritas*, by virtue of his experience in affairs of state, had given him the informal recognition of one whose opinion and judgment garnered the most respect. Augustus was careful to cultivate a less regal demeanor than Julius Caesar before him, hence the choice of *princeps* as opposed to *dictator*.

8   **sub imperium** "under his command"; one of the key aspects of Augustus' settlement was his privilege of *maius imperium*, which exceeded the *imperium* of any provincial governor or army commander, and served as the legal and constitutional foundation of his rule.

8–9 **prospera vel adversa** Both are substantives.

9   **claris scriptoribus** abl. of agent; Tacitus thinks no doubt of Sallust and Livy, who wrote about the Republic.

9–10 **temporibusque ... dicendis** "for relating the times," a gerundive

10   **defuere** = *defuerunt*

decora ingenia These will have included Livy, Cremutius Cordus, and Asinius Pollio, though Cremutius and Pollio may have been somewhat critical; for history under Augustus and the early emperors also see Tac. *Hist.* 1.1, *postquam bellatum apud Actium ... magna illa ingenia cessere.*

11   **gliscente adulatione** an abl. absolute indicating causality. He may have in mind writers such as Velleius Paterculus, who wrote a history of Rome with an overtly flattering portrayal

of Tiberius (see Kraus and Woodman 1997, 82–84). *adulatio* and its role in the disintegration of the Roman character, particularly within the Senate, is a key theme in Tacitus' work; cf. *Hist.* 1.1, *simul veritas pluribus modis infracta, primum inscitia rei publicae ut alienae, mox libidine <u>assentandi</u>*.

deterrerentur Tacitus will use a subjunctive indicating an actual fact with *donec*; cf. *Ann.* 2.6, *donec . . . misceatur*.

11–12 **Tiberii . . . Neronis** The connectives in *Gaiique et Claudii* divide the two Julian from the two Claudian emperors, and likely reflect the *Annales*' structure too, the first eight books covering the two Julians, the last ten, the two Claudians (see Syme 1958, 256).

12 **res** "histories," "affairs." *falsae* modifies it; supply *erant* to complete the clause.

florentibus ipsis an abl. absolute referring to the four emperors

falsae "falsified"

13 **recentibus odiis** an abl. absolute describing the condition under which their histories were composed

14 **inde consilium mihi** Supply *est*.

pauca . . . et extrema Both are substantives referring to Tacitus' very brief treatment of Augustus that takes up only chapters 2–5 and 9–10.

tradere a complementary infinitive after *consilium mihi*

15 **sine ira et studio** "without anger or partisanship"; the precise meaning of this phrase has received ample attention from scholars; see, e.g., Luce (1989, 16–31); for an excellent discussion about distortion and bias in ancient writers in general, including Tacitus, see Wiseman (1993, 122–46).

15–16 **quorum causas procul habeo** Tacitus chooses his subject carefully and thereby establishes his authority and the veracity of its treatment, something that was essential for Roman historians (see, e.g., Sall. *Cat.* 3.3–5). Tacitus has here distanced himself from his subject, since he was not born until early in Nero's reign, and only entered political life under Vespasian. For his attempt to establish his credentials as an authoritative and "objective" historian cf. *Hist.* 1.1.

∾ *ANNALES 1.9–10*
The funeral of Augustus and two views of his principate

The first order of business upon Tiberius' succession was the funeral of his predecessor. Tacitus here presents two views of Augustus that also serve effectively to summarize his rule. In the first section Tacitus presents the "positive view" of Augustus' tenure. The second section proceeds to deconstruct that view and to expand on the more negative side of Augustus' reign, which is given far greater weight and space. The passage represents a fine and expansive example of the "loaded alternative," concerning which see pp. xxxiii–iv. It also exemplifies the application in a literary work of a *controversia*, a rhetorical exercise that was a part of a young Roman man's education in which he took a controversial subject and argued either side of it. Tacitus gives us a lively summation of Augustus' principate, which established, as becomes clear in the passage below, some of the inherently negative characteristics of imperial rule, including vanity, treachery, and cruelty. In addition, the passage deconstructs Augustus' own *res gestae* (his memoirs) that stood in front of his mausoleum in the Campus Martius, which Tacitus simultaneously summarizes and refutes here (Haverfield 1912, 197–99; Kraus and Woodman 1997, 98). Tacitus further damns Augustus from the outset by not giving him a formal obituary, something the reader would have expected. It should be noted that in this passage I refer to Augustus also as Octavian, the name by which he was known prior to 27 BCE.

1   **at** The intensifier here is intended to contrast the "wise" against those who were discussing the more superficial aspects of Augustus' reign.

2   **eius** i.e., Augustus'

3   **hi** refers to those who were apologists for Augustus and the establishment of the Principate. Understand a verb of speaking after *hi* following the verbs *extollebatur arguebaturve* in the previous line; what follows in the remainder of the paragraph will be in indirect discourse.

pietate . . . necessitudine Both are abl. of means indicating causality.

erga parentem The *parentem* in question is Julius Caesar, who had adopted his grand-nephew Octavian (as he was known before he adopted the name Augustus in 27 BCE) as his son and heir in his will.

3–4   **in . . . locus** Supply *esset*.

4   **ad arma civilia** a compact reference; Tacitus refers here to Octavian's initial command against Antony in 43 BCE, their subsequent joint campaign against Sex. Pompeius, and Augustus' ultimate break and conflict with Antony.

actum Supply *esse*; the subject is Augustus.

5   **neque parari . . . neque haberi** "neither to be levied . . . nor to be conducted"

possent an impf. subjunctive in a subordinate clause in indirect discourse

bonas artis "by honorable methods" (so Furneaux *ad loc.*), "good behavior" (Woodman 2004, 7); *artis* is acc. pl.

5–6   **multa . . . multa** Both are substantives in the acc. pl., direct objects of *concessisse*.

6   **interfectores** especially C. Cassius and M. Brutus, whom Antony and Octavian defeated at Philippi in 42 BCE

ulcisceretur an impf. subjunctive with *dum*, which is either temporal or = *dummodo*, "provided that"; i.e., Augustus permitted behavior that he would otherwise have felt unacceptable, and used Lepidus and Antony only as convenient weapons against Caesar's murderers. Augustus commemorated his revenge against the assassins in his construction of the Temple of Mars Ultor, vowed on the eve of Philippi.

7   **hic socordia senuerit** *hic* refers to Lepidus; *socordia* is abl. of means with a causal sense; *senuerit* is the pf. subjunctive in a subordinate clause in indirect discourse

ille i.e., Antony

7–8 **per libidines pessum datus sit** *pessum dare* is an idiom meaning "to ruin" or "to destroy"; Tacitus uses here as in the previous clause *per* + the acc. for variation instead of an abl. of means. The reference is to Antony as a hard-living man who had a reputation for heavy drinking and amorous escapades.

9   **regeretur** The subject of *regeretur* understood is the *patriae* from the previous clause; *regeretur* is subjunctive in a result clause.

9–10 **regno ... dictatura ... nomine** All three are abl. of means describing how the state was reconstituted under Augustus. The acceptance of this argument by some repeats the "party line" espoused by Augustus in his *Res Gestae*. Cassius Dio (52.1.1), on the other hand, refers to it as a time when monarchy was established.

10   **constitutam rem publicam** The subject of this clause is the *rem publicam*; Tacitus has dropped the verb *esse* with *constitutam*. After Actium normal government appeared to return, and in 27 BCE Augustus declared the *res publica* restored; to maintain his grip on the state, as Tacitus notes (see *Ann.* 1.2), Augustus assumed a series of powers through special mandates and styled himself as *princeps* (see p. xxiii).

11   **mari Oceano ... amnibus longinquis** abl. of means; *mari Oceano* here is hendiadys; cf. *Hist.* 4.12. Such usage is poetic (see, e.g., Verg. *Aen.* 7.38, *advena exercitus*). The reference to *mari Oceano* is to Augustus' consolidation of Roman governance in Gaul and Spain in the first instance, while *amnibus longinquis* refers to his establishment of Rome's northern boundaries on the Danube and the Rhine (which had to be settled for, rather than the Elbe, after Varus' defeat in 9 CE, see p. 48).

saeptum Supply *esse*; the subject is *imperium*.

12   **classis** acc. pl.

        cuncta inter se conexa Note that *cuncta* is an acc. n. pl. sub-
        stantive in apposition to the nouns that proceed it, despite
        their being f., and determines the gender of *conexa* (supply
        esse).

13   **ius . . . socios** Supply *esse* in both clauses.

        civis acc. pl.

13–14   **magnifico ornatu** an abl. of quality; supply *esse*. Augustus
        famously entered Rome "a city of brick" and left it "a city of
        marble" (Suet. *Aug.* 28.3). Some of his more impressive build-
        ing projects included the Temple of Apollo on the Palatine,
        the Temple of Mars Ultor and its forum, the Portico of Octa-
        via, the Theater of Marcellus, the Temple of the Divine Julius
        Caesar in the Forum, and numerous other projects (some un-
        dertaken by Agrippa or other nobles) throughout the Campus
        Martius.

14   **pauca admodum vi tractata** *pauca* here is a substantive,
        the subject of *tractata*, and refers to the several conspiracies
        against Augustus; the adj. itself is frequently modified in Taci-
        tus with the adv. *admodum*, see, e.g., *Agr.* 14.2, *Germ.* 18.1,
        Ann. 4.51. The translation of *admodum* depends on whether it
        is intended in a negative or corroborative sense; if the former,
        it should be translated "only," "just," but if the latter, trans-
        lated "indeed," "to be sure." *vi* is an abl. of means.

        quo "by which"; introduces a purpose clause

16–46   Tacitus here delivers an extended rebuttal of the previous ar-
        guments and a litany of Augustus' morally duplicitous actions
        in establishing what was, in fact, a military dictatorship that
        also set the foundations for future tyrants. His detractors em-
        phasize the murder, treachery, and scandals that plagued his
        personal affairs.

16   **contra** Translate as an adv., "on the contrary"; note the direct
        response of lines 16–17 to line 3 above.

17   **obtentui** "as a pretext"; dat. of purpose; cf. above, p. 65 line 26

ceterum here with an adversative sense after *obtentui*, "but in fact"; this use of *ceterum* is particularly Tacitean; cf., e.g., *Ann.* 1.14.

cupidine abl. of means or cause

18   **veteranos** i.e., Caesar's veterans who had been discharged but were induced by bribery to support Octavian; see Cic. *Att.* 16.8.1; cf. Vell. Pat. 2.61.1.

18–20   **concitos . . . paratum . . . corruptas . . . simulatam** All are the pf. pass. infinitive in indirect discourse with the verb *esse* omitted; the relentless piling on of four clauses in asyndeton supports the description of Augustus as motivated *cupidine dominandi*.

19   **adulescente privato** Octavian was nineteen in 44 BCE when Caesar was assassinated, and not yet a senator, though he did have some experience, including military service on campaign with Caesar in Spain.

    corruptas consulis legiones i.e., those of Antony summoned from the East to Italy; see Cic. *Phil.* 3.3.6, App. *BCiv.* 2.45.

20   **simulatam Pompeianarum gratiam partium** "favor towards the Pompeian party had been feigned"; the reference is to Octavian's association, due to Antony's rebuff, with the senatorial party immediately after Caesar's assassination.

20–27   Talk turns to Octavian's actions during the campaign at Mutina in 43 BCE. He was given the rank of senator and propraetor and sent with the consuls, C. Pansa and A. Hirtius, against the forces of Antony. Although they won the war, both consuls perished and Octavian was suspected in their deaths. Octavian, however, grew suspicious that he was being used as a tool by the Senate to help defeat Antony. Consequently, Octavian later that year formed an alliance with Antony and Lepidus, the so-called second triumvirate, after which they fought and defeated in the campaign at Philippi in 42 BCE the forces of the Republic and the Senate led by M. Brutus and C. Cassius.

20-24 **mox . . . occupavisse** The structure of this difficult sentence is as follows: *ubi mox, Hirtio et Pansa caesis* [sc. *Octavianum*] *occupavisse copias utriusque, sive hostis* [understand *abstulerat*] *illos, seu* [sc. *Caesar abstulerat*] *Pansam venenum adfusum vulneri, sui milites et Caesar, machinator doli, abstulerat Hirtium,* [sc. *Octavius*] *fascis et ius praetoris invaserit decreto patrum.*

20-21 **decreto patrum fascis et ius praetoris** *decreto* is abl. of means; *patrum* is an archaism used here instead of *senatus*. *fascis* is acc. pl. and refers to his joint command with the consuls against Antony (Suet. *Aug.* 10; *RG* 1). The rank of propraetor with military *imperium* and senatorial status was decreed to him simultaneously on Cicero's motion on January 1, 43 BCE (Cic. *Phil.* 5.46). He never relinquished his *imperium* after that date.

21 **invaserit** The verb often has undertones of seizing violently or by force.

caesis abl. in an absolute construction; modifies *Hirtio et Pansa*, the two consuls, mentioned above, with whom he held command. On the suspicion of Octavian's involvement in their deaths see Suet. *Aug.* 11. Hirtius is Aulus Hirtius, the author of the eighth book of Caesar's Gallic War commentaries, and although victorious, was killed at Mutina on April 27.

22 **Pansa** He was attacked and wounded by Antony's men on his way to Mutina, and later died from his injuries.

sive . . . seu a classic loaded alterative in which the more nefarious possibility is given greater expansion and weight; Tacitus' use of brachylogy in both clauses and his economical use of the finite verb makes this one of the more difficult sentences in his corpus.

vulneri dat. after *adfusum*

23 **machinator doli** a striking Vergilian echo recalling Sinon's treachery at Troy, *Aen.* 2.264–67; see Putnam (1989, 563–64) for discussion.

abstulerat Tacitus will use indicative verbs in indirect discourse in parenthetical or explanatory relative clauses; it is singular by attraction to *Caesar* although the subjects are *venenum . . . adfusum, sui milites,* and *Caesar.*

24 **senatu** is in fact a dat. of disadvantage with *extortum,* supply *esse;* for the form cf. *Ann.* 3.47. The reference is to the allegation that after Mutina the Senate was reluctant to grant Octavian the consulship, which he supposedly wrested out of the Senate's hands with an army at his back (see Suet. *Aug.* 26).

24-26 **extortum . . . consulatum, armaque . . . versa** an extended chiasmus

25 **acceperit** pf. subjunctive in a subordinate clause in indirect discourse

26 **rem publicam versa** Supply *esse* for *versa,* which is an infinitive in indirect discourse; *rem publicam* refers to the forces that favored senatorial rule, represented by Brutus and Cassius, who held commands in the East.

proscriptionem civium During the Second Triumvirate Octavian, Antony, and Lepidus executed their political enemies and confiscated their lands in the same way Sulla had in 82 BCE (Cass. Dio 47.3–13). Their most famous victim was Cicero.

26-27 **divisiones agrorum** Confiscated land was divided up and the veterans from the campaigns of Octavian and Antony against Brutus and Cassius were settled on it in 41 BCE. The confiscations are referred to in Verg. *Ecl.* 1 and 9.

27 **ipsis** abl. of agent

fecere = *fecerunt;* the indicative is often used in a relative clause in indirect discourse if it constitutes the paraphrase of a noun.

laudatas pf. pass. infinitive in indirect discourse; supply *esse.*

sane here in a concessive sense; cf. *Ann.* 1.3, *rudem sane bonarum artium*

28 **exitus** acc. pl.; while *Casii* is sing., *Brutorum* is pl., referring both to M. Brutus and Decimus Brutus; Decimus had fought against Antony at Mutina in 43 BCE and was executed in northern Italy later that year.

29 **sit** subjunctive in a concessive clause with *quamquam*

  remittere complementary infinitive with *fas sit*

29-30 **sed . . . sed** Tacitus here uses anaphora for rhetorical emphasis.

  Pompeium In 40 BCE Octavian married Scribonia, a relation of Sex. Pompeius (Pompey the Great's son); in the next year he struck the Pact of Misenum with Pompeius giving him control of Sicily, Sardinia, Corsica, and Achaea (Cass. Dio 48.36.4). In that same year Octavian divorced Scribonia, by whom he had his only child, a daughter named Julia. By 38 BCE the pact was broken and in 36 BCE Sex. Pompeius was defeated at the Battle of Naulochus, after which he fled to Asia where he was executed by M. Titius.

30 **imagine . . . specie** both abl. of means; for Lepidus see p. 72.

  deceptos Supply *esse*.

31 **Tarentino Brundisinoque foedere** abl. of means. The pact at Tarentum was made in 37 BCE, that of Brundisium in 40 BCE. The pact at Brundisium included Antony's agreement to a marriage with Octavia, Octavian's sister. The pact at Tarentum confirmed the triumviral powers of Antony and Octavian for another five years.

32 **inlectum** a pf. pass. infinitive in indirect discourse

  subdolae . . . exsolvisse "had paid the punishment of the treacherous marriage alliance with death"

33-48 Tacitus now turns to Augustus' tenure as *princeps* after Antony's demise. Scorn is heaped first on the disasters brought on by his foreign adventures before Tacitus turns his barbs against Augustus' domestic circumstances (for the emperor's family see the stemmata on p. 153), with Livia and Tiberius the subjects of particular criticism.

33 **pacem . . . cruentam** Supply *esse*.

34   **Lollianas Varianasque cladis** *cladis* is acc. pl. Lollius was defeated in Germany in 16 BCE with the loss of a legion and a standard (Cass. Dio 54.20); for Varus see p. 48.

    Romae locative

34–35   **Varrones, Egnatios, Iullos** All are in the pl. for rhetorical effect. Varro was Terentius Varro Murena, executed with Fannius Caepio in 23 or 22 BCE for conspiracy against Augustus' life (see Cass. Dio 54.3; Vell. Pat. 2.91). Egnatius Rufus was aedile, then praetor in the next year; when he failed to win the consulship he plotted against Augustus and was caught and executed in 19 BCE (Vell. Pat. 2.91). Iullus was M. Antony's son by Fulvia; although promoted to high office and married to Marcella, one of Octavia's daughters, he was forced to suicide for adultery with Augustus' daughter Julia in 2 BCE (Vell. Pat. 2.100.4).

35   **nec domesticis abstinebatur** lit. "nor was it abstained from his personal affairs"; or freely, "nor were his personal affairs spared"; for this impersonal use of *abstineo* see, e.g., Livy 3.10.7, *ut seditionibus abstineretur*.

    domesticis an abl. with *abstinebatur*

    abducta A verb such as *memorabatur* is understood.

36   **per ludibrium** "in mockery"; cf. *Ann.* 1.20, (*milites praefectum*) *per ludibrium rogitantes an tam immense onera . . . libenter ferret*

    Neroni uxor *Neroni* is a dat. of separation. The reference is to Livia Drusilla, who had been married to Ti. Claudius Nero, and who married Octavian in 38 BCE.

36–37   **concepto necdum edito partu** an abl. absolute; *partu* is a metonym, translate "offspring." The child in question is Drusus, Tiberius' younger brother, who was father of the emperor Claudius and died in 9 BCE.

37   **nuberet** impf. subjunctive in an indirect question. *M.* reads *nuberetque tedii et*, connecting it immediately with *Vedii*; there have been numerous though unsatisfactory suggestions for emendation, and I have here omitted the corrupt text (see p. 2).

38   **Vedii Pollionis luxus** Supply *erat*. Vedius became a virtual paradigm for cruelty, known for throwing slaves alive to his lampreys (see, e.g., Sen. *Ira* 3.40; cf. Plin. *HN* 9.77, 167); Augustus was forced to disassociate himself from his former friend.

38–39   **postremo . . . noverca** Tacitus here uses anaphora with a variation (*gravis* + *in* + the acc., then *gravis* + the dat.). Already Tacitus has implicated Livia in the death of Gaius Caesar (Augustus' grandson by his daughter Julia and his trusted advisor, M. Agrippa, and Augustus' own son by adoption [1.3]), accused her of putting Tiberius into Augustus' good graces to secure his succession, and of seeing to it that Augustus' sole remaining grandson by blood, Agrippa Postumus, was sent into exile (he was executed in 14 CE upon Tiberius' succession). Tacitus also plays on the tradition of the wicked stepmother to malign her character further; for discussion of the use of *gravis* in this passage see Santoro L'Hoir (2006, 59).

40   **relictum** Tacitus falls back into indirect discourse here. Supply *esse*; the subject is *nihil*. This is one of the more grossly exaggerated criticisms against Augustus, given his extensive restoration of temples and his interest in reorganizing by various means the religious life of the state.

        cum here causal

        templis et effigie Both are abl. of means. While true, temples to Augustus within the city itself were set up only after his death, and prior to that only in the provinces.

42   **caritate . . . cura** abl. of cause

        adscitum Supply *esse*.

43   **quoniam . . . introspexerit** an explanatory clause in indirect discourse with the verb in the pf. subjunctive; *adrogantiam* and *saevitiam* will prove two of Tiberius' chief characteristics. Suetonius does not accept Augustus' cynicism as an explanation for his adoption (*Tib.* 21).

43-44 **comparatione deterrima** The phrase is compressed; Tacitus means *comparatione cum deterrimo homine*. Woodman (2004, 8) translates it "by the basest of comparisons."

44 **sibi** i.e., Augustus

45 **paucis ante annis** abl. of degree of difference

tribuniciam potestatem an important power that rendered the person of the *princeps* sacrosanct and gave him the right to introduce legislation before the Senate. Tiberius was first granted *tribunicia potestas* in 6 BCE but then abruptly retired to Rhodes; the date referred to here is probably 4 CE when Tiberius held the power a second time; it was renewed in 13 CE for another ten years.

46 **a . . . postularet** *postularet* is the impf. subjunctive in a *cum* clause; the verb takes the acc. of what is asked + *ab* with the abl. (from whom something is asked).

honora oratione either an abl. absolute or an abl. of description; *honora* is strictly poetic—found in Valerius Flaccus (e.g., 4.342) and Statius (e.g., *Theb.* 2.629)—and first used in prose by Tacitus.

47 **de habitu cultuque et institutis** "concerning his deportment, his style of dress, and his manners"; for his *habitus* also see Suet. *Tib.* 68.

iecerat "had dropped remarks," though perhaps the modern idiom "had let fly" is a more apt capturing of the sense here

47-48 **quae . . . exprobaret** *quae* is a rel. pron. introducing a purpose clause.

48 **velut excusando** The gerund is an abl. of instrument used to express attendant circumstance.

✺ *ANNALES* 1.74

Romanius Hispo's prosecution of Granius Marcellus and the rise of the DELATORES

Over the course of the *Annales*, as Tiberius' rule deteriorates, *delatores* will emerge ever more powerful; these were vicious prosecutors whose ambition, desire for political prestige, and lucrative remuneration led them to accuse fellow senators of crimes ranging from astrological consultations concerning the life of the *princeps* to provincial maladministration. Although their activities were often essential in maintaining justice and good governance, in Tacitus' view there were times when they exceeded their mandates, and served as lackeys in fulfilling the desires, often viewed as malevolent, of the emperor. For Tacitus, they were central in creating an atmosphere of fear and intimidation that pervaded the Senate under Tiberius (and subsequent emperors), and made political life under the early emperors treacherous. Tacitus first introduces them here with the typological depiction of either Caepio Crispinus or Romanius Hispo (and most likely the latter), who prosecuted Granius Marcellus in 15 CE. It is worth noting that in the end the charge of *impietas* and speaking ill of the *princeps* only served to arouse Tiberius' anger at the prosecutor, while the more serious charge concerning provincial maladministration was sent to a lower court. Concerning this passage see Sinclair's excellent discussion (1995, 118–19); for *delatores* in general see Rutledge (2001).

1   **nec multo post** The present accusation immediately follows another Tacitus related in 1.73, concerning which see below, lines 15–16.

Granium Marcellum praetorem His rank was in fact higher, since Bithynia was a senatorial province and as such governed by a proconsul. *praetor* is a term commonly applied to provincial governors. On Granius' relevance to the contemporary scene see Woodman (2009, 35).

2   **quaestor ipsius** *quaestor* is in apposition to *Caepio Crispinus*, the subject of *postulavit*; the *quaestor* was often a very close

and trusted appointee (see Cic. *Div. in Caec.* 61), hence the deep sense of betrayal.

maiestatis This gen. of the charge with *postulavit* is found only in Tacitus.

3 **subscribente Romanio Hispone** an abl. absolute. Hispo as *subscriptor* would have been Caepio's co-prosecutor; Romanius Hispo's name is in fact problematic with an alternative reading of Romanus; the former is accepted by most editors and commentators.

qui The antecedent, as has been noted by several scholars, is deliberately ambiguous: Hispo or Caepio? The result of such ambiguity is to typologize the *delator* as a recognizable "species" under the Principate (see Sinclair 1995, 118–19).

4 **celebrem** modifies *quam*, whose antecedent is *formam*; it is the direct object of *fecerunt*. Translate "infamous."

miseriae . . . audaciae nom. pl., the subjects of *fecerunt*

5 **egens, ignotus** The phrase recalls Aeneas' self-description at Verg. *Aen.* 1.384; cf. Ter. *Phorm.* 751.

5–6 **occultis libellis** abl. of means; the meaning of *libellis* here is problematic. Woodman (2004, 38) translates it "secret documents," although Goodyear (1981, 160) argues for simply "accusations."

saevitiae dat. after *adrepit*

adrepit "wormed his way into" (in reference to personal feelings or confidence)

6–7 **clarissimo cuique** *periculum facessit* takes the dat.

7 **periculum facessit** "accused"; cf. Tac. *Hist.* 4.43

potentiam . . . odium direct object of *adeptus*, a pf. act. pple. from *adipiscor*

8–10 **quod . . . invenere** The phrase constitutes a compact statement; translate, "which, those having followed, (made them) rich men out of poor, men to be feared instead of men to be despised, discovered destruction for others and, in the end, for themselves."

quod The antecedent is *exemplum*.

9   **metuendi** the pass. periphrastic here used substantively, "men who ought to be feared"

10   **invenere** = *invenerunt*

   insimulabat This verb can take several constructions, including the acc. with an infinitive as it does here.

11   **inevitabile crimen** The phrase is in apposition to the preceeding clause.

12   **cum . . . accusator** i.e., the prosecutor was singling out each of the emperor's worst vices.

   deligeret impf. subjunctive in a *cum* clause

13   **obiectaretque reo** "and was charging the defendant" (sc. "with broadcasting them"); *obiectaretque* takes the dat.

13–14   **nam . . . credebantur** The meaning here is that because the *foedissima quaeque* were true, they were consequently believed to have been said by the defendant.

15–16   Tacitus turns briefly to a crime he had already noted prosecutors had tried unsuccessfully to introduce, that of *impietas* against the emperor and his family. At *Ann.* 1.73 Tacitus relates the case of Falanius, a Roman equestrian who was charged with desecrating an image of Augustus by allowing an actor of mimes in the presence of the now deified emperor's image kept in his house; in addition, Falanius was accused of selling an image of Augustus along with his house and gardens. Another equestrian, Rubrius, was charged with violating the *numen* of Augustus through perjury. Tiberius ordered both cases, as well as the one in the present passage, dismissed.

15   **sitam** Understand *esse* with *sitam*, a pf. pass. infinitive in indirect discourse after *addidit*; the subject is *statuam*.

   alia in statua *alia* modifies *statua*.

   amputato capite abl. absolute; it was not uncommon, in fact, to replace the heads on statues.

16   **inditam** Understand *esse*, a pf. pass. infinitive in indirect dis-
        course; the subject again is *statuam*.

∾ ANNALES 2.69

Witchcraft, poison, and magic spells used against Germanicus

Fear, jealousy, and its murderous consequences are central elements
for Tacitus of the imperial tyranny. A key illustration of this is the
troubled relationship between Tiberius and Germanicus. Tacitus ostensibly portrays Germanicus as a popular leader who would have restored republican government but put his duty to the emperor before
personal ambition, as illustrated in his crushing of the mutinies in
Germany upon Tiberius' accession. According to Tacitus, however,
Germanicus' popularity provoked the envy of his morose uncle, who
sent him to deal with affairs in the East, where he hoped he would
meet an untimely end (Tac. *Ann.* 2.5; Tiberius' motives reflect those
of Micipsa in sending Jugurtha to Numantia, Sall. *Iug.* 6.1–7.2). Germanicus had been given *maius imperium* over all governors whose
provinces he might visit. His mandate was to stabilize the situation
in Armenia, which was without a king, and to do the same in the
client kingdoms of Cappadocia, Commagene, and Amanus, whose
rulers had all recently died and were all ripe for Roman annexation;
in addition, Syria and Judaea were asking for relief from burden-
some taxation (see *Ann.* 2.42). Germanicus crowned Artaxias III
king of Armenia, oversaw the annexation of Cappadocia, and made
Commagene part of the province of Syria (*Ann.* 2.58). He clashed,
however, with the governor of Syria, Cn. Calpurnius Piso, a man
of ancient, noble lineage whom Tacitus portrays as proud, violent,
and recalcitrant. When Germanicus died in Antioch after falling ill
there, rumors abounded that poison and magic arts had been used
against him; Piso, Livia, and Tiberius were all suspected of complicity in his death (cf. *Ann.* 3.3). Piso was tried for treason and murder,
but ultimately acquitted of the latter charge. Recent discovery of an
inscription in Spain concerning Piso's punishment has cast new light

onto this particular case, and Tacitus' treatment of it. For discussion see Kraus and Woodman (1997, 99–102), Damon and Takács (1999, especially Damon, 143–62), and Griffin (2009, 177–80).

1   **Aegypto** abl. of place from which; strictly speaking, a province requires a prep., which Tacitus omits. Germanicus had been visiting in Egypt, where he met with Tiberius' displeasure for entering the province without his consent (Augustus established the rule whereby no one of the rank of equestrian or higher could enter the province without imperial permission).

     cuncta an acc. substantive, the subject of *abolita* and *versa*; it refers to everything Germanicus had done among the cities and armies of the East prior to traveling to Egypt.

     apud *apud* + acc. = "among"

2   **abolita . . . versa** Both are infinitives in indirect discourse after *cognoscit*, with *esse* understood.

     in contrarium "to the contrary" (i.e., "reversed")

3   **hinc** "for this reason"

3–4 **nec . . . intentabantur** lit. "nor were less bitter the things which were aimed by that one (i.e., Piso) against Caesar"; the phrase has caused commentators difficulties; the verb *intento* in Tacitus frequently has the sense of stretching forth weapons in a menacing manner (see, e.g., *Hist.* 1.69, *tela ac manus in ora legatorum intentant*); here the verb could simply mean to "aim" or "threaten."

4   **acerba quae** the subject of *intentabantur*

5   **Syria** as with *Aegypto* above, an abl. of place from which without a prep.

     adversa . . . valetudine abl. of means with a causal sense after *detentus*

6   **recreatum** a pf. pass. infinitive in indirect discourse after *accepit*, with *esse* and the subject *Germanicum* understood

     accepit The subject is Piso.

     pro incolumnitate "on behalf of his safety"

7   **solvebantur** "paid as due"; the subject is *vota*.

       admotas hostias direct object of *proturbat*; refers to the victims brought for sacrifice to the altars, hence *admotas*

       sacrificalem apparatum "materials for sacrifice"

7–8   **festam Antiochensium plebem** "the plebeians of Antioch celebrating a holiday"

8   **per lictores** *per* here indicates agency.

       proturbat "he drives off"

       Seleuciam acc. place to which

9   **degreditur** The subject is Piso.

       opperiens modifies the understood subject.

       aegritudinem i.e., the ultimate outcome of his illness

9–10   **Germanico acciderat** "had befallen Germanicus"; *acciderat* takes the dat.

10–11   **persuasio ... accepti** constitutes the subject of *augebat*.

10   **persuasio** "a conviction"; it was a figment of Germanicus' imagination, and the charge of poisoning was ultimately dismissed at Piso's trial (*Ann.* 3.14).

       saevam vim morbi the direct object of *augebat*

11   **accepti** "of being the recipient of"; here a pf. pass. pple. acting as a substantive

       solo ac parietibus "in the floor and in the walls"; both are locative.

11–14   **et reperiebantur ... aliaque malefica** *erutae ... reliquiae, carmina et devotiones ... nomen ... insculptum, semusti cineres ... obliti aliaque malefica* all constitute the subject of *reperiebantur*; the *et* here affirms the actuality of the discovery.

12   **erutae ... reliquiae** "the exhumed remains"; the remains of the dead were used as curses against the living or for magic practices in general; for the most vivid example see Lucan 6.624–53 with Braund's commentary in this series (*A Lucan Reader* 2009); the same story concerning the use of curses and spells to bewitch Germanicus is related in Cassius Dio 57.18.9.

carmina et devotiones *carmina* here refers to incantations and curses of the sort that had long been prohibited by the Twelve Tables; *devotiones* sometimes refer more strictly to curses addressing the dead.

13 **nomen Germanici plumbeis tabulis insculptum** *insculptum* modifies *nomen* and takes the abl., hence *plumbeis tabulis*; one form of cursing was to inscribe the curse onto a lead tablet and to bury it with the presumption that the spirits of the underworld would receive the curse.

14 **tabo obliti** "smeared with foul matter," because they are dragged *semusti* from the funeral pyre

malefica Goodyear (1981, 411) translates the word substantively as "devices of black magic."

quis an abl. of means in the pl.; *aliaque malefica* is the antecedant.

15 **animas** acc. in indirect discourse after *creditur*, the subject of *sacrari*

numinibus infernis dat., indirect object

missi "men who had been sent"; pf. pass. pple. acting as a substantive

16 **ut** "as," "on the grounds that"

valetudinis adversa rimantes *adversa* is a substantive in the n. acc. pl.; Furneaux *ad loc.* translates it, "prying into the bad symptoms of the disease."

∾ *ANNALES 4.1–2, 4.3*

The rise of Sejanus

Under Augustus and Tiberius the Praetorian Guard turned into a powerful force in Rome, and the Praetorian Praefect grew to become one of the most prestigious offices of the state. Sejanus represents the first in a line of praefects who were of dubious moral character, including Sertorius Macro under Caligula and Ofonius Tigellinus under Nero, and he is one of Tacitus' greatest villains.

For Tacitus, his rise and fall constitute a central component in the tragedy of Tiberius' reign (see p. xxiv). The following passage introduces Sejanus and gives a brief character sketch based on Sallust's of Catiline, and on Livy's of Hannibal (see p. xxxiv). Indeed, Tacitus recalls Sallust here more pointedly than at any other point in his works, and it has been argued that Books 4 and 5 were intended to be read as a monograph, like Sallust's *Bellum Catilinam*, since the narrative recounts the rise and fall of a dangerous usurper (Kraus 2009, 104). The Sallustian reference thus marks the halfway point in the Tiberian hexad, and recalls a similar reference at the opening of Tacitus' work (see p. 70 line 1).

1   **C. Asinio C. Antistio consulibus** an abl. absolute

      Tiberio dat. of possession with a copulative verb

2   **compositae rei publicae** "of a state that was peaceful"

3   **prospera** "prosperous events"; a n. pl. substantive

      ducebat "reckoned"; as Martin and Woodman (1989, 78) note, the parenthetical aside in Tacitus is sometimes used, as it is here, to express cynicism, paradox, or both.

      turbare a complementary infinitive with *coepit*

4   **saevire . . . praebere** Both are complementary infinitives with *coepit*, but the subject of *coepit* shifts from *fortuna* to *ipse* (i.e., Tiberius).

      saevientibus a substantive in the dat. after *praebere*

      viris "powers"; pl. of *vis*

5   **initium et causa** Supply *erant*.

      penes Aelium Seianum *penes* + acc. = "with"

5–6   **cohortibus praetoriis praefectum** *praefectum* here functions as a substantive and takes the dat.

6   **supra memoravi** i.e., at *Ann.* 1.24, 69; 3.29, 35, 72

7   **quo facinore** "by what crime"; the phrase echoes the commencement of Tiberius' reign at *Ann.* 1.6, see p. xxviii.

      dominationem the direct object of *raptum*

7–8   **raptum ierit** "went to seize"; *ierit* is pf. subjunctive in an indirect question with *raptum* as a supine; for similar use of the supine see, e.g., *Ann*. 4.66, 73

8   **Vulsiniis** a locative; the place is modern Bolsena.

     patre Seio Strabone an abl. of origin with *genitus*. Sejanus' father had been Augustus' Praetorian Praefect (see Tac. *Ann*. 1.7) and later was put in the trusted position of Praefect of Egypt (Cass. Dio 57.19); Velleius refers to him as the *princeps equestris ordinis* (2.127.3).

8–9   **equite Romano** an abl. in apposition to *patre Seio Strabone*

9   **prima iuventa** an abl. of time

10   **sectatus** "having followed eagerly"

     Apicio diviti et prodigo M. Gavius Apicius, not to be confused with the famous gourmand and author of the celebrated cookbook (though Tacitus' description would suit such a character), who lived later.

11   **stuprum** Here the word implies disgrace or dishonor stemming from sexual impropriety.

     veno dedisse *dare* + *veno* or *venum* = "to give for sale"; the infinitive is in indirect discourse after the phrase *non sine rumore*.

     variis artibus an abl. of means

11–12   **mox Tiberium variis artibus devinxit adeo ut** cf. *Ann*. 1.3 (said of Livia's control over Augustus and her conniving at Agrippa Postumus' exile): *nam senem Augustum devinxerat adeo uti*, etc. For a good discussion of the similarities between the two passages see Santoro L'Hoir (2006, 150–52).

12   **obscurum** The adj. here has several possible meanings: "reserved," "secretive," and "unintelligible," all of which are key aspects of Tiberius' character and administration; for Tiberius' "obscurity" see *Ann*. 1.7, 13.3; on the secretive nature of his administration see 1.6. Tiberius' inscrutability always made him a difficult person to "read"; see O'Gorman (2000, 78–105).

adversum "towards"; here a prep.

sibi uni i.e., to Sejanus

12–13   **ut . . . efficeret** "so that he rendered him obtuse in regard to others, while in regard to himself alone he was careless and let down his guard"

13   **sollertia** abl. of means with a causal sense

    isdem artibus abl. of means

13–14   **non tam . . . quam** "not so much . . . than"

14   **victus est** The subject is Sejanus.

    deum gen. pl. of *deus*

    ira abl. of means, again as with *sollertia* in line 13, with a causal sense, "due to"; for a similar sentiment cf. Tac. *Hist.* 1.3, *adprobatum est non esse curae deis securitatem nostram, esse ultionem.* See Griffin (2009, 169–72) for a discussion of Tacitus' metaphysical explanations for historical events.

    in rem Romanam acc. with *in*; *res* can = "the state" when *publica* is omitted; cf. Tac. *Hist.* 1.29, *res sine discordia translatae.*

14–15   **cuius pari exitio viguit ceciditque** The phrase is an example of Tacitean obscurity. The antecedent of *cuius* is *rem Romanam*; *pari exitio* is an abl. of attendant circumstance and *pari* can be translated adverbially: "by whose destruction he equally flourished and fell." Tacitus here means that Sejanus rose through means destructive to the state, and that likewise left destruction in his path after his demise (see, e.g., *Ann.* 5.6–9, 11).

15–20   These lines constitute a brief character sketch of the sort at which Tacitus excelled (see p. xxxiv). This particular passage draws heavily on Sallust's characterization of Catiline (*Cat.* 5), and, as Martin and Woodman (1989, 84) note, "is the closest and most sustained imitation of Sallust in the whole of Tacitus." Keitel (1984, 322–23) has argued the connection between Sejanus and Catiline is intended to suggest that the Principate is no more stable politically than the late Republic.

15   **illi** dat. of possession with the verb *erat* omitted, as it is for the remainder of the sentence

    tolerans modifies *corpus.*

16   **sui obtegens** *obtegens* as a pple. uses the gen. only here.

    criminator a rare noun until later Latin; Tacitus for variation will occasionally combine a pple. with a noun; cf. *Ann.* 6.38, *ostentans et contemptor*

    iuxta "(were) side by side"

17   **palam ... intus** "openly ... within," constituting an antithesis

    compositus pudor "a quiet modesty"; Woodman (2004, 122) translates the phrase "a calm reserve."

17–18 **summa apiscendi libido** *summa* is a n. pl. substantive after the gerund *apiscendi*, which is gen. after *libido* and also an archaic form of *adpiscendi*

18   **eiusque causa** "and for its sake." The *eiusque* refers to the previous clause; *causa* is usually preceded by the noun it governs in the gen. case.

    modo ... saepius "now ... more often"

19   **noxiae** an adj. modifying *industria ac vigilantia*; translate "no less harmful."

19–20 **parando regno finguntur** *finguntur* has the sense of conceiving something for some purpose but also of fabricating or inventing.

    parando regno a gerundive in the dat. expressing purpose; stylistically it constitutes an archaism that Tacitus enjoys using.

21   **vim praefecturae modicam antea** *antea* modifies *vim ... modicam*; the meaning here is that the power of the Prae-fect had previously been moderate but that Sejanus would strengthen it as a path to power.

    intendit "aimed at"

    dispersas modifies *cohortis* in line 22, which is acc. pl.; both are the direct object of *conducendo.*

22   **una in castra** *una* modifies *castra*, and is acc. motion towards; for *unus* in the pl. cf., e.g., Ter. *Eun.* 367, *aderit una in unis aedibus.* Here *una* = "in one place," "together."

conducendo a gerund, abl. of means

23   **imperia** "orders," "commands"

acciperent The subjunctive is ambiguous and could be either in a result or purpose clause.

numeroque . . . robore . . . visu All are abl. of means.

inter se Take with *visu*; translate "by seeing each other," The notion here is that familiarity and intimacy would give rise to a greater camaraderie.

24   **ipsis** refers here to the soldiery.

fiducia . . . metus Both are the subject of *oreretur.*

oreretur See *acciperent* in line 23.

praetendebat "He was holding out as a pretext"

lascivire infinitive in indirect discourse after *praetendebat*

25   **diductum** "dispersed"; modifies *militem*

si quid subitum *quid* here functions as an indef. pron. after *si*, modified by *subitum.*

ingruat a subjunctive in a subordinate clause in indirect discourse indicating potential; its tense (pres. rather than impf. after *praetendebat*) violates the rule concerning sequence of tenses.

25–26   **maiore auxilio pariter subveniri** an example of Tacitus' compressed phrasing; translate "their support as one body would offer greater assistance," *maiore auxilio* is an abl. of means, modified by *pariter.*

26   **subveniri** an infinitive in indirect discourse after *praetendebat*; it is pass. and its usage here is impersonal.

severius "more strictly"; a compar. adv. The notion is that the Praetorians would behave with greater military discipline if the place were made to look and feel like a military encampment.

acturos sc. *esse*; a fut. act. infinitive in indirect discourse; the subject is the soldiery.

vallum A fortification of the sort that would be set up around a military encampment.

27   **statuatur** a pres. subjunctive; see *ingruat* above, line 25.

inlecebris abl. of separation

ut "when"

28   **inrepere** a historical infinitive

militaris animos the direct object of *inrepere*

adeundo appellando Both are gerunds and are abl. of means; understand *eos* (i.e., *milites*).

29   **ipse** i.e., Sejanus

deligere a historical infinitive

29–31   **senatorio ambitu . . . ornandi** abl. of separation with *abstinebat*; *senatorio ambitu* needs to be understood in close conjunction with *ornandi*. Martin and Woodman (1989, 89) translate the phrase "nor did he refrain from courting popularity amongst senators by honouring . . ."

30   **clientes suos** direct object of *ornandi*

honoribus aut provinciis abl. of means; *honoribus* can refer either to monetary awards for services rendered or to offices.

31   **ornandi** a gerund in the gen.

facili Tiberio atque ita prono an abl. absolute. Both this phrase and Sejanus' bestowal (as an equestrian) of honors to senators (lines 29–31) suggest the inferiority of both the *princeps* and Senate to him.

32   **apud** "among"

patres cf. *Ann.* 1.10, line 21

celebraret "celebrated the praises of"; impf. subjunctive in a result clause

33–34   **interque principia legionum** the headquarters of the legionary camps where the standards were also kept along with the images of the emperors

34   **sineret** subjunctive in a result clause

35-46   The first six lines of 4.3 are omitted, in which Tacitus notes
        that Sejanus conveniently had a personal grudge against Ti-
        berius' son Drusus. He gives this as a partial motive for Seja-
        nus' seduction of Drusus' wife, Livilla (sister of Germanicus
        and Claudius), and further states that it was Sejanus' first step
        in a series of moves against the imperial house.

35   **cuncta temptanti** *cuncta* is n. pl. substantive, the direct object
        of *temptanti*, a pple. in the dat. after *promptissimum visum*
        and referring to Sejanus

35-36   **promptissimum visum** Understand *est* with *visum*.

36   **Liviam** also known as Livilla

        convertere complementary infinitive with *visum*

37   **formae . . . indecorae** a gen. of description

        initio aetatis "at the start of her life"

        pulchritudine abl. of means

38   **ut** "as if"

        amore an abl. of means; this sentence picks up on the theme
        of sexual dereliction noted above (line 11).

        adulterio an abl. of means

39   **primi flagitii** a gen. with *potitus est* and an archaism

39-40   **neque . . . abnuerit** the pf. subjunctive here indicating a past
        generalization; the precise sense of the phrase is problem-
        atic; see Martin and Woodman (1989, 92–93) for discussion.
        Woodman (2004, 123) translates the phrase, "(and, with her
        modesty lost, a female was unlikely to reject other things)."

        amissa pudicitia an abl. absolute

40   **alia** n. substantive, the direct object of *abnuerit*

        abnuerit a pf. potential subjunctive

40-41   **ad coniungii . . . necem mariti** The first two phrases are chi-
        astic, the final phrase parallel to the second, hence also chias-
        tic with the first.

41   **illa** i.e., Livilla

cui a dat. of possession with *avunculus, socer,* and *liberi* in line 42

41–42   **avunculus . . . posteros** constitutes two tricolons for climactic effect.

42   **seque** i.e., Livilla (again)

43   **municipali adultero** an abl. of means. The sneer against Sejanus' origins from the municipalities is pejorative.

        pro honestis et praesentibus Translate *pro* "instead of"; both *honestis* and *praesentibus* are substantives in the abl. case. The latter refers to Livilla's comfortable and privileged position as empress heir apparent in her capacity as Drusus' wife.

44   **flagitiosa et incerta** n. substantive, the direct object of *expectaret*

        expectaret subjunctive in a purpose clause

        conscientiam an acc. of motion towards, with *in*

45   **specie artis** "under the pretense of his skill"

45–46   **frequens secretis** "was frequently at hand for her secrets"; *frequens* has the sense of "being frequently" or "assiduously" at a place and takes the dat. Understand *erat*.

✑ *ANNALES 6.1*
Tiberius' debauchery on Capri

In 26 CE Tiberius, disgusted with life in Rome, left the city at Sejanus' urging and governed afterward from his imperial villa on the island of Capri. From then until his fall in October of 31, Sejanus controlled access to Tiberius, during which he effected the removal of Agrippina and her sons (see p. xxiv). After Sejanus' downfall, Tiberius still showed no interest in returning to the city, and remained in Campania while the persecution of Sejanus' adherents continued. In the last years of his life, rumors abounded that Tiberius surrendered himself to sensuous depravity of the worst sort, with the most salacious reports found in Suetonius (*Tib.* 42–45). The free reign given to sexual passions, recounted here, is among

the most outstanding characteristics of the tyrant for Tacitus, as
we also find in his portrayal of
Nero (see, e.g., *Ann.* 16.19–20).
See Dunkle (1971, 15–18) for
discussion of *libido* as an aspect
of tyranny in antiquity; also see
Houston (1985, 179–96) whose
discussion gives a more balanced
and complex picture of Tiberius'
life on Capri.

Fig. 2. Tiberius, Augustus' successor,
is one of Tacitus' most complex and
tragic characters. Glyptotek, Munich.
Wikimedia Commons.

1   **Cn. Domitius** father of the
emperor Nero, his cogno-
men was Ahenobarbus;
Suet. *Ner.* 5.1 says that
he was *omni parte vitae
detestabilis.*

Camillus Scribonianus His full name was L. Arruntius Ca-
millus Scribonianus, and he subsequently rebelled against
Claudius in 42 while legate in Dalmatia (Cass. Dio 60.15–16;
Suet. *Claud.* 13.1–2).

2–3   **tramisso ... freto** an abl. absolute

2   **quod** The antecedent is *freto.*

Capreas modern Capri, located opposite the Surrentine peninsula in the southernmost part of the Bay of Naples. Augustus purchased it from the Neopolitans and built an imperial
villa on the island; see Cass. Dio 52.43.2; cf. Suet. *Aug.* 92.2.

3   **praelegebat** "he was coasting along"

4   **intraret** an impf. subjunctive in an indirect question introduced by *ambiguus*

seu corresponds to the *an*, formulating an alternative indirect
question not with another verb in the subjunctive but in the
participular mood, *simulans.*

speciem *speciem* picks up yet again the theme of Tiberius' dissimulation.

5   **venturi** "of one about to come"

in propinqua "to the vicinities"; *propinqua* is acc. place to which, with *in*

5–6   **aditis . . . hortis** an abl. absolute

6   **iuxta Tiberim** probably refers to the gardens left by Caesar to the Roman people on the western and northern side of the Tiber (Suet. *Caes.* 83.2).

7   **pudore** abl. of cause

quibus . . . indomitis an abl. of means; *indomitis* should be translated adverbially and taken closely with *adeo.*

8   **exarserat** an instance of Tacitean metaphor

more regio an abl. of manner

ingenuam The word can mean both "noble" and "freeborn," and here may have the sense of both; Tacitus follows up the remark by noting that the ancestry of those Tiberius defiled incited his lust further, while at the same time the reference to his regal behavior (*more regio*) is accentuated by the contrast with those who are "freeborn."

pollueret an impf. subjunctive in a result clause

9   **nec . . . tantum . . . set** "not only . . . but"; these function to create a coordinating conj.

10   **imagines . . . incitamentum** *incitatmentum* is in apposition to *imagines* as well as *formam* and *corpora*, all of which he had "as an incentive," "an incitement." Normally *imagines* were paraded at funerals to rouse the audience to emulate the virtues of the *maiores* (see, e.g., Polyb. 6.53; Sall. *Iug.* 4.5–6; Tac. *Agr.* 46.1–3); here Tacitus has turned the convention on its head.

11   **habebat** The subject is Tiberius.

12   **vocabula** "names"

sellariorum et spintriarum Both are gen. pl.; take with *vocabula*. The meaning of the first is uncertain but derives from *sellarium* = "privy"; cf. Schol. *ad Juv.* 3.136, by which time the word had come to mean "a public courtesan." The latter has the alternative form of *sphintria* and is translated "male prostitute"; for both also see Suet. *Tib.* 43.1.

12-13   **ex foeditate loci ac multiplici patientia** a difficult phrase; Woodman (2004, 166) translates it "from the foulness of their place and their multifarious passivity." For the meaning here of *patientia* cf. Petr. 9, 25; Cic *Ver.* 2.5.13, 34.

13   **qui conquirerent** The rel. *qui* here introduces a purpose clause, hence the subjunctive.

14   **pertraherent** The verb can mean both "to allure (to a place)" and "to conduct to a place (by force)"; what follows indicates Tacitus has in mind both meanings.

14-15   **dona in promptos, minas adversum abnuentis** *dona* and *minas* are the direct objects of *exercebant* in line 16. Both *promptos* and *abnuentis* are acc. participles and substantantives; note the varying construction of *in* and *adversum*; translate *in* "towards" or (more idiomatically) "for."

15   **retinerent** an impf. subjunctive acting as a frequentative; translate "if a parent or relative was holding them back"; cf. above, p. 7 line 2 for an identical construction.

16   **raptus** like *vim* (as well as *dona* and *minas*), a direct object of *exercebant*, here in the acc. pl.

suaque . . . libita a n. pl. substantive from *libet*; translate "their own pleasure"; for *libita* with this sense cf. Tac. *Ann.* 12.6, 14.2.

ipsi refers here to the *servi*.

in captos a substantive in the acc. pl. with *in* (translate "against"). No doubt one of the more galling aspects of Tiberius' depravity was the reversal of roles in which nobles found themselves, as imperial servants employed their will against them.

exercebant "were using"

∾ *ANNALES* 6.50–51

Tiberius' death and obituary, and the succession of Caligula

Tiberius died on March 16, 37 CE, at a villa once owned by Lucullus on Cape Misenum in the northern mainland of the Bay of Naples. Despite his advanced age, Tiberius was still slow to choose an heir. It was only very late, and in part through the designs of his new Praetorian Praefect, Sertorius Macro, that Tiberius chose Gaius Caligula, the sole remaining son of Agrippina and Germanicus, to succeed him. Tacitus gives a vivid account of Tiberius' tragic, murderous end—not without a touch of dark humor that highlights the inevitably awkward and dangerous nature of imperial succession (see Mellor 1993, 130; see 129–36 for his general discussion of Tacitean irony and humor). Suetonius (*Tib.* 73; cf. *Calig.* 12.2) recounts a similar version, but also gives two other alternatives (one that Caligula poisoned Tiberius, the other that he died a natural death) that Tacitus omits. Tacitus follows this episode with Tiberius' obituary, which includes summary of his life, reign, and gradual slide into corruption, for an analysis of which see Woodman (1989, 197–205).

1–2   **septimum decimum kal. Aprilis** i.e., the seventeenth day before the kalends of April: March 16; cf. Suet. *Tib.* 73.1. Tacitus has dropped the usual inclusion of *a.d.* here with the date, as he does elsewhere, e.g., *Ann.* 6.25.

2   **interclusa anima** an abl. absolute

    creditus est The subject is Tiberius.

3   **explevisse** a complementary infinitive with *creditus est*; the phrase is first here with Tacitus; Martin (2001, 93) translates it "completed his mortal span."

    multo gratantum concursu an abl. of manner constituting a virtual abl. of accompaniment with *gratantum*, a gen. pl. substantive; translate "well-wishers." *gratantum* is a distinctly poetic verb (see, e.g., Verg. *Aen.* 5.40).

3–4 **ad capienda imperii primordia** a gerundive of purpose with a verb of motion, *egrediebatur*

5 **adfertur** "it is reported"; indicative in a temporal *cum* clause

redire an infinitive in indirect discourse

vocem ac visus Both are subject acc. in indirect discourse.

vocarique here a pass. infinitive used impersonally

qui functions here as an indef. pron. and introduces a purpose clause.

5–6 **recreandae defectioni** a gerundive in the dat. indicating purpose

6 **hinc** "on this account"

in omnis *omnis* is acc. pl.; translate *in* "to," "for."

7 **dispergi** a historical infinitive

7–8 **se quisque . . . fingere** "each one to represent himself"; *fingere* is a historical infinitive; cf. *Ann.* 1.7 where the Senate tries to guess the best face to put forward on the occasion of Tiberius' succession.

8 **in silentium fixus** *fixus* is from *figo* and takes *in* + either the abl. or acc.; translate "affixed into silence." Caligula is taken by surprise and scarcely hides his shock; according to Tacitus (*Ann.* 6.20), however, he was usually a master of dissimulation.

8–9 **a summa spe novissima expetabat** "from the highest hope awaiting the worst"; the prep. *a* here has the sense of "instead of." *novissima* as a substantive literally means "the uttermost," cf. Tac. *Ann.* 12.20; 15.44.

9 **Macro** Q. Naevius Cordus Sertorius Macro was instrumental in Sejanus' overthrow and was his successor as Praetorian Praefect. He went on to become Praefect of Egypt, but Caligula forced him to suicide. Cassius Dio (58.28.2–3) explicitly blames Caligula for Tiberius' murder.

opprimi "to be smothered"

10 **discedique** an infinitive in the pres. pass. used impersonally

finivit "died"

10–11 **octavo et septuagesimo aetatis anno** abl. of time when; he was born November 16, 42 BCE.

12 **ei** dat. of possession with the verb *esse* understood. His father was Tib. Claudius Nero; see Suet. *Tib.* 4 for his life and career.

13 **in Liviam et mox Iuliam familiam** Both *Liviam* and *Iuliam familiam* are acc. with *in* = "into." Livia was adopted into the Julian clan under the terms of Augustus' will; see Tac. *Ann.* 1.8; also see Suet. *Tib.* 3.

  adoptionibus abl. of means

14 **transierit** a pf. subjunctive in a concessive clause governed by *quamquam*

  casus . . . ancipites Supply *erant*.

15 **proscriptum** The reference is likely to his being outlawed after his assistance to Lucius Antonius in the Perusine War of 41 BCE, after which he fled first to Sex. Pompeius in Sicily and then to Marc Antony in Achaea; shortly after the Pact of Misenum in 39 BCE he returned to favor with Octavian, who soon after appropriated his wife Livia.

16 **multis aemulis** abl. of means

  Marcellus See above, p. 59 line 8.

17 **Agrippa** Concerning whom see above, p. 59.

  Gaius Luciusque two favored sons of Agrippa and Julia. Gaius was born in 20 BCE; he died on February 21, 4 CE, in Lycia while acting with proconsular authority in the eastern provinces. Lucius was born in 17 BCE and died on August 20, 2 CE, in Massilia while traveling to Spain. For their third son Agrippa Postumus, see p. 84.

  viguere = *viguerunt*

18 **Drusus** see above, pp. 48, 59. He was the father of Germanicus, Livilla, and Claudius.

  prosperiore civium amore *prosperiore . . . amore* is an abl. of description. The reference to *civium* and their feelings towards Drusus refers to the rumor of his desire to restore the Republic; see Tac. *Ann.* 1.33; cf. Suet. *Claud.* 1.1.

19   **in lubrico** "in a slippery spot," "in a hazardous place"

egit The verb *ago* can sometimes be translated virtually equivalent to the verb "to be," as is the case here; cf. *Ann.* 3.19, 3.38 for similar usage

accepta in matrimonium Iulia an abl. absolute

impudicitiam Julia, Augustus' only daughter by his first wife, Scribonia, was banished when Augustus discovered her immoral behavior in 2 BCE. She died in 14, and Tacitus gives her obituary at *Ann.* 1.53.

20   **declinans** "avoiding." For Tiberius' exile in Rhodes see above, p. xxiii; for ancient explanations for his long stay see Vell. Pat. 2.99; Cass. Dio 55.9.5.

Rhodo abl. place from which

21   **vacuos principis penatis** For *penatis* see above, p. 58 line 3. Tacitus' assertion that the house of the *princeps* was *vacuos* is not entirely true, since Gaius did not die until 4 CE.

duodecim annis i.e., from 2 to 14 CE

rei Romanae for this phrase in reference to the Roman state cf. *Ann.* 4.1, p. 93

22   **tribus ferme et viginti** *viginti* is indeclinable, but one would normally expect an acc. duration of time; instead Tacitus here uses the abl.

22–23   **morum quoque tempora illi diversa** The difficulty of the precise meaning of this phrase hinges on the interpretation of *tempora*, which can refer to a particular period of time in the life of a person, the conditions affecting a person, or, as is most likely here, a particular season or phase, since in such instances *tempus* will take a gen. See, e.g., Quint. *Inst.* 12.11.13: *si aetatem nostrum non spatio senectutis sed tempore adulescentiae metiamur.* Translate "The phases of his character were various."

23   **egregium** Understand *tempus*.

vita famaque Both are abl. of specification with *egregium*; cf. *Agr.* 14.1, *uterque bello egregius.*

24 **in imperiis sub Augusto** The reference is to the imperial commands he held in the course of an illustrious military career under Augustus. Between 12 and 9 BCE he reduced Pannonia; from 9 to 7 BCE and from 4 to 6 CE he campaigned in Germania; between 6 and 9 CE he put down revolts in Pannonia and Illyricum.

occultum ac subdolum For both understand *tempus*, as for *egregium* in line 23.

25 **fingendis virtutibus** a gerundive construction in the dat. case indicating purpose, and to be taken closely with *occultum ac subdolum*

donec "so long as"

Germanicus ac Drusus For Germanicus' death see p. 89; Drusus, Tiberius' son, died in 23 CE.

superfuere = *superfuerunt*

26 **idem . . . mixtus** When modified by a predicate *idem* can be translated as "likewise"; supply *est.*

bona malaque n. pl. substantives

incolumni matre an abl. absolute. Livia died in 29 CE, and Tacitus gives her obituary at *Ann.* 5.1; of Tiberius' reign after her death Tacitus states, *tunc velut frenis exsoluti* [sc. *Tiberius et Seianus*] *proruperunt* (*Ann.* 5.3).

27 **intestabilis saevitia** Supply *erat*; note the shift from the nom. to the abl. in the following phrase.

obtectis libidinibus an abl. absolute

28 **postremo** "at last"

prorupit The metaphor of bursting is one Tacitus applies periodically to Tiberius; see, e.g., *Ann.* 1.4, *multaque indicia saevitiae, quamquam premantur, erumpere*; cf. above line 26.

29   **remoto pudore et metu** Take the whole phrase together as an abl. absolute; *pudore* refers to his inclination towards modesty while still in Rome and with his mother still living; *metu* refers to the restraint he felt during Sejanus' ascendancy. Martin (2001, 93–95) notes the parallel here with Sall. *Hist.* 1.12, *postquam remoto metu Punico*. As Rome's morals remained in check as long as Carthage loomed as a threat, Tiberius' character was similarly restrained by those around him.

suo . . . ingenio Our understanding of this phrase is problematic. The ancients held that character was fixed at birth; for Tacitus, Tiberius' character was bad from the start, and only hypocrisy and the restraints imposed by those around him hid his true nature. Martin (2001, 93–5) thus translates the phrase, "he followed his own inclination"; Woodman (1989, 197–205; 2004, 194), however, suggests that the word *ingenium* here means "behavior," not character, and that we should translate the phrase, "he had only himself to rely on."

ꙮ *ANNALES 11.24*
Claudius' speech on allowing Gauls into the Senate

Tacitus' manuscript breaks off with the death of Tiberius in 37 CE and does not resume until six years into the reign of Claudius in 47 (see p. xxiv), when the empress Messalina and Claudius' courtiers reign supreme. In the next year Claudius delivered a speech to the Senate concerning the admission of Gauls into its order; it supported Claudius' request, although opposed by some, to expand admission to include Gallic chieftains from Gallia Comata. Caesar and Augustus had both supported and undertaken similar expansion, and Claudius now sought senatorial support for his policy. The speech stands as the sole example in antiquity of an oration whose text still survives in an inscription from Lyons, France (ancient Lugdunum). It offers a rare opportunity for us to assess how ancient historians reworked and manipulated their source material through direct comparison with the epigraphic record (also see p. xxxii).

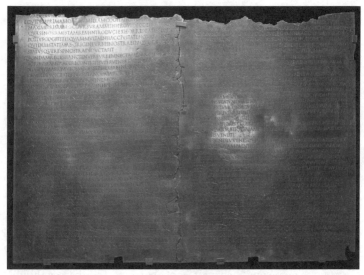

Fig. 3. The Lyons Tablet records Claudius' speech on the admission of Gauls to the Senate, and is the only inscription from antiquity that allows for comparison in an oration recorded by an ancient historian. Gallo-Roman Museum of Lyon. Wikimedia Commons.

Tacitus has, in fact, made substantial changes to the speech: his version is reworked to be considerably shorter than the surviving inscription (it represents less than one-third of the extant original); prolix points in the original, such as the various ethnicities allowed into Rome, are condensed; the personal asides Claudius made referring to family and courtiers are eschewed; the long point about new arrivals obtaining magistracies is abbreviated to a single sentence near the end; and no single Gallic city receives any special mention, as they did in Claudius' oration. These are just some of the more striking differences between Tacitus and the original, which also includes a number of Graecisms and archaic language, which Tacitus here avoids. For detailed comparative analysis of Tacitus' version of the speech with the inscription see Malloch (2009, 124–26) and Griffin (1982, 404–18; cf. 2009, 180–81).

1–10   Claudius here discusses the earliest period of Rome's past, from its mythological origins to the conquest of Italy, and notes the tradition from the start of inclusion of others within the state and within its political sphere.

2   **Clausus** For his Sabine origin see Livy 2.16; Verg. *Aen.* 7.706–9. According to Livy, Attus (or Attius) Clausus came to Rome in 505 BCE from Regillus; cf. Suet. *Tib.* 1.1; Tac. *Ann.* 4.9.

       origine Sabina abl. of description

3   **civitatem . . . familias** Both are acc. with *in* + *adscitus est*.

       patriciorum *civitatem . . . patriciorum* recalls Livy 4.3.14; see Kraus and Woodman (1997, 99); the *gens Claudia* was among the most ancient of the aristocratic families in Rome.

4   **uti** infinitive with *hortantur* where a iussive noun clause would be expected; *hortor* + the infinitive is a poetic construction and used by Tacitus only in the *Annales*.

       paribus consiliis abl. with *uti*

5   **transferendo** gerund, abl. of means

       huc adv. of place to which

       quod . . . fuerit The *quod* is modified by *egregium*, and the subjunctive is in a rel. clause of characteristic.

6–8   **ignoro . . . accitos** After *ignoro* the speech goes into indirect discourse, with *accitos* as the main verb and *esse* omitted.

6   **Iulios . . . Coruncanios . . . Porcios** all subjects acc. in indirect discourse; the *gens Iulia* traced its origins back to Anchises and Venus, whose grandson, Ascanius, son of Aeneas, was the first king of Alba Longa. The best known of the Coruncanii were perhaps Gaius and Lucius, two brothers, one of whom, Lucius, was killed on an embassy to Queen Teuta in 230 BCE, which precipitated the First Illyrian War. The Porcii came fom Tusculum; the *novus homo* ("new man"), M. Porcius Cato the Elder (Cato the Censor, 234–149 BCE), was the first in his family to hold the consulship, thereby ennobling the clan. None of these are mentioned in the extant portion of Claudius' speech.

Alba . . . Camerio . . . Tusculo all are abl. of origin; Camerium was a Latin city destroyed early in Rome's history.

7   **vetera** acc. pl. substantive

scrutemur subjunctive in a purpose clause

Etruria Lucaniaque abl. of place from which. Etruria would have been inhabited by the Etruscans, from whom, to cite but one example, Augustus' minister Maecenas traced his origins; Lucania was inhabited by the Samnites.

omni Italia abl. of place from which; Claudius is referring to the Italians who eventually shared the same rights as Romans, though not until after the Social War (90–88 BCE).

7–8   **Etruria . . . accitos** Understand as the subject of this clause *alios*.

8   **ipsam . . . promotam** *ipsam* is the subject acc. in indirect discourse of *promotam* and refers back to *omni Italia*; citizenship was extended to the Alps when Caesar granted it to the people of Transpadane Gaul in 49 BCE.

Alpis acc. with *in*

9   **singuli viritim** Tacitus captures some of Claudius' somewhat prolix style here, imitating his use of pleonasms and fulsomeness of expression.

9–10   **in nomen nostrum** with *coalescerent*

10   **coalescerent** subjunctive in a result clause

10–20   Tacitus now has Claudius turn to the period of the late Republic and the Augustan era, when Caesar first allowed those beyond Rome's boundaries into the Senate, and when the civil wars necessitated a revision of its numbers.

10   **solida . . . quies** Understand *erat*.

domi locative

11   **externa** acc. pl. substantive with *adversus*

Transpadani See above, line 8.

recepti Understand *sunt*.

12–13   **specie . . . subventum est** Veteran legions were settled in colonies throughout the empire and intermarried with local provincial women, whose children offered a steady supply of manpower for the army.

12   **specie** abl. of means

      deductarum modifies *legionum*.

12–13   **additis . . . validissimis** abl. absolute or an abl. of means

13   **provincialium . . . imperio** Note the chiasmus Tacitus uses here with emphasis on the two contrasting adjectives.

      fesso imperio dat. with *subventum est*

      subventum est an impersonal use; cf. p. 97 line 26. Translate, "there was help for our exhausted empire."

      num particle, expects a negative response

14   **paenitet** an impersonal that takes the acc. + infinitive

      Balbos L. Cornelius Balbus came from Gades in Spain and was enfranchised by Pompey (Cic. *Balb.* 19); he later was a Caesarian adherent and subsequently consul in 40 BCE (Cass. Dio 48.32.2).

      minus an adv. modifying *insignis*, which in turn is acc., modifying *viros*

14–15   **e Gallia Narbonensi** abl. place from which; Gallia Narbonensis was possibly Tacitus' place of origin and Agricola's as well (see p. xvi, 13). Individual cities in Gaul had long since been granted the privilege of senatorial membership; see Suet. *Caes.* 80.2. In the Lyons Tablet Claudius notes that Vienna, Lugdunum, and men *ultra fines Narbonensis* had long since sent senators to Rome.

15   **transivisse** pf. act. infinitive with *paenitet*

      posteri eorum i.e., of those allowed into the Senate by Caesar and his successors

      amore abl. of respect

      in "towards"

16   **exitio** a dat. of tendency indicating the result produced; translate "resulted in destruction."

16–17   **Lacedaemoniis et Atheniensibus** The Spartans reduced the conquered Messenians to serfdom and also had the institution of *xenelasia*, the occasional expulsion of foreigners, while Athens was very strict in its definition of "citizen," and eventually even forced its allies to pay tribute. No such comparison is made in the surviving portion of the Lyons Tablet.

17   **armis** abl. of means

        pollerent impf. subjunctive in a concessive clause

18   **nisi quod** "except for the fact that"

        pro alienigenis "as foreigners"; cf. above, p. 38 line 14 for this use of *pro*

19   **tantum** an adv. with *valuit*

        sapientia abl. of means

20   **hostis . . . civis** most famously the Sabines; see Livy 1.13.

        habuerit A pf. subjunctive here is used after *valuit* to indicate the actuality of the result that took place.

        advenae Tacitus here condenses the original speech where the origins of some of the early kings, who were outsiders, such as Numa Pompilius, Tarquinius Priscus, and Servius Tullius, are given greater expansion in Claudius' original oration.

21   **libertinorum filiis** something of an exaggeration; the practice was not common until the time of Caesar; Claudius made a similar argument on another occasion, citing as precedent his ancestor Appius Claudius Caecus (Suet. *Claud.* 24.1), who admitted sons of freedmen into the Senate.

        magistratus acc. pl. after *mandare*

        mandare historical infinitive; understand as the subject "we," "our people."

21–22   **ut plerique falluntur** "as most mistakenly assume"

22   **repens** = *recens*

priori populo dat. of agent; *priori* here = *vetus*

factitatum est Tacitus uses the frequentative here, both an archaic and poetic use.

23   **Senonibus** the tribe that captured and sacked Rome in 390 BCE, under the leadership of Brennus

scilicet Tacitus has Claudius indulge in some mildly pedantic sarcasm here.

Vulsci a people who occupied the Liris Valley and the regions southeast of the Alban Hills (whose language was Umbrian). They were allies of the Hernici, Latini, and Aequi; the Vulsci periodically fought with the Romans from the regal period until 304 BCE when they were defeated once and for all and quickly integrated into the Roman state.

Aequi An Italic tribe (who spoke Oscan) that occupied southern Latium and the Alban Hills, from which they were expelled in 431 BCE; they proved a tough opponent against Rome (see Livy 6.12), which fought its last war against them in 304 BCE and established Latin colonies on their territory (including Alba Fucens); the remaining Aequi were granted *civitas sine suffragio* and integrated into the Roman state (Livy 9.45; 10.1).

24   **adversam** takes the dat.

instruxere = *instruxerunt*

a Gallis another reference to the Senones

25   **Tuscis** in reference to Lars Porsena, king of the Etruscans, and his successes against Rome; see *Hist*. 3.72; Livy 2.13.

Samnitium iugum see above, p. 45 line 7.

26–27 **nullum . . . confectum** Supply *est* and understand *bellum*; Claudius is here referring to Caesar's conquest of Gaul, as the Lyons Tablet makes explicit.

26   **breviore spatio** abl. of time within which

27   **quam** with the compar. *breviore*

inde "from that time"

fide abl. of description, although there is an argument to be made for specification with *pax*. Both here and in the actual speech the revolt of Julius and Florus Sacrovir (Tac. *Ann.* 3.40–47) in 21 CE goes unmentioned as it does in the Lyons Tablet.

28   **moribus artibus adfinitatibus nostris** abl. with *mixti*

29   **inferant** a iussive subjunctive

potius . . . habeant "rather than possess them apart from us"

separati here an adj. that can be translated adverbially

omnia a substantive modified by *vetustissima* and *nova* in line 30

30   **fuere** = *fuerunt*

31–32   **plebeii . . . Latinos** "the plebians entered the magistracies after the nobles; after the plebians, the Latins; after the Latins, the rest of the peoples of Italy"; *plebeii* and *Latini* are both nom. pl., while *ceterarum Italiae gentium* is gen. for variation.

31   **plebeii** The plebians, according to our ancient sources, were allowed into patrician magistracies only after a long struggle. L. Sextius Lateranus and C. Licinius Stolo were supposedly the authors of the legislation granting plebians such rights (the *leges Liciniae Sextiae*), and L. Sextius the first plebian consul in 367 BCE. The historicity of the struggle itself is questioned by modern scholars (see Raaflaub 2006, 139–41). By the mid-third century plebians were allowed to hold all official magistracies.

Latini See above, line 6.

32   **ceterarum Italiae gentium** in the wake of the Social War 90–88 BCE; L. Julius Caesar passed the *lex Julia de civitate Latinis et sociis danda* in 90 BCE and it was supplemented by the *lex Plautia Papiria* in 89 BCE that offered citizenship to rebels who ceased from their insurrection; Italians are subsequently found in Roman magistracies.

inveterascet "will start to grow old"; an inchoative

hoc i.e., the presence of Gauls as senators

33   **exemplis** abl. of means

ᴄᴠ *ANNALES 11.29–30*
Messalina's fall, Part I: Her adulteries and conspiracy revealed

According to our sources, the same year Claudius delivered his speech on the Gauls (in 48 CE) his third wife, Valeria Messalina, conspired his overthrow. Tacitus (as well as our other sources) tells us that Messalina, whose adulteries were notorious to all but her husband, plotted to marry C. Silius, a handsome nobleman, and to depose the *princeps* while he was in Ostia dedicating his new harbor. Claudius' freedmen, who now reigned supreme, recognized the danger to their own position were Messalina to succeed, and thus denounced the conspiracy to Claudius. Indeed, in Cassius Dio's account of the episode (61.31) her downfall was the result of her destruction of the imperial freedman Polybius, which provoked alarm amongst the rest of Claudius' *liberti*.

For Tacitus, the entire episode of Messalina's denunciation and execution is paradigmatic of Claudius' character and his reign, marked by a lonely ruler easily swayed by his wives and imperial minions, a toxic blend of weakness and cruelty. The episode is among the most ironic in all of Tacitus, since it follows Claudius' censorship; the state's foremost overseer of morals was apparently incapable of looking after his own house. As Dickison has noted (1977, 634–47), her fall highlights the theatrical elements of Claudius' reign: the *senex amator*, the wise and sympathetic *meretrices*, and the imperial slaves who run the show are all elements of a Roman farce (also see Santoro L'Hoir 2006, 234–38 for Euripidean influence on this episode). The entire "conspiracy" as related in Tacitus and other sources is viewed with skepticism, and one current theory holds that rather than a wedding and conspiracy we have a simple instance of adultery, something that rarely ended well for women of the imperial house; see Fagan (2002, 566–79).

1   **ipse** The subject is Narcissus, the freedman who is the driving force behind Messalina's denunciation and execution.

1–2   **ad occasiones intentus** for *intentus* with *ad* see, e.g., *Ann.* 4.67, *Tiberius . . . quanto intentus olim publicas ad curas*. Narcissus was no doubt concerned that a change in regime would jeopardize his personal safety and position at court, and felt compelled to move once Messalina took the drastic step of marriage. He was forced to suicide upon Nero's accession in 54 (*Ann.* 13.1).

2   **longa . . . mora** abl. absolute; the delay allowed Messalina to carry out her plot.

      apud Ostiam Claudius renovated and dedicated a new port at Ostia in this year in order to enlarge capacity for commercial activity; Trajan subsequently expanded it.

2–3   **duas paelices** the direct object of *perpulit* in line 4; a *paelix* is specifically the mistress of a married man or a kept mistress, and at the imperial court were often freedwomen, such as Vespasian's mistress Caenis (Suet. *Vesp.* 3).

3   **is** i.e., Claudius

      corpori dat. with *insueverat*; take with *quarum*.

      largitione abl. of means

4   **promissis** abl. of means

      uxore deiecta an abl. absolute of attendant circumstance, dependent on the phrase *plus potentia ostentando*

      plus potentiae *plus* is the direct object of *ostendando*, which is a gerund and an abl. of means; *potentiae* here is a partitive gen. The promise was a dubious one, since Claudius soon married his niece, Agrippina the Younger.

5   **delationem subire** *subire* has the meaning here of "to take upon oneself"; cf. *Hist.* 4.42, *sponte . . . accusationem subisse iuvenis admodum*.

6   **id paelici nomen** *nomen* is predicative with *id*, the verb *erat* understood; *paelici* is dat. of possession. Nothing further is known about Calpurnia.

6-7 **ubi datum secretum** "when a private audience had been granted" (the verb *est* is understood); for *secretum* with this meaning cf. *Hist.* 4.2, *petito secreto futura aperit*

7 **genibus Caesaris provoluta** *provoluta* is middle or reflex. in meaning and can take either *ad* + the acc. or the dat.; see, e.g., *Ann.* 12.18, *genibus eius provolutus*; Livy 34.11, *ad genua consulis provoluntur.*

7-8 **nupsisse Messalinam Silio exclamat** *nupsisse* is a pf. act. infinitive in indirect discourse after *exclamat*; *Messalinam* is the subject acc.; *Silio* is dat. after *nupsisse*.

8 **Silio** C. Silius was consul designate for 48; he was grandson of P. Silius Nerva, consul in 20 BCE, and purportedly one of the most handsome men in Rome (*iuventutis Romanae pulcherrimus*, Tac. *Ann.* 11.12).

   Cleopatram the second of the two *paelices*; nothing further is known about her.

9 **comperisset** the plpf. subjunctive in an indirect question; the subject is Cleopatra.

   interrogat The subject is Claudius.

   illa adnuente i.e., Cleopatra; the construction is an abl. absolute.

9-10 **cieri Narcissum postulat** *cieri* is a pres. pass. infinitive in indirect discourse; the subject of *postulat* is Claudius; Tacitus uses the infinitive instead of a iussive noun clause (cf. above, p. 111 line 4).

10 **is** i.e., Narcissus

   veniam the direct object of *petens*

   in praeteritum "for the past"; for the construction cf. Suet. *Dom.* 9.3, *negotiantes venia in praeteritum donavit*

11 **ei** *ei* is an uncommon use of the dat. with *dissimulavisset*; it can best be translate "kept hidden/secret from him."

   Vettios, Plautios the direct object of *dissimulavisset*. A short list of Messalina's paramours is provided by Tacitus at *Ann.* 12.35–36. Plautius Lateranus was spared; Vettius Valens (a noted physician according to Pliny *HN* 29.8) was less fortunate. Plautius returned to favor under Nero, was consul designate in 65, but executed for involvement in the Pisonian conspiracy.

dissimulavisset a subjunctive in a *quod* clause

12 **obiecturum** a fut. act. infinitive in indirect discourse with the *esse* dropped; translate "would expose," with *adulteria* as the direct object.

12–13 **ne . . . reposceret** The text is problematic, with an alternate reading of *nedum*, "much less" for *ne*, which some commentators take as an equivalent of *nedum*, or as a purpose clause whose subject is Claudius. Woodman (2004, 210) translates *ne . . . reposceret*, "he [i.e., Claudius] should not reclaim."

domum servitia et ceteros fortunae paratus The *domum* refers to Claudius' house now taken over by Silius and Messalina; the *ceteros* refer to the household slaves and the other accoutrements of imperial power; *paratus* is acc. pl.

13 **frueretur . . . redderet** Both are iussive subjunctive; the subject is Silius.

his abl. with *frueretur*; it refers to the material perquisites noted here and in line 12.

14–15 **an . . . nam** The manner in which Tacitus has Narcissus frame the question highlights Claudius' ignorance of Messalina's notorious behavior (cf. *Ann.* 11.26–28).

14 **rumperetque** a iussive subjunctive; the subject is Silius once again.

an here an interrogative particle without an implied alternative; the transition to direct speech heightens the urgency of the situation.

15 **nosti** an irregular form of the pf. of *nosco* that can be translated as a pres.; the verb takes a direct object and can mean "acknowledge."

15–16 **populus et senatus et miles** Three of the pillars of imperial power are given in ascending order of importance, with *miles* a particularly evocative image for Claudius, since they raised him to power.

16   **agis, tenet** The juxtaposition of both verbs in the pres. act. indicative highlights the urgency of the situation.

∾ *ANNALES 11.31–32*
Messalina's fall, Part II: Her nuptial celebrations with Silius

In the brief section omitted between this and the previous passage, Claudius confirms and assesses the situation through discussions with the *praefectus annonae*, C. Turranius, and the Praetorian Praefect, Lusius Geta. They prepare to secure Claudius' position by hastening to the Praetorian camp to reaffirm the loyalty of the soldiery. The scene then shifts to Messalina's and Silius' nuptial celebrations, which resemble Bacchic worship; the worship of that deity was famously suppressed and regulated after 186 BCE (see Jaeger's volume in this series, *A Livy Reader* 2011), and Marc Antony (in)famously associated himself with Bacchus.

1   **non alias** "never"

    solutior luxu "more unbridled in her luxury"

    adulto autumno "with autumn advanced," an abl. absolute

2   **simulacrum vindemiae** just the appearance of a vintage through presses and wine

2–3 **urgeri . . . fluere** Tacitus here uses the historic infinitive.

3   **lacus** "vats"; nom. pl.

    pellibus abl. of means; Bacchants were often associated with rites involving the wearing of skins, as creatures close to nature.

    adsultabant Bacchic rites were also associated with ecstatic dancing.

4   **sacrificantes vel insanientes** Both modify *Bacchae*.

    ipsa i.e., Messalina

crine fluxo an abl. of description. Bacchants are frequently shown in visual representations with their hair let down or disheveled.

5   **thyrsum** a wand wielded in Bacchic rites by its celebrants, often adorned with filets of wool

hedera abl. of means

gerere a historical infinitive

6   **cothurnos** a type of legging worn by actors

iacere a historical infinitive; Tacitus' description of Silius is highly evocative of Velleius Paterculus' description of Marc Antony (2.82.4).

strepente . . . choro an abl. absolute

circum here an adv.

7   **Vettium Valentem** subject acc. in indirect discourse

lascivia abl. of manner, which Tacitus here uses without a prep., despite the absence of a modifying adj.

7-8   **in praealtam arborem conisum** "having struggled into a very high tree"

8   **interrogantibus** dat. with *respondisse*

aspiceret impf. subjunctive in indirect question

8-9   **tempestatem . . . atrocem** an elliptical phrase; sc. "responded that he saw"

9   **ea species** i.e., the view or sight of danger

forte "by chance"

10   **lapsa vox** "an unfortunate utterance"

in praesagium acc. of motion towards, with *in*

11-12   Until now there were just rumors of the emperor's approach. Now messengers will confirm that he is returning to the city.

11   **undique** "from every quarter"

11-12   **qui . . . adferrent** The *qui* is a rel. that forms a purpose clause, hence *adferrent* is in the subjunctive; everything in between is governed by *adferrent*, and therefore in indirect discourse.

12   **gnara . . . cuncta** *cuncta* is a substantive modified by *gnara* (here = *nota*), the subject acc. in indirect discourse with the verb *esse* understood.

Claudio dat. with *gnara*

venire The subject is Claudius.

promptum modifies the understood subject *Claudium*, which now shifts to the acc.

ultioni dat. with *promptum*

13   **Lucullianos in hortos** acc. motion towards with the adjectival element preceding the prep. The *horti Luculliani* (Gardens of Lucullus) were the first major public gardens in Rome, and a part of Lucullus' sumptuous villa on the Pincian Hill descending into the Campus Martius. There is a real sense of irony here, since Messalina, according to Tacitus, engineered the destruction of Valerius Asiaticus, the previous owner of the estate, in order to obtain the gardens (Tac. *Ann.* 11.1).

13–14 **dissimulando metu** The phrase is problematic if taken in the abl., and scholars have suggested the two alternative readings of *metui* or *metum* for *metu*; the alternative readings would mean that *dissimulando* is either a gerund (if we accept *metum*) or gerundive in the dat. indicating purpose (if we accept *metui*); translate "to conceal his fear."

14   **ad munia fori** "to the duties of the forum"

digrediuntur Messalina and Silius are the subjects here.

ceteris . . . dilabentibus an abl. absolute

15   **adfuere** = *adfuerunt*

ut with repeated past actions = "whenever"; cf. Caes. *BGall.* 3.4

quis an indef. pron., "someone"

16–20 This lengthy sentence represents a last-ditch effort by Messalina to save herself by sending her children to plead her case. The structure of the sentence is broken up by two subordinate clauses, with the main line of thought as follows: *Messalina tamen haud segniter intendit ire obviam et aspici a marito misitque ut Britannicus et Octavia pergerent in complexum patris.*

16   **in publico aut per latebras** Note the variation in construction with the use of one prep. with the abl. then another with the acc.

17   **eximerent** subjunctive in a concessive clause with *quamquam*

ire obviam et aspici "to go to meet and be seen"; both are complementary infinitive with *intendit*. Such a meeting between Claudius and Messalina is precisely what the freedmen were intent on avoiding.

18   **quod** refers to the entire preceding clause.

saepe subsidium habuerat The subject is Messalina. What the phrase means is that she had often communicated her desires to her husband in person if things were not about to go her way; see, e.g., Cass. Dio 60.22.4.

haud segniter intendit "she decided quickly"; *haud segniter* is litotes while *intendit* here has a meaning similar to *constituere*.

19   **misitque** Understand "orders" or "a message."

Britannicus et Octavia the son and daughter of Claudius with Messalina

in complexum *complexum* is acc. of motion towards, with *in*.

20   **pergerent** an impf. subjunctive in a iussive noun clause

Vibidiam, virginum Vestalium vetustissimam Note Tacitus' fine use of alliteration here. Vibidia, as the oldest of the Vestals, will have been the head of the order and possibly will have had some sway with Claudius in his capacity as *pontifex maximus*. For the intercession of the Vestals in moments of crisis cf. *Hist.* 3.81; there is a delicious irony here, however, that the only one to come to Messalina's assistance is a Vestal.

21   **adire . . . expetere** Both are infinitive after *oravit*, which usually takes the subjunctive; cf. *Ann.* 12.9.

22   **tribus . . . comitantibus** an abl. absolute

omnino "only," an adv.

22–23 **id . . . solitudinis** a rare substitute for *tanta solitudo*

23 **spatium** the direct object of *emensa*; i.e., she walked through the whole space of the city from the Gardens of Lucullus in the north to the Via Ostiensis in the south.

 pedibus an abl. of means

 emensa "having traversed"; a pf. act. pple. from *emetior*

 vehiculo abl. of means

24 **quo** abl. of means, *vehiculo* is the antecedent.

 purgamenta pl. for sing.; the detail adds a lurid touch underscoring Messalina's final degradation, since she is about to be discarded as part of the detritus of empire.

 Ostiensem viam intrat The *via Ostiensis* was the main road along the Tiber connecting the city with Ostia.

25 **nulla cuiusquam misericordia** "with no one showing any pity"; an abl. absolute

 flagitiorum deformitas "the vile nature of her disgraces"

26 **praevalebat** "carried more weight" (sc. than her position as empress); cf. *Hist.* 2.65; the use of the indicative with *quia* indicates the certainty with which people judged her misdeeds.

∾ *ANNALES 11.37–38*
Messalina's fall, Part III: Her execution

In *Annales* 11.34–36 Tacitus recounts how Narcissus acted quickly as Messalina and others sympathetic to her tried to win Claudius' ear. Tacitus also relates that arrests and executions of Messalina's supporters and paramours, including C. Silius, were swiftly carried out. Messalina, now denied access to the emperor, undertakes a last-ditch effort to save herself. In this passage Tacitus gives an account of the empress' final downfall that is both sordid and pathetic; her lack of an obituary is indicative of Tacitus' negative opinion.

1 **Lucullianis in hortis** See above, p. 123.

 prolatare "was prolonging"; a historical infinitive

2 **vitam** the direct object of *prolatare*

Fig. 4. Claudius was Tiberius' nephew, successor to his mad nephew Caligula, and an unlikely candidate for the imperial throne. National Archaeological Museum of Tarragona. Wikimedia Commons.

componere a historical infinitive

preces "petitions"

nulla spe . . . ira Both are abl. of manner, explaining *componere preces.*

3   **tantum . . . superbiae** a partitive gen. construction

inter extrema "in the midst of her extremities"; cf. Tac. *Hist.* 2.46, *ipsos extrema passuros ausurosque*

gerebat "show," "have," "entertain"

eius i.e., Messalina's

4   **properavisset** a plpf. subjunctive indicating potential; cf. p. 103 line 15

      in accusatorem *in* here = "against" + acc.; the *accusatorem* is Narcissus.

5   **nam** introduces further explanation for the previous sentence, i.e., the motive for Narcissus' quick action.

      domum acc. place to which

      tempestivis epulis abl. of means

6   **vino** abl. of means

      iri . . . nuntiarique Both are complementary infinitive with *iubet*.

      miserae i.e., Messalina; the term of endearment confirms Narcissus' suspicions about Claudius' sentimentality and leniency, which would mean destruction for himself and his fellow freedmen.

6–7   **hoc . . . verbo** abl. after *usum*

7   **usum** pf. act. infinitive in indirect discourse after *ferunt*, with *esse* omitted

      dicendam ad causam a gerundive construction indicating purpose; translate *causam* "case."

      postera die abl. of time when

8   **adesset** a subjunctive in an indirect command

8–11 The passage is a difficult one, varying between the historic infinitive, the impf., the pf., and the pres. The variation in grammatical construction, however, helps to convey the sense of alarm on the part of the freedmen at the possibility of Claudius' clemency.

8   **quod ubi auditum** i.e., Claudius' remark about the *miserae* and his desire to give her a hearing

      languescere ira, redire amor These are not infinitives in indirect discourse, but rather the historical infinitive with *ira* and *amor* as subject.

9   **cunctarentur** an impf. subjunctive of a deponent verb indicating potential; translate, "if they should delay."

propinqua nox "the night at hand"

10 **timebantur** The two subjects are *nox* and *memoria* in line 9.

prorumpit . . . denuntiatque both are in the pres.; translate *denuntiatque* "commands."

10–11 **centurionibus et tribuno** *denuntiatque* takes the dat.

11 **qui** i.e., the *tribuno*

exequi caedem *exequi* is an alternative form of *exsequi*, "to effect her execution"; *denuntiatque* takes an infinitive construction.

11–12 **imperatorem iubere** a subject acc. with the infinitive in indirect discourse after an implied verb of speaking

12 **e libertis** a partitive use of the abl.

13 **fusam** i.e., Messalina; the pf. pass. pple. of this verb can mean "prostrate," "lying down"

humi locative, "on the ground"

13–14 **adsidente matre Lepida** abl. absolute. Domitia Lepida was the daughter of L. Domitius Ahenobarbus and Antonia Maior, hence Claudius' cousin, as well as Nero's aunt since her brother was Cn. Domitius Ahenobarbus, Nero's natural father.

14 **florenti filiae** dat. with *concors*

haud concors because Messalina had effected the death of her husband C. Appius Junius Silanus, Cass. Dio 60.14.3; Suet. *Claud.* 37.2. Silanus had been consul in 28 CE, see Tac. *Ann.* 4.68.

14–15 **supremis . . . necessitatibus** abl. of time when; translate "in her final extremities"; cf. *Hist.* 1.3, *supremae clarorum virorum necessitates fortiter toleratae.*

15 **evicta erat** "had been induced," "had been moved"

16 **opperiretur** subjunctive in a iussive noun clause

transisse a pf. act. infinitive in indirect discourse with an implied verb of speaking

vitam direct object of *transisse*

16-17   **neque aliud quam morti decus quaerendum** "nor ought any other honor be sought than death"

16   **aliud** modifies *decus*.

17   **quam** Take closely with *aliud*.

        morti a dat. of agency that is virtually equivalent to an abl. of means here

        quaerendum a pass. periphrastic in indirect discourse with the verb *esse* dropped

17-18   **animo ... corrupto** an abl. absolute

18   **honestum** modifies *nihil*.

        inerat "was contained within"

        questus m. nom. pl.

        inriti predicative adj. with adverbial force, modifying both *lacrimae* and *questus*, hence m.

19   **ducebantur** "were being prolonged," "extended"; cf., e.g., Caes. *BGall.* 1.38

        impetu abl. of means

        venientium gen. pl. pple. substantive, referring to the guards arriving for her execution

        pulsae Supply *sunt*.

        fores the subject of *pulsae*

20   **at** provides a stark contrast with the vindictive freedman who is *increpans*, as opposed to the tribune who stands by in silence.

        libertus i.e., Euodus

20-21   **multis et servilibus probris** an abl. of means

22-24   Messalina had not been fully aware of the precariousness of her position. It takes the reproaches of a lowly freedman and the menacing presence of the centurion to awaken her, too late, to the reality of her situation.

22   **tunc primum** the conjunction of these two adverbs gives added power to her shock.

fortunam suam introspexit "she looked her own fate in the face"

23 **quod** *ferrum* is the antecedent.

iugulo aut pectori dat. with *admovens*

per trepidationem Tacitus prefers this construction at times as opposed to the abl.; cf. *per inquisitiones*, p. 33 line 12.

24 **ictu** abl. of means

transigitur The meaning here is that she was transfixed by a blow from the tribune's sword.

matri i.e., Lepida

concessum The verb *esse* is dropped; the brevity of the sentence and the lack of words expended by Tacitus on the empress is a powerful statement concerning his own thoughts about Messalina; cf. the damning absence of a formal obituary for Augustus.

25 **nuntiatumque** Supply *est*.

Claudio epulanti dat. after *nuntiatumque*

perisse pf. act. infinitive in indirect discourse

Messalinam subject acc. in indirect discourse

25-30 Claudius' emotional absence here highlights one of the most peculiar examples of human behavior in all of the *Annales*, although it is in keeping with his own "absence" throughout Tacitus' Claudian narrative (see Malloch 2009, 116–19).

25-26 **non distincto** an abl. absolute introducing an indirect question

26 **sua an aliena manu** an abl. of means; the *an* indicates two alternatives, with the *utrum* and the verb *esset* understood.

27 **solita** "the things that are normal/customary"; a n. substantive

convivio a dat. to be taken with *solita*

ne . . . quidem negates *secutis . . . diebus*, which phrase itself collectively negates *dedit* in line 29.

27-28 **secutis . . . diebus** abl. of time when

28–29   **odii gaudii, irae tristiae . . . adfectus** All are gen. with *signa*.

29   **laetantis** a pple. in the acc. pl. modifying *accusatores*

    accusatores i.e., Narcissus and his fellow freedmen

    aspiceret an impf. subjunctive in a *cum* clause

30   **cum** a brachylogy since the verb from the preceding *cum* clause is understood

    filios i.e., Octavia and Britannicus

    maerentis a pple. in the acc. pl. modifying *filios*

∾ *ANNALES 14.4–6*
Nero's matricide, Part I: The collapsible boat

Nero succeeded Claudius in 54 with the help of his mother, Agrippina the Younger (see p. xxv). By 59 relations between the two had soured and he decided upon her elimination (see p. xxvi). To that end, feigning a motive of reconciliation, he lured her down to Baiae, deciding on the elaborate contrivance of a collapsible boat to make her death appear an accident (cf. Suet. *Ner.* 34.2–3; Cass. Dio 62.13). When that fails, fearful of his own safety, he sends his guards to execute her. The whole episode has an air of the theatrical about it: the elaborate mechanism of the collapsible boat is reminiscent of stage machinery; the murder of Acerronia is darkly comic (see Mellor 1993, 129–33); and the whole episode is sandwiched first by Nero's, then by Agrippina's acting out feigned ignorance of the crime. All of this merely serves to underscore Nero's love of theater, of which this is a lethal example. For excellent discussions of the theatrical both in Tacitus and in the reign of Nero see Woodman (1993, 104–28), Bartsch (1994, 20–22, and 1–62 for theatricality in the context of Nero's reign), and, as concerns this passage, Champlin (2003, 84–111).

1   **iam** The scene opens as Agrippina and Nero are conversing over dinner at an imperial villa on the Bay of Naples.

    pluribus sermonibus an abl. of means explaining *tracto convictu* in line 3

1–2   **modo . . . et rursus** "now . . . and again"

2   **familiaritate iuvenili** an abl. of means

adductus modifies *Nero*; note the variation of construction in the use of description; *adductus* here = *grave*.

seria "serious matters," n. substantive

3   **consociaret** an impf. subjunctive with *quasi*

tracto . . . convictu an abl. absolute

in longum "for a long time"; a poetic expression, see Verg. *Ecl.* 9.56

abeuntem i.e., Agrippina

4   **oculis et pectori** Both are dat. with *haerens* in zeugma; translate "clinging closely to her gaze and breast." For similar details see Cass. Dio 61.13.2; Suet. *Ner.* 34.

explenda simulatione Furneaux takes this difficult phrase as an abl. absolute or causal abl., although Woodcock takes it as a "quasi-instrumental," translating it "putting the finishing touches to his hypocrisy."

5   **periturae** a fut. act. pple. modifying *matris*

quamvis Take closely with *ferum*; translate "albeit," "however much."

7   **sideribus . . . placido mari** Both are abl. of specification.

8   **convincendum ad scelus** a gerundive or gerund indicating purpose

multum "far," an adv.

9–10   **duobus . . . Agrippinam comitantibus** an abl. absolute; *Agrippinam* is the direct object of *comitantibus*.

9   **e numero familiarium** a partitive use of the abl. in conjunction with the gen.

10   **ex quis** a partitive use of the abl.; *quis* = *quibus*

10–11   **haud procul gubernaculis adstabat** "was standing nearby not far from the helm"; take *haud procul* with *gubernaculis*, an abl. of separation.

11-12 **Acerronia . . . reclinis** Woodman (2004, 277) translates this phrase, "Acerronia leaning over the feet of her reclining mistress."

11 **cubitantis** a pres. act. pple. in the gen. acting as a substantive

12 **reciperatam matris gratiam** "the favor of his mother regained"; Agrippina had tried to exercise power through her son, and Tacitus reports that Cluvius Rufus and Fabius Rusticus assert that she even resorted to incest to retain her influence, *Ann.* 14.2; cf. Cass. Dio 61.11.3–4.

12-13 **per gaudium** "joyously"

13 **dato signo** an abl. absolute

ruere a historical infinitive in a temporal *cum* clause

tectum loci lit., "the shelter of the place," i.e., the area where they were conversing

14 **multo plumbo** an abl. of specification

grave modifies *tectum*.

pressusque a simple for a compound (*oppressus*) verb; understand *est.*

15-16 **eminentibus lecti parietibus . . . validioribus** an abl. absolute that describes the *lecti*; what we need to imagine is that they were on couches with a framework akin to a poster bed. The framework was sufficiently strong to resist the weight of the collapse.

16 **quam . . . cederent** here a result clause; lit. "stronger than that they yield"; translate, "too strong to yield."

oneri dat. with *cederent*

16-17 **protectae sunt** The subjects are Agrippina and Acerronia.

17-18 These lines detail the confusion that follows in the wake of the failure to collapse the boat, with those who were not party to the conspiracy hindering those involved.

17 **turbatis omnibus** an abl. absolute

18 **impediebant** The indicative here with *quod* attests to the reality of the statement.

visum Supply *est*.

19   **unum in latus** the acc. of motion towards, with *in*

20   **submergere** complementary infinitive with *visum*

   ipsis i.e., the rowers

   in rem subitam "for the emergency"; *in* + the acc. here has virtually the force of a dat.

21   **et alii** "and some"

   contra nitentes i.e., there were others who tried to balance the ship by going to the opposite side

   dedere = *dederunt*

   lenioris gen. sing., modifying *iactus*

21–22   **in mare** acc. with *in*, motion towards

22   **imprudentia** an abl. of cause

22–23   **Acerronia . . . se Agrippinam esse . . . clamitat** The subject of *clamitat* is Acerronia; the *se* is subject acc. in indirect discourse referring to Acerronia. Suetonius excludes this episode from his account, though Cassius Dio includes it.

23   **subveniretur** "assistance be rendered," a subjunctive in a iussive noun clause after *clamitat*; for the pass. use of *subveniretur* see above, p. 97 line 26.

   matri *subveniretur* takes the dat.

   clamitat here the iterative

24   **contis et remis . . . navalibus telis** All are abl. of instrument; translate *navalibus telis* "naval projectiles," i.e., any implements of the ship that came to hand.

   quae its antecedent is *telis*

   conficitur "was finished off," "was killed"; the pres. is used for vividness.

25   **eoque** "and for this reason," an abl. of means or cause

   adgnita an alternative form of *agnita*, pf. pass. pple. of *agnosco*

26   **umero** abl. of specification or respect

nando a gerund; abl. of means

occursu lenunculorum take as an abl. of means

27   **Lucrinum in lacum vecta** acc. of place to which, with *vecta*; the place was famous for its oysters in antiquity.

villae suae infertur *infertur* frequently takes the dat. The villa will have been one of many that dotted the Bay of Naples, stretching from Misenum to the Surrentine peninsula and belonging to Roman aristocrats; cf. above, p. 104.

28   **reputans** The subject is Agrippina.

se . . . accitam acc. in indirect discourse after *reputans*, with the verb *esse* dropped

fallacibus litteris abl. of means

29   **honore praecipuo** abl. of manner

habitam Supply *esse*; pf. pass. infinitive in indirect discourse.

quodque here introducing a substantival clause, the direct object of *reputans*

iuxta a prep. that governs *litus*

ventis abl. of means

30   **acta . . . impulsa** both modify *navis*; translate *acta* "having been driven."

saxis dat. with *impulsa*

summa sui parte "had collapsed in its highest part"; *sui* here is partitive.

30–31   **veluti terreste machinamentum** i.e., a piece of siege machinery, or a similar sort of contrivance; the reference also underscores the theatricality of the episode since it can also refer to stage machinery, and in fact, Cassius Dio (61.12.2) says that Nero conceived of the idea when he saw a collapsible boat in a theater production.

31   **concidisset** a subjunctive after *quodque*; it indicates not actual causality but deduction based on the other factors in the "accident."

32–33   **solum insidiarum remedium esse** Editors and commentators generally understand *sensit* as an introductory verb for this clause; *esse* is an infinitive in indirect discourse.

33   **intellegerentur** The subject is *insidiae* (understood), taken from *insidiarum* in the previous line; the verb is subjunctive in a subordinate clause in indirect discourse.

34   **nuntiaret** a subjunctive in a *qui* clause indicating purpose

        benignitate abl. of means indicating causality

        deum gen. pl.; cf. p. 95 line 14

34–35   **fortuna eius** *fortuna* is abl. of means; *eius* refers to Nero. Agrippina, dissembling her knowledge of his crime, makes out her rescue to be a fortunate outcome for him.

35   **evasisse** pf. act. infinitive in indirect discourse; undertstand *se* (Agrippina).

        gravem casum the direct object of *evasisse*

        periculo abl. of means or cause

36   **visendi** a gerund in the gen. with *curam*

        differret a subjunctive in a iussive noun clause

        ad praesens "for the present"

36–37   **sibi . . . opus** Supply *est*; for the idiom *opus est* see above, p. 52 lines 14–15; the dat. *sibi* here refers to Agrippina.

ও *ANNALES 14.8*

Nero's matricide, Part II: Agrippina's murder

Nero is horror-stricken when he receives word that the plot has failed (*Ann.* 14.7). His ministers now realize that either they must do away with Nero or involve themselves in the open murder of Agrippina. Agerinus, Agrippina's freedman who brings news of her safety, now offers a convenient pretext for her execution; when brought before Nero he is accused on a trumped-up charge of acting as Agrippina's agent in an attempt to assassinate him. Anicetus, the head of the fleet at Misenum, is then hastily sent to execute Agrippina. The final scene of her execution in the dim light of the *cubiculum*, taken with her last words, make this among the more lurid scenes in the Tacitean corpus. Tacitus (*Ann.* 14.9) insists on the veracity of this particular version of events; he is more dubious about whether Nero viewed her corpse afterwards, praising her form and appearance.

Fig. 5. Claudius' son by adoption, Nero was the last of the Julio-Claudians to rule in Rome. Glyptotek, Munich. Wikimedia Commons.

1   **circumdat** The verb takes an acc. of the thing being surrounded with an abl. of that which surrounds it.

statione "with a posting of guards"

2   **refractaque ianua** an abl. absolute; note the entrance is more violent here than the simple *impetus venientium* encountered in Messalina's execution above (p. 125).

obvios here a substantive with a partitive gen. construction; translate "the servants he encountered."

3   **foris** acc. pl., place to which, with *ad*

       veniret a subjunctive in a temporal clause with *donec*

       cui dat. after *adstabant*; its antecedent is *cubiculi*.

3–4   **ceteris . . . exterritis** an abl. absolute; *terrore* makes the phrase
       a pleonasm.

4   **inrumpentium** a pres. pple. in the gen. as a substantive

       cubiculo dat. after *inerat*

5   **anxia Agrippina** an abl. absolute

5–6   **quod** introduces a causal clause; the verb *venisset* is under-
       stood (Woodcock 1939, *ad loc.*).

6–8   **aliam . . . indicia** Supply an introductory phrase such as "She
       was thinking," implied by the abl. absolute in line 5 indicating
       Agrippina's state of mind.

6–7   **aliam . . faciem** subject acc. in indirect discourse

6   **fore** the fut. infinitive of the verb *esse*

       laetae rei "of a happy situation"; Woodman (2004, 278) trans-
       lates it "Welcome circumstances."

7   **solitudinem** a subject acc. in indirect discourse; supply *esse*.
       For solitude as an indication of one's final demise before the
       breaking of the storm cf. Vitellius' end, *Hist.* 3.84, and see
       above, p. 124 lines 22–23 during Messalina's fall.

       repetinos strepetus subject acc. in indirect discourse

8   **indicia** subject acc. in indirect discourse

       abeunte dehinc ancilla an abl. absolute

9–10   **Anicetum . . . comitatum** *comitatum* is not from the more
       common *comitor* but from *comito*, hence a pf. pass. pple.;
       translate "attended," "followed."

       trierarcho . . . classiario abl. with *comitatum*

10–12 **ac . . . parricidium** sc. "she said"; understand a verb of speak-
       ing after *ac*.

10   **visendum** gerund of purpose with *ad*

venisset plpf. subjunctive in the protasis of a past contrary to fact condition; the subject is Anicetus.

11   **refotam** Supply *esse*; a pf. pass. infinitive in indirect discourse after *nuntiaret*

    nuntiaret Woodman (2004, 278) translates this as a potential subjunctive, "he might report."

    sin "but if"

    patraturus a periphrastic construction; supply *esset*.

11–12   **nihil . . . credere** "she would not believe it of her son"; i.e., she believed Anicetus was acting on his own initiative

11   **nihil** here an intensive form of *non*

    se a subject acc. in indirect discourse referring to Agrippina

    de filio Supply an understood *id* or *hoc*.

12   **credere** infinitive in indirect discourse

    imperatum infinitive in indirect discourse with the *esse* dropped

    parricidium the subject of *imperatum*

13   **fusti** This is an irregular form of the abl., here the instrumental; cf., e.g., Val. Max. 6.3.9.

    caput eius i.e., Agrippina's

14   **in mortem** *in* + acc. here indicates intent or result.

15   Agrippina's final command is particularly shocking. It is worth noting that Tacitus reports that astrologers told Agrippa that Nero was destined to murder her, to which she replied, "*occidat, dum imperet*" (*Ann.* 14.9).

    ventrem not the stomach but the womb; cf. Cass. Dio 61.13.5; for this usage see Juv. 6.596.

    feri a sing. imperative; Cassius Dio gives a virtually identical account of Agrippina's last words in Greek.

    multisque vulneribus abl. of means

    confecta est the same verb Tacitus used to describe the death of her friend Acerronia

✨ *ANNALES 15.38*

The great fire of 64 CE

Five years after Agrippina's death Rome was devastated by one of the most damaging fires in its history (see p. xxvi). Suetonius (*Ner.* 38.2) and Cassius Dio (62.16–18) directly blame Nero for the fire, and report rumors (as does Tacitus, *Ann.* 15.39) that Nero sang of the burning of Troy during the conflagration (although he afterward looked to the relief of those adversely affected by the fire). Tacitus, on the other hand, uses innuendo to impute blame to Nero, both setting up before and expanding afterwards a scenario by which the reader finds it more plausible to fix the blame on the emperor: at 15.37 Tacitus states that Nero was using the whole city as his own house. The fire, Tacitus subsequently implies, created a convenient pretext for Nero to clear out the city and build his palatial *Domus Aurea* (15.40–42). In addition, a suspicious fresh outbreak of fire on the estate of the Praetorian Praefect, Ofonius Tigellinus, gave rise to rumors that Nero was looking to re-found the city (15.40). The episode is also part of a larger theme expounded on by Tacitus, that of Neronian extravagance, highlighted in the previous chapter (15.37), ironically, by a huge water festival staged on the *Stagnum Agrippae* in the Campus Martius. For an excellent discussion of the fire and the construction of the *Domus Aurea*, see Champlin (2003, 178–209).

1–3 The structure of this phrase, were we to put it into English word order, is as follows: *clades gravior atque atrocior omnibus quae acciderunt huic urbi per violentiam ignium sequitur, incertum forte an dolo principis (nam auctores prodidere utrumque).*

1 **forte** "by chance"

an introducing an indirect alternative question with *utrum* omitted; supply *esset*. The phrase is a classic example of innuendo based on a loaded alternative, in which the deck is stacked heavily against the emperor.

incertum Supply *est*.

2   **utrumque** i.e., both versions explaining the fire's outbreak

prodidere = *prodiderunt*

omnibus sc. *clades*; a compar. abl. with *gravior* and *atrocior*

quae The antecedent is *clades*.

2–3   **huic urbi** dat. with *acciderunt*

3   **per violentiam** For *per* indicating agency; cf. p. 91 line 8.

4   **initium** sc. of the fire

in ea parte "in that part"

circi The reference is to the Circus Maximus, evident from the more specific location between the Palatine and Caelian hills. There were several structures that went by the name *circus*; this and the Circus Flaminius in the southwestern Campus Martius were the best known in Nero's day, although the punishment of the Christians in the fire's wake would take place in the Circus of Gaius near the Mons Vaticanus, now occupied by St. Peter's Square and Basilica.

ortum Supply *est*.

quae The antecedent is *parte*.

4–5   **Palatino Caelioque montibus** dat. with *contigua*; the eastern end of the circus near where the Arch of Constantine still stands today

5   **quibus** dat. with *inerat*

id here a demonstrative modifying *mercimonium*

mercimonium an archaism found primarily in Plautus (see p. xxxix)

6–7   **simul ... et statim ... ac** Tacitus' quick succession of adverbs and connectives reflects the fire's swift movement.

6   **quo** abl. of means

simul coeptus ignis "as soon as the fire started"

7   **vento** abl. of means

citus a pf. pass. pple.

8   **domus** nom. pl.

munimentis abl. of means

saeptae Supply *sunt*; the subject is *domus*.

8–9   **templa muris cincta** Understand *sunt* with *cincta*; *muris* is an abl. of means; *templa per se* were the precincts themselves that contained the *aedes* for housing the cult statue. The Portico of Octavia, the Forum of Caesar, and the Forum of Augustus, with large open areas containing *aedes* either in the back or in the center, would have been among such precincts and would have formed firebreaks throughout the city.

9   **aut quid aliud morae interiacebat** "or was any other hindrance intervening"; *quid* here is an indef. pron. modified by *aliud*; *morae* is partitive gen.

impetu abl. of specification with *pervagatum*; translate "widespread in its attack."

10   **plana primum** sc. *corripuit*; *plana* here is an acc. pl. n. substantive

edita acc. pl. n. substantive; acc. of place to which, with *in*

adsurgens modifies *incendium*.

11   **inferiora** acc. pl. n. substantive, direct object of *populando*

populando gerund, abl. of means; Tacitus will occasionally use a gerund in close conjunction with a pres. act. pple. to modify the same subject for the sake of *variatio*.

antiit The subject is *incendium*.

velocitate abl. of means or cause

mali "of the evil," a n. gen. sing. substantive

12   **obnoxia urbe** abl. absolute; translate *obnoxia* "exposed," "subject to injury."

artis itineribus . . . flexis abl. of cause explaining *obnoxia*. Rome's modern Campo Marzio, with its meandering and narrow streets, may give a sense of what the city was like in antiquity before the fire.

hucque et illuc "hither and thither"

13   **enormibus vicis** "irregular blocks"

qualis ... fuit "such as was old Rome," "so was old Rome constituted"

ad hoc "in addition," "besides"

lamenta Supply *erant*.

14   **fessa aetate aut rudis pueritiae** another instance of variation; *fessa aetate* is an abl. of description, *rudis pueritiae* a gen. of description; both describe *quique sibi quique aliis* in line 15.

15   **sibi ... aliis** Both are dat. with *consulebant*.

16   **pars ... pars** "some ... some"

mora ... festinans *mora* is abl. of means indicating causality; note the juxtaposition of a noun in the abl. with a pres. act. pple. in the nom. for variation.

cuncta an acc. pl. n. substantive

17   **impediebant** subject = *pars ... pars*

17–19   **et saepe ... correptis** The passage describes the horrors of those trying to escape a firestorm and has the feel of a city at war taken by an enemy, complete with terms we would expect in battle, such as *in tergum*, *lateribus*, and *fronte circumveniebantur*, and already employed by the term *populando* above. The metaphorical language recalls that elsewhere (at, e.g., *Ann.* 13.25, 15.58), by which Tacitus implies Nero makes war against Rome itself; see Keitel (1984, 307–9, 319–20) for discussion.

17   **in tergum** "behind," "to the rear"

17–18   **lateribus aut fronte** Both are abl. functioning as the locative.

18   **proxima** "places that were nearby," acc. n. pl. substantive

19   **illis ... correptis** abl. absolute

igni here an abl. of means

quae longinqua i.e., from the fire; supply "places" (the pl. of either the n. or m. is preferred for regions or neighborhoods); cf. Tac. *Ann.* 1.61, *incedunt maestos locos*.

20–21   **vitarent ... peterent** Both are impf. subjunctive in an indirect question introduced by the adj. *ambigui*.

21 **complere . . . sterni** Both are the historical infinitive; translate *sterni* "were scattered."

quidam picked up by the *alii* in line 22

22 **amissis . . . fortunis** abl. absolute

diurni quoque victus a gen. closely connected with *amissis* in the preceding abl. absolute; translate "and with the loss of their daily sustenance."

caritate abl. of cause

23 **suorum** "of their kin," an objective gen.

patente effugio i.e., despite the possibility of refuge they chose suicide

24–27 The passage contributes to the notion that the fire was deliberately set by Nero. The blaze was ultimately controlled by tearing down large swaths of flammable structures to create firebreaks.

24 **interiere** = *interierunt*

24–25 **cebris . . . minis** abl. absolute indicating causality, with *quia* corresponding as an alternate explanation

multorum . . . prohibentium Supply *eos*; *restinguere* is a complementary infinitive with *prohibentium*.

26 **esse sibi auctorem** *esse* is an infinitive in indirect discourse after *vociferabantur*, while *sibi* is a dat. of possession after a copulative verb; Woodman (2004, 323) translates it "they had authorization."

27 **raptus** acc. pl., direct object of *exercerent*

exercerent subjunctive in a purpose clause

iussu abl. of means or cause; another fine instance of Tacitean variation in which a purpose clause and a phrase in the abl. create an alternative explanation

∾ *ANNALES 15.44*

The persecution of the Christians after the fire

To dispel rumors that he was responsible for the disaster, Nero cast about for a scapegoat, and targeted the Christians. It is clear from Tacitus' introduction that this is his first mention of the Christians in his works, while it is only the second reference in our Roman literary sources (Pliny mentioned them a few years earlier in his letters to Trajan, *Ep.* 10.96; cf. 10.97 for Trajan's reply). The passage is typical of how Tacitus, and for that matter, other Romans, tend to discuss religions considered outside the sphere of traditional Roman religious practice (cf. Tac. *Hist.* 5.2–5 on Jewish history, culture, and religion). In Suetonius' discussion of the Neronian persecution (*Ner.* 16.2) he states Christians were punished due to a conspiracy driven by *superstitio nova et malefica*, while Pliny refers to Christians as practicing a *prava superstitio*. This was by no means an attitude the Romans held towards the Christians alone, as the suppression of the cult of Bacchus in 186 BCE illustrates (see Mary Jaeger's commentary on Livy in this series, *A Livy Reader* 2011). But cultural dynamics are not exclusively in play here. The nature of the persecution was yet another example of Nero's extravagance, cruelty, and theatricality that Tacitus found abhorrent.

1–2   **ope humana . . . largitionibus . . . placamentis** All are abl. of means.

2   **deum** an archaic gen. pl., cf. p. 95 line 14

3   **quin** Translate here as a clause of hindering.

        iussum infinitive with *esse* dropped in indirect discourse. Tacitus, as in 15.38, here keeps alive in the reader's mind the possibility that Nero was guilty of arson.

        crederetur subjunctive after *quin*

3–4   **abolendo rumori** gerundive, dat. indicating purpose

4   **subdidit** The verb can mean "supply" but also has the sense of making a fraudulent substitution

quaesitissimis poenis *adfecit* takes the acc. + the abl.; cf., e.g., *Ann.* 1.6, *ne cunctaretur Agrippam morte adficere*; Woodman (2004, 325) translates *quaesitissimis* "choicest." *quaesitissimis* appears in the superl. only here and in *Ann.* 2.53.

5   **per** here + acc. = "on account of," taken with *invisos*

Christianos first given this appellation, according to *Acts* 11:25–28, in Antioch in the reign of Claudius

6   Tacitus now takes the opportunity to explain the cult's origins, indicating that, at least for Tacitus and his circle, this group was not very well known in the city at the time of writing. Pliny some years before (probably 111 or 112 CE) also found it necessary to explain in his missive to Trajan just who the Christians were and what practices they followed as well.

per "through," "by," indicating agency

7   **Pontium Pilatum** mentioned only here among Roman historians, but finding a place also in the works of Josephus (*AJ* 18.4.2), Philo (*Leg.* 38), and Eusebius (*Hist. Eccl.* 2.7). Josephus and Philo held very negative views of Pilate, much at odds with the more neutral take on him in the New Testament.

supplicio adfectus erat "had been put to death"; cf. Plin. *Ep.* 10.96.3, *supplicium minatus*

8   **in praesens** "for the present"

exitiabilis Perhaps the two most plausible explanations for Tacitus' use of this adj. here are, (a) he may have been aware of Christian martyrdom such as Pliny had experienced as governor of Bithynia, (b) he may have thought the religion pernicious in nature (and the adj. here is very strong, as Furneaux points out, more akin to Suetonius' use of *malefica* than to Pliny's *prava*).

9   **per Iudaeam, originem eius mali** Tacitus is very likely looking forward here since the province was to break into open revolt in 66, which he almost certainly will have treated in the lost portion of Book 16 or 17 (although he had already written a brief Jewish ethnography and discussed some background of the revolt at *Hist.* 5.1–12).

9-10   **non modo . . . sed** a coordinating conj.

10   **quo** "where"

10-11 **cuncta . . . atrocia . . . pudenda** *cuncta* is a substantive modified by *atrocia* and *pudenda*; *cuncta* could refer to other foreign rites of which Tacitus may not have approved, such as those of Isis or the Magna Mater.

11-14 Arrests take place, then confessions, then a denunciation of others who are in turn rounded up for punishment; the action mirrors Pliny's own experience, although he was careful to investigate those initially denounced and to allow them the opportunity to renounce their faith.

11   **celebranturque** "practiced"; in reference to religious rites, see Tac. *Germ.* 39.2.

       correpti i.e., brought to trial

12   **indicio** abl. of means

       eorum i.e., those who were arrested as *Christiani*

13   **proinde** "in the same manner"

       in crimine . . . odio Note the variation, the first abl. using a prep., the second an abl. of means or cause. Translate *crimine* "charge"; cf. *Hist.* 5.5 for Tacitus' similar charge against the Jews

14   **convicti sunt** The subject is both the *correpti* and the *multitudo ingens*.

       pereuntibus substantive in the dat. with *addita*

       addita ludibria "jests were added"; the Romans were not averse to making games out of executions, occasionally with a mythological element added in for good measure (see, e.g., Suet. *Ner.* 12.2; for a good discussion of this phenomenon see Bartsch 1994, 50–62).

15   **tergis contecti** "covered in the hides"

       laniatu abl. of means

       crucibus dat. with *adfixi*; the punishment visited on Peter in the persecutions and one visited on non-citizens and low-born criminals in general

interirent a subjunctive in a result clause dependent on *addita* in line 14

16   **flammandi** The text here may be corrupt and is controversial, with an alternative reading suggested of *flammati*; Woodman (2004, 325) keeps the gerundive and translates the phrase "made flammable."

defecisset plpf. subjunctive that indicates frequency of occurrence

16–17 **in usum** the *in* + acc. indicates purpose

17   **nocturni luminis** Night games were particularly impressive spectacles, taken here to a gruesome apex.

ei a demonstrative adj. here modifying *spectaculo*

18   **edebat** used in general of games and spectacles of various sorts; see, e.g., *Ann.* 1.15, *ederent ludos.*

habitu abl. of description with *aurigae*; see Suet. *Ner.* 22–25 for his lengthy discussion of the emperor's proclivity for chariot racing.

19   **plebi** dat. with *permixtus*

curriculo "racing-chariot"; dat. with *insistens*

unde "whence," "from which," i.e., the vicious punishments

20   **sontis** acc. substantive after a prep.

novissima exempla "the most extreme penalties," the direct object of *meritos*; cf. *Ann.* 12.20, *meritum quidem novissima exempla Mithridaten*

meritos i.e., the Christians

21   **tamquam** "on the grounds that"

utilitate publica an abl. of cause; on relinquishing personal grievances for the sake of public good, see p. 13 line 29.

in saevitiam Here *in* with the acc. indicates causality.

22   **absumerentur** subjunctive with *tamquam*

Appendix A:
Maps

❧ *The Mediterranean region*

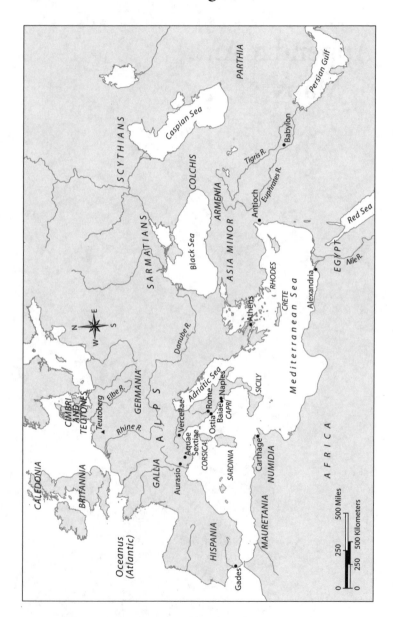

❧ *The city of Rome*

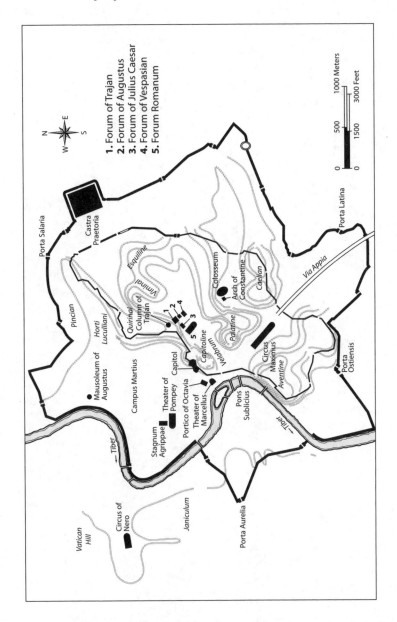

1. Forum of Trajan
2. Forum of Augustus
3. Forum of Julius Caesar
4. Forum of Vespasian
5. Forum Romanum

Appendix B: Genealogical charts

∽ 1. The family of Tiberius

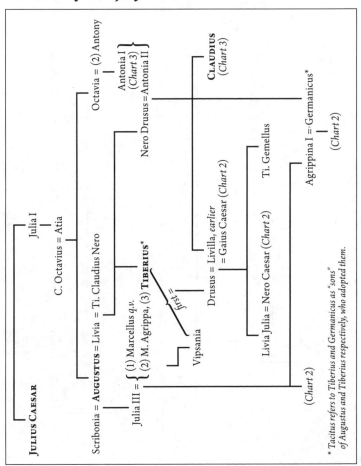

* Tacitus refers to Tiberius and Germanicus as "sons" of Augustus and Tiberius respectively, who adopted them.

❧ 2. The heirs

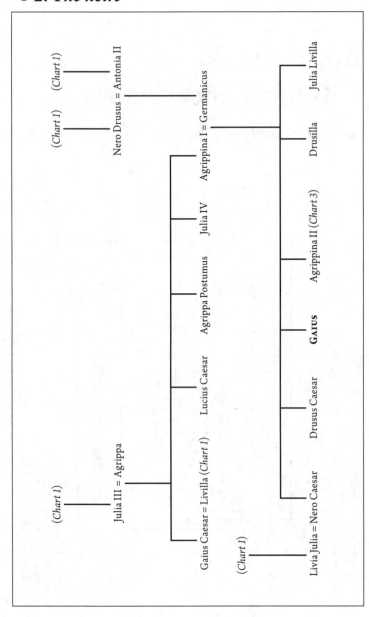

❧ 3. *The family of Claudius and Nero*

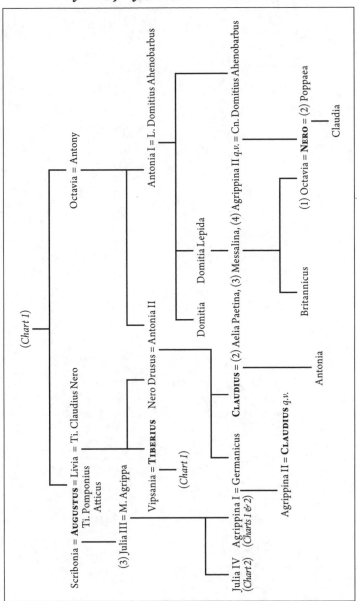

Complete Vocabulary

ā *or* ab, *prep.* + *abl.*, from, by

abdō, -ere, -idī, -itum, to put
away, remove, withdraw,
hide, conceal

abdūcō, -ere, -duxī, -ductum,
to lead away, seduce

abeō, -īre, -īvī, -itum, to go
away, depart from

abnuō, -ere, -nuī, -nuitum, to
refuse, deny

aboleō, -ēre, -ēvī, -itum, to
obliterate, put to an end,
abolish

abripiō, -ere, -ripuī, -reptum,
to tear or drag away, remove

abstineō, -ēre, -uī, -tentum, +
abl., to keep off, refrain

absūmō, -ere, -sumpsī,
-sumptum, to annihilate,
kill, ruin

ac, *conj.*, and

accēdō, -ere, -cessī, -cessum, to
approach, add

Acceronia, -ae, *f.*, Acceronia (a
woman's name)

accidō, -ere, -cidī, -cisum, +
dat., to befall, happen

accingō, -ere, -cinxī, -cinctum,
to gird about

acciō, -īre, -īvī, -ītum, to call,
summon

accipiō, -ere, -cēpī, -ceptum, to
take, receive, accept, learn

accūsātor, -ōris, *m.*, informer,
accuser

acer, -cris, -cre, *adj.*, sharp,
keen, fierce

acerbus, -a, -um, *adj.*, bitter

aciēs, -ēī, *f.*, line of battle, battle

ad, *prep.* + *acc.*, to, toward; +
hoc, in addition, besides

addō, -ere, -idī, -itum, to add

addūcō, -ere, -duxī, -ductum,
to draw tight

adductus, -a, -um, *adj.*, serious,
severe

adeō, *adv.*, so, so much, so very

adeō, -īre, -īvī, -itum, to go
to, approach; to undertake,
enter upon

adeptus, -a, -um. *See* adipiscor

adfectō (1), to aim at

adfectus, -ūs, *m.*, mood,
feeling, emotion

adferō, -ferre, attulī, adlātum,
to bring forward, report

adficiō, -ere, -fēcī, -fectum, to
treat, afflict, inflict

adfīgō, -ere, -fixī, -fixum, to fix, attach to

adfinitās, -ātis, *f.,* alliance by marriage, relationship, affinity

adfīrmō (1), to strengthen, confirm, affirm

adfligō, -ere, -flixī, -flictum, to throw down; to strike, beat

adfundō, -ere, -fūdī, -fūsum, to pour into

adgnita. *See* **agnoscō**

adiciō, -ere, -iēcī, -iectum, to throw or put near; to add, increase

adimō, -ere, adēmī, -emptum, to take away

adipiscor, -ī, adeptus sum, to get, obtain, inherit, win

adminiculum, -ī, *n.,* support

admīrātiō, -ōnis, *f.,* admiration

admodum, *adv.,* to be sure; only, just, very, indeed

admoneō, -ēre, -uī, -itum, to warn

admoveō, -ēre, -mōvī, -mōtum, to bring near

adnuō, -ere, -uī, -ūtum, to nod assent

adolescō, -ere, adolēvī, adultum, to grow, mature, advance, reach its peak

adoptiō, -ōnis, *f.,* adoption

adoptō (1), to choose, select, adopt

adpetens, -entis, *adj.,* greedy, desirous of

adrepō, -ere, -sī, -tum, to worm one's way into

adsciscō, -ere, -scīvī, -scītum, to adopt

adsector, -ārī, -ātus sum, to accompany

adsequor, -ī, -secūtus sum, to pursue, overtake, rival

adsideō, -ēre, -sēdī, -sessum, to sit near, attend

adsīgnō (1), to mark out, allot, assign, award

adsistō, -ere, -stitī, —, to stand by

adspiciō, -ere, aspexī, aspectum, to catch sight of, spot

adstō (1), to stand at/near

adsultō (1), to jump

adsum, -esse, -fuī, —, to be present/at/near; to come, appear

adsūmō, -ere, -psī, -ptum, take up, adopt

adsurgō, -ere, -surrexī, -surrectum, to rise up

adūlātiō, -ōnis, *f.,* flattery

adulescens, -entis, *m. and f.,* youth

adulter, -erī, *m.,* adulterer

adulterium, -ī, *n.,* adultery

advehō, -ere, -vexī, -vectum, to conduct, convey, bear, bring

advena, -ae, *m.,* foreigner

adventus, -ūs, *m.,* invasion, arrival, approach

adversum, *prep. + acc.,* against, towards

adversus, -a, -um, *adj.,* against, facing, unfavorable, hostile

advocātus, -ī, *m.,* advocate, one who pleads cases

aegritūdō, -inis, *f.,* disease, sickness

Aegyptus, -ī, *f.,* Egypt

Aelius, -ī, *m.,* Aelius (a man's name)

aemulus, -ī, *m.,* rival

Aequī, -ōrum, *m. pl.,* the Aequi (an Italic tribe)

aestimō (1), to assess, consider

aetās, -ātis, *f.,* age, life

aevum, -ī, *n.,* time, life, age

Āfrica, -ae, *f.,* Africa (Libya and the territory of Carthage)

ager, agrī, *m.,* field

Agerinus, -ī, *m.,* Agerinus (a man's name)

agmen, agminis, *n.,* an army column, a train (of men on the march)

agnoscō, -ere, -nōvī, -nitum, to recognize

agō, -ere, ēgī, actum, to drive, do, act

Agrippa, -ae, *m.,* Agrippa (a man's name)

Agrippīna, -ae, *f.,* Agrippina (a woman's name)

āiō, *defective verb,* to say, affirm

Alba, -ae, *f.,* Alba (a city in Latium)

alias, *adv.,* at another time

alibī, *adv.,* elsewhere, in/at another place, in one place . . . in another, here . . . there

aliēnigena, -ae, *m.,* foreign-born

aliēnus, -a, -um, *adj.,* not one's own, belonging to others, foreign, strange

aliquandō, *adv.,* at any time, ever, finally

alius , -a, -ud, *adj.,* another, other

alō, -ere, -uī, -itum, feed, nourish, strengthen

Alpes, -ium, *f. pl.,* the Alps

alter, -tera, -terum, *pron.,* another, other

altus, -a, -um, *adj.,* high, deep

ambiguus, -a, -um, *adj.,* uncertain, wavering

ambiō, -īre, -īvī, -itum, to surround

ambitiō, -ōnis, *f.,* desire for honor

ambitiōsus, -a, -um, *adj.,* ambitious

ambitus, -ūs, *m.,* corrupt canvassing

amīcitia, -ae, *f.,* friendship, alliance

amīcus, -ī, *m.,* friend

āmittō, -ere, -mīsī, -missum, to send away, dismiss, lose

amnis, -is, *m.,* river

amō (1), to love

amor, -ōris, *m.,* love, affection, desire

amputō (1), to amputate, cut off

an, *conj.,* or; **an . . . an,** whether . . . or

anceps, ancipitis, *adj.,* double, twofold, doubtful

ancilla, -ae, *f.*, maidservant, female slave

Anicetus, -ī, *m.*, Anicetus (a man's name)

anima, -ae, *f.*, soul, spirit, breath

animus, -ī, *m.*, spirit, courage; mind, opinion

annāles, -ium, *m. pl.*, annals, history

annālis, -e, *adj.*, annual

annus, -ī, *m.*, year

ante, *adv. and prep.* + *acc.*, before

anteā, *adv.*, before, formerly

anteeō, -īre, -īvī, -itum, go faster than, precede, forestall

Antiochensis, -e, *adj.*, of/belonging to the people of Antioch

Antiochensis, -is, *m.*, an inhabitant of Antioch

antīquus, -a, -um, *adj.*, of old, belonging to ancient times

Antistius, -ī, *m.*, Antistius (a man's name)

Antōnius, -ī, *m.*, Antonius (a man's name)

anxius, -a, -um, *adj.*, distressed, anxious

Aper, -prī, *m.*, Aper (a man's name)

aperiō, -īre, -uī, -tum, to reveal, open

Apīcius, -ī, *m.*, Apicius (a man's name)

apiscor, -ī, aptus sum, to pursue; to obtain

apparātus, -ūs, *m.*, trappings, paraphanelia, equipment

apparō (1), to prepare

appellātio, -ōnis, *f.*, address, calling by name, name

appellō (1), to call

Āprīlis, -is, *m.*, April

apud, *prep.* + *acc.*, with, among, at, before, near; + *person*, in the presence of, in the house of

arbītrium, -ī, *n.*, judgement, mastery, dominion

arbitror, -ārī, -ātus sum, to judge, think

arbor, arboris, *f.*, tree

arcanum, -ī, *n.*, secret

arceō, -ēre, -uī, -tum, to hold off, keep at a distance

ardor, -ōris, *m.*, ardor, intensity

argumentum, -ī, *n.*, plot

arguō, -ere, -uī, -ūtum, to show; to accuse, complain of

arma, -ōrum, *n. pl.*, armor, arms; force, war

armātus, -a, -um, *adj.*, armed

armō (1), to arm, equip

arrogantia, -ae, *f.*, arrogance

ars, artis, *f.*, skill, art, trade, stratagem

Arsacēs, -is, *m.*, Arsaces (first king of the Parthians)

artus, -a, -um, *adj.*, close, narrow, small

Āsia, -ae, *f.*, Asia Minor

Asinius, -ī, *m.*, Asinius (a man's name)

aspectus, -ūs, *m.*, sight, look, appearance

asper, -era, -erum, *adj.*, rough, uneven, harsh, severe

aspiciō. *See* adspiciō

at, *conj.*, but, yet

Athēniēnsēs, -ium, *m. pl.*, the Athenians

Atilius, -ī, *m.*, Atilius (a man's name)

atque *or* ac, *conj.*, and

ātrox, -ōcis, *adj.*, horrible

auctor, -ōris, *m.*, author, cause

audācia, -ae, *f.*, boldness

audax, -ācis, *adj.*, daring, bold, rash

audeō, -ēre, ausus sum, —, to intend; to dare

audiō, -īre, -īvī, -ītum, to hear, listen

auferō, -ferre, -abstúlī, -ablātum, to carry off, remove, steal

augeō, -ere, auxī, auctus, to grow, increase

augescō, -ere, —, —, to begin to grow, increase, prosper

Augustus, -ī, *m.*, Augustus (and the title of succeeding emperors)

Aurelius, -ī, *m.*, Aurelius (a man's name)

aurīga, -ae, *m./f.*, charioteer

auris, -is, *f.*, ear

Aurulenus, -ī, *m.*, Aurulenus (a man's name)

aurum, -ī, *n.*, gold

aut, *conj.*, or; aut . . . aut, *coordinating conj.*, either . . . or

autem, *particle*, moreover, on the other hand, furthermore

autumnus, -ī, *m.*, autumn

auxilium, -ī, *n.*, help, aid, assistance

avārus, -a, -um, *adj.*, greedy

avunculus, -ī, *m.*, mother's brother, maternal uncle

Baccha, -ae, *f.*, a Bacchant, female attendant of Bacchus

Balbus, -ī, *m.*, Balbus (a man's name)

balinea, -ae, *f.*, bathhouses

balineum, -ī, *n.*, bath

beātus, -a, -um, *adj.*, happy

bellum, -ī, *n.*, war

benignitās, -ātis, *f.*, kindness, benevolence

biennis, -e, *adj.*, two years old, lasting two years

biennium, -ī, *n.*, a two-year period

bis, *adv.*, twice

Bīthӯnia, -ae, *f.*, Roman province of Bithynia in Asia Minor

bonus, -a, -um, *adj.*, good, honest

brachium, -ī, *n.*, arm

brevis, -e, *adj.*, short, brief

Britannia, -ae, *f.*, Britain

Britannicus, -ī, *m.*, Britannicus

Brundisīnus, -a, -um, *adj.*, of Brundisium

Brutus, -ī, *m.*, Brutus (a man's name)

cadō, -ere, cecidī, cāsum, to fall

Caecilius, -ī, *m.*, Caecilius (a man's name)

caedēs, -is, *f.*, murder, slaughter, massacre, execution

caedō, -ere, cecīdī, caesum, to cut down, murder

Caelius, -a, -um, *adj.*, Caelian

caelum, -ī, *n.*, sky, heavens; climate

Caepiō, -ōnis, *m.*, Caepio (a man's name)

Caesar, -aris, *m.*, Caesar (later a title of emperors and designated heirs of the imperial house)

Calpurnia, -ae, *f.*, Calpurnia (a woman's name)

Camerium, -ī, *n.*, Camerium (a town in Latium)

Camillus, -ī, *m.*, Camillus (a man's name)

Campānia, -ae, *f.*, Campania (the region south of Latium)

campus, -ī, *m.*, plain, field

Camurius, -ī, *m.*, Camurius (a man's name)

canis, -is, *m. and f.*, dog

capax, -ācis, *adj.*, capable, competent

capessō, -ere, -īvī, —, to seize; + **consilium,** to form a purpose/plan

capiō, -ere, cēpī, captum, to capture, take, seize

capitāle, -is, *n.*, capital offense

Capreae, -ārum, *f. pl.*, Capri (an island)

captīvitās, -ātis, *f.*, captivity, capture

caput, capitis, *n.*, head, life

Carbō, -ōnis, *m.*, Carbo (a man's name)

cāritās, -ātis, *f.*, regard, affection

carmen, -inis, *n.*, song, poem; spell

Cassius, -ī, *m.*, Cassius (a man's name)

castra, -ōrum, *n. pl.*, camp

cāsus, -ūs, *m.*, chance, calamity, plight, fate

Catō, -ōnis, *m.*, Cato (a man's name)

causa, -ae, *f.*, cause, legal case

causidicus, -ī, *m.*, pleader of a case

cēdō, -ere, cessī, cessum, to go away from, withdraw, yield; to grant, allow; to be inferior to

celeber, -bris, -e, *adj.*, celebrated, famous

celēbrō (1), to frequent, throng; to celebrate, honor, make known

centuriō, -ōnis, *m.*, commander of a century, centurion

certāmen, -inis, *n.*, contest, struggle, combat

certō (1), to contest, contend, struggle

cēterus, -a, -um, *adj.*, the other, the rest; *acc. n. sing. as adv.*, moreover

chorus, -ī, *m.*, dance in a ring, a troop of dancers and singers, a chorus

Christiānus, -a, -um, *adj.*, Christian

Christus, -ī, *m.,* Christ

cibus, -ī, *m.,* food, sustenance

cieō, -ēre, -īvī, -itum, to set in motion; to call upon

Cimbrī, -ōrum, *m. pl.,* the Cimbri (a north German tribe)

cingō, -ere, cinxī, cinctum, to surround, gird

cinis, -eris, *m.,* ash

Cinna, -ae, *m.,* Cinna (a man's name)

circensis, -e, *adj.,* of the circus/racetrack

circum, *adv.,* all around

circumdō, -dare, -dedī, -datum, to place around, surround, enclose

circumsistō, -ere, -stetī, —, to stand around, surround

circumveniō, -īre, -vēnī, -ventum, to surround, encircle, beset

circus, -ī, *m.,* circle, race-track

citerior, -ius, *compar. adj.,* nearer

cito, *adv.,* quickly

citus, -a, -um, *adj.,* quick

cīvīlis, -e, *adj.,* civil, affecting citizens, public

cīvis, -is, *m.,* citizen

cīvitās, -ātis, *f.,* city, the body-politic; the state

clādes, -is, *f.,* disaster, defeat, massacre

clāmitō (1), to cry out

clāmor, -ōris, *m.,* shout, battle cry, noise

claritās, -ātis, *f.,* brightness, celebrity

clārus, -a, -um, *adj.,* famous

classiārius, -a, -um, *adj.,* of the fleet or marines

classis, -is, *f.,* class, army, fleet

Claudius, -a, -um, *adj.,* of the Claudian clan

Claudius, -ī, *m.,* Claudius (a man's name)

Clausus, -ī, *m.,* Clausus (a man's name)

clēmenter, *adv.,* leniently, gently

clēmentia, -ae, *f.,* clemency, mercy

Cleopātra, -ae, *f.,* Cleopatra (a woman's name)

cliens, -entis, *m.,* client

coalescō, -ere, -aluī, -alitum, to unite

coeō, -īre, -īvī, -itum, to meet, assemble, go/come together, rally

coepiō, -ere, coepī, coeptum, to begin, start, commence, undertake

cogitō (1), to think, think on

cognoscō, -ere, -nōvī, -nitum, to learn, become aware of

cohors, -hortis, *f.,* cohort, band of armed men

colligō, -ere, -ēgī, -ectum, to collect, add up

colō, -ere, -uī, cultum, to worship

comitātus, -a, -um, *adj. + abl.,* accompanied

comitium, -ī, *n.,* place in forum where assemblies or elections were held

comitō (1), to accompany, attend

commercium, -ī, *n.*, right of exchange, relations

comminus, *adv.*, near/close at hand

comparātiō, -ōnis, *f.*, comparison

comperiō, -īre, -ī, -tum, to find out, learn

complector, -ī, complexus sum, to twine around, embrace

compleō, -ēre, -ēvī, -ētum, to fill up

complexus, -ūs, *m.*, embrace

compōnō, -ere, -posuī, -positum, to compose, order, encompass, include, calm

compositus, -a, -um, *adj.*, ordered

computō (1), to count

concēdō, -ere, -cessī, -cessum, to give up to, concede

concidō, -ere, -ī, to collapse, fall down

concieō, -ēre, -cīvī, -cītum, to set in motion, rouse, provoke

concipiō, -ere, -cēpī, -ceptum, to conceive

concors, -dis, *adj.*, agreeing

concupiscō, -ere, -cupīvī, -cupītum, to covet

concurrō, -ere, -currī, -cursum, to run/flock together; to join battle

concursus, -ūs, *m.*, flocking/ running together

conditor, -ōris, *m.*, maker, builder, founder, author

condūcō, -ere, -duxī, -ductum, to bring together

cōnectō, -ere, -nexī, -nexum, to join, connect

conferō, -ferre, -tulī, collātum, to bring/carry together, collect; to confer

conficiō, -ere, -fēcī, -fectum, to make, complete, finish off; to execute, kill

conflictō (1), to torment, vex

conflīgō, -ere, -flixī, -flictum, to come into conflict, clash, contend

confluō, -ere, -xī, —, to flow/ run together, crowd together

congregō (1), to collect into a flock, assemble, regroup

cōnītor, -ī, -nixus sum, to struggle toward, strive to reach

coniugium, -ī, *n.*, marriage, wedlock

conlocō (1), to arrange, put, place, set, station

conquīrō, -ere, -quīsīvī, -quīsītum, to search for, seek after

conscientia, -ae, *f.*, conscience; joint knowledge

conscius, -a, -um, *adj.*, knowing, privy to

conscius, -ī, *m.*, accomplice

conscrībō, -ere, -scripsī, -scriptum, to enroll

consensus, -ūs, *m.*, agreement, combined action

consequor, -ī, consecūtus sum to follow, understand

consilium, -ī, *n.*, plan, intention

consociō (1), to join in

consortium, -ī, *n.*, partnership

constituō, -ere, -uī, -ūtum, to establish, lay down, put in order

constō, -āre, -itī, -atum, to agree

consul, -ulis, *m.*, consul

consularis, -e, *adj.*, consular

consulātus, -ūs, *m.*, consulship

consulō, -ere, -suluī, -sultum, + *dat.*, to consult, take care for

consultum, -ī, *n.*, deliberation, decree

contactus, -ūs, *m.*, contagion, touch

contegō, -ere, -texī, -tectum, to cover up

contemnō, -ere, -tempsī, -temptum, to think little of, despise

contiguus, -a, -um, *adj.*, bordering upon, neighboring

contineō, -ere, -uī, contentum, to maintain

continuus, -a, -um, *adj.*, continuous

contrā, *adv. and prep.* + *acc.*, opposite, on the contrary; against

contrarium, -ī, *n.*, contrary, opposite

contumēlia, -ae, *f.*, insult, abuse

contus, -ī, *m.*, pole, pike

convertō, -ere, -vertī, -versum, to turn around, reverse, direct

convictus, -ūs, *m.*, banquet, entertainment; intimacy

convincō, -ere, -vīcī, -victum, to overcome; to show clearly, prove incontestably

convīvium, -ī, *n.*, feast, banquet

cōpia, -ae, *f.*, abundance, resources; *f. pl.*, troops

corpus, -oris, *n.*, body, substance

corripiō, -ere, -ripuī, -reptum, to take hold of, seize, plunder

corrumpō, -ere, -rūpī, -ruptum, to destroy, corrupt

Coruncānius, -ī, *m.*, Coruncanius (a man's name)

cothurnus, -ī, *m.*, high shoe/ buskin worn by tragic actors

cōtīdiē, *adv.*, daily

Crassus, -ī, *m.*, Crassus (a man's name)

crēber, -bra, -brum, *adj.*, thick, frequent, numerous, repeated

crēdō, -ere, -idī, -itum, + *dat.*, to trust, have confidence in; to believe

Crepereius, -ī, *m.*, Crepereius (a man's name)

crīmen, -inis, *n.*, crime, charge

crīminātor, -ōris, *m.*, accuser

crīnis, -is, *m.*, hair

Crispinus, -ī, *m.*, Crispinus (a man's name)

crūdēlitās, -ātis, *f.*, severity, cruelty

cruentus, -a, -um, *adj.*, bloody

cruor, -ōris, *m.*, blood, bloodshed

crūs, crūris, *n.*, leg

crux, crucis, *f.*, cross

cubiculum, -ī, *n.*, apartment, bedchamber

cubitō (1), to lie down

culpa, -ae, *f.*, fault

cultus, -ūs, *m.*, care, cultivation, culture, way of life

cum, *conj.*, when, since; *prep.* + *abl.*, with

cunctor, -ārī, -ātus sum, to delay, hesitate

cunctus, -a, -um, *adj.*, all, the whole

cupiditās, -ātis, *f.*, enthusiasm, passion, desire

cupīdō, -inis, *f.*, desire, passion

cūr, *adv.*, why

cūra, -ae, *f.*, care, concern, trouble

Curiatius, -ī, *m.*, Curiatius (a man's name)

cūriātus, -a, -um, *adj.*, of/pertaining to the curia

curriculum, -ī, *n.*, racing-chariot

Curtius, -ī, *m.*, Curtius (a man's name)

custōs, -ōdis, *m.*, guard

Dācī, -ōrum, *m. pl.*, the Dacians

damnum, -ī, *n.*, loss

Dānuvius, -ī, *m.*, the Danube

dē, *prep.* + *abl.*, down from, concerning, of

dēcēdō, -ere, -cessī, -cessum, to go away, subside

decem, *indecl. number*, ten

decemvirālis, -e, *adj.*, of/belonging to a council of ten men, decemviral

decimus, -a, -um, *adj.*, tenth

dēcipiō, -ere, -cēpī, -ceptum, to deceive, cheat

dēclīnō (1), to avoid

decorus, -a, -um, *adj.*, graceful, elegant

dēcrētum, -ī, *n.*, decree

decus, -oris, *n.*, ornament, grace, splendor, glory, honor

dēdecus, -oris, *n.*, disgrace, vice

dēdūcō, -ere, -duxī, -ductum, to lead away, withdraw, settle

dēfectiō, -ōnis, *f.*, weakness, faintness; rebellion, revolt

dēfendō, -ere, -fendī, -fensum, to defend, put out (flames)

dēficiō, -ere, -fēcī, -fectum, to withdraw, leave, cease

dēformis, -e, *adj.*, ugly, loathsome, misshapen

dēformitās, -ātis, *f.*, ugliness, vile nature, vileness

dēgredior, -ī, degressus sum, to march down, depart

dehinc, *adv.*, after this/that, from now on, next, then

dēiciō, -ere, -iēcī, -iectum, to eject, bring down, cause to fall

dēiectus, -a, -um, *adj.*, downcast

dein *or* deinde, *adv.*, then, henceforth, next; from that place

dēlātiō, -ōnis, *f.*, accusation, denunciation

delegō (1), to appoint

dēlēniō, -īre, -īvī, -ītum, to soothe, charm

dēligō, -ere, -lēgī, -lectum, to select

dēmum, *adv.,* at last, finally

dēnique, *adv.,* finally

dēnuntiō (1) + *dat.,* to command

dēprecor, -ārī, -ātus sum, to beg for mercy

derupiō, -ere, -upuī, -eptum, to tear away/down

dēserō, -ere, -uī, -tum, to leave, forsake

desertus, -a, -um, *adj.,* deserted, abandoned

dēsidia, -ae, *f.,* idleness

dēspērātiō, -ōnis, *f.,* desperation, despair

dēstinō (1), to resolve; to appoint, choose

dēstringō, -ere, -strinxī, -strictum, to strip off, draw

dēsum, -esse, -fuī, —, to be lacking/needing

dētentus, -a, -um. *See* **dētineō**

dēterreō, -ēre, -uī, -itum, to deter, discourage from

dēterrimus, -a, -um, *adj.,* worst

dētineō, -ēre, -uī, -entum, to hold back

deus, -ī, *m.,* god

dēvinciō, -īre, -vinxī, -vinctum, to bind (emotionally), lay under obligation, subjugate

dēvōtiō, -ōnis, *f.,* curse

dīcō, -ere, dixī, dictum, to say, pronounce

dictātūra, -ae, *f.,* dictatorship

dictiō, -ōnis, *f.,* saying, pleading or defense, language

dictō (1), to compose

dīdūcō, -ere, -duxī, -ductum, to draw apart, divide, scatter

diēs, -ēī, *m. and f.,* day

differō, -ferre, distulī, dīlātum, to scatter, spread abroad; to postpone, defer

dignus, -a, -um, *adj.,* worthy, deserving, suitable

dīgredior, -ī, -gressus sum, to depart

dīlābor, -ī, -lapsus sum, to disperse, scatter

dīligō, -ere, -lexī, -lectum, to esteem, love

discēdō, -ere, -cessī, -cessum, to depart

discidium, -ī, *n.,* discord, disagreement; divorce

discordia, -ae, *f.,* disagreement, discord

discordō (1), to quarrel

disertus, -a, -um, *adj.,* eloquent

dispergō, -ere, -persī, -persum, to scatter, distribute, spread

disputātiō, -ōnis, *f.,* discussion, argument, debate

dissimulō (1), to keep secret, conceal

dissociabilis, -e, *adj.,* incompatible

dissolūtiō, -ōnis, *f.,* dissolution, destruction

distinguō, -ere, -tinxī, -tinctum, to separate, divide, distinguish

diū, *adv.*, for a long time

diurnus, -a, -um, *adj.*, of the day, daytime, daily

dīus -a, -um. *See* **dīvus**

dīversus, -a, -um, *adj.*, opposite, diverse

dīves, -itis, *adj.*, rich

dīvīsiō, -ōnis, *f.*, division, allotment

dīvus, -a, -um, *adj.*, divine, deified, godlike

dō, dare, dedī, datum, to give

documentum, -ī, *n.*, evidence, example, proof

dolus, -ī, *m.*, deceit, trick, device; evil intent, wrongdoing

domesticus, -a, -um, *adj.*, personal, private, one's own

dominātiō, -ōnis, *f.*, rule, tyranny

dominor, -ārī, -ātus sum, to have dominion, rule

Domitius, -ī, *m.*, Domitius (a man's name)

domus, -ūs *or* **-ī**, *f.*, house, home

dōnātīvum, -ī, *n.*, gratuity, donative

dōnec, *conj.*, while, until, so long as

dōnum, -ī, *n.*, gift

Drūsus, -ī, *m.*, Drusus (a man's name)

dubitō (1), doubt, be hesitant

dubius, -a, -um, *adj.*, doubtful

ducentī, -ae, -a, two hundred

dūcō, -ere, -duxī, -ductum, to lead, conduct; to reckon; to prolong, extend

dulcēdō, -dinis, *f.*, pleasantness

dum, *conj.*, while, provided that

duo, -ae, -o, *cardinal number*, two

duodecim, *cardinal number*, twelve

ē. *See* **ex**

eādem, *adv.*, at the same time

ēditus, -a, -um, *adj.*, high, elevated; *substantive*, heights

ēdō, -ere, -idī, -itum, to give forth, beget; to publish

efficiō, -ere, -fēcī, -fectum, to bring to pass, make

effigies, -ēī, *f.*, likeness, image, portrait

effigiō (1), to form, fashion

effugiō, -ere, -ī, -itum, to escape

effugium, -ī, *n.*, flight, means of escape

effundō, -ere, -fudī, -fusum, to pour out, flow out

egens, -entis, *adj.*, poor

Egnātius, -ī, *m.*, Egnatius (a man's name)

ego, meī, *pron.*, I

ēgredior, -ī, -gressus sum, to go out, come out

ēgregius, -a, -um, *adj.*, distinguished, outstanding, excellent

ēligō, -ere, -lēgī, -lectum, to pick out, choose, elect

ēloquentia, -ae, *f.*, eloquence

ēmētior, -īrī, emensus sum, to pass through; to measure out

ēminens, -entis, *adj.,* eminent, distinguished

ēmineō, -ēre, -uī, —, to stand out, project, be prominent

enim, *conj.,* for

ēnormis, -e, *adj.,* enormous, vast, of irregular shape

eō, īre, īvī, itum, to go

epulor, -ārī, -ātus sum, to feast

epulum, -ī, *n.,* banquet, feast

eques, -itis, *m.,* horseman, equestrian

ergā, *prep. + acc.,* in respect to, towards

ergō, *adv.,* consequently

ēripiō, -ere, -ripuī, -reptum, to snatch away, carry away, wrest

ērudītiō, -ōnis, *f.,* learning, taught knowledge

ērumpō, -ere, -rūpī, -ruptum, to break out, burst forth, erupt

ēruō, -ere, -ī, -tum, to throw out, dig up, root out, overthrow, destroy

et, *adv. and conj.,* also, and

etenim, *conj.,* for, since

etiam, *adv. and conj.,* and also, even

Etrūria, -ae, *f.,* Etruria (a region in central Italy north of Rome)

Eudemus, -ī, *m.,* Eudemus (a man's name)

Euodus, -ī, *m.,* Euodus (a man's name)

ēvādō, -ere, -vāsī, -vāsum, to go/come out, escape

ēvincō, -ere, -vīcī, -victum, to overcome entirely, induce, move

ēvocātus, -ī, *m.,* veteran, volunteer

ex, *prep. + abl.,* out of, from, due to

exactor, -ōris, *m.,* executioner

exactus, -a, -um, *adj.,* exact, accurate

exanimō (1), to kill

exardeō, -ēre, —, —, to burn, be inflamed

excipiō, -ere, -cēpī, -ceptum, to follow, take off, relieve, except

exclāmō (1), to call out

excogitō (1), to think out, devise, invent, contrive

excūsō (1), to excuse

exemplum, -ī, *n.,* example, model, precedent

exequor, -ī, execūtus sum, to effect, carry out

exerceō, -ēre, -uī, -itum, to keep busy, administer, carry into effect, use

exercitus, -ūs, *m.,* army

exigō, -ere, -ēgī, -actum, to drive out

exilium, -ī, *n.,* exile

exim, *adv.,* from there, after that

eximō, -ere, -ēmī, -emptum, to take away, remove

existimō (1), to think, suppose

exitiābilis, -e, *adj.*, destructive, fatal, deadly

exitium, -ī, *n.*, exit, destruction, ruin

exitus, -ūs, *m.*, exit, death, departure

exolvō, -ere, -solvī, -solūtum. *See* **exsolvō**

expectō (1), to await, anticipate, hope for

expediō, -īre, -īvī, -ītum, to disclose, explain

expellō, -ere, -pulsī, -pulsum, to expel, banish

expers, -ertis, *adj.* + *gen.*, to be free from

expetō, -ere, -petīvī, -petītum, to seek after

expleō, -ēre, -plēvī, -plētum, to fill up, complete, finish

expostulō (1), to demand, call for, vehemently/urgently require

exprōbrō (1), to reproach

expugnō (1), to assault, conquer

exsolvō, -ere, -solvī, -solūtum, to pay (a penalty)

externus, -a, -um, *adj.*, foreign

exterreō, -ēre, -uī, -itum, to strike with terror, frighten

extinguō, -ere, -tinxī, -tinctum, to kill, destroy

extollō, -ere, —, —, to elevate, extol

extorqueō, -ēre, -sī, -tum, to wrest away, extort

extrā, *prep.* + *acc.*, without

extrēmum, -ī, *n.*, edge, outer parts, extremity

extrēmus, -a, -um, *adj.*, utmost, furthest, last

exul, -ulis, *m. and f.*, exile

exultō (1), to revel, run riot, let oneself go

Fabius, -ī, *m.*, Fabius (a man's name)

fabula, -ae, *f.*, story

facessō, -ere, -īvī, -ītum, to do, perpetrate

faciēs, -ēī, *f.*, form, shape; face, appearance

facilis, -e, *adj.*, easy, ready, easily managed, compliant

facinus, -oris, *n.*, deed, crime

faciō, -ere, fēcī, factum, to make, do

factitō (1), to do frequently/habitually, make habitually

facultās, -ātis, *f.*, opportunity; ability

fallax, -ācis, *adj.*, deceitful, deceptive

fallō, -ere, fefellī, falsum, to deceive, trick; *impers.*, to be mistaken

falsus, -a, -um, *adj.*, false

fāma, -ae, *f.*, rumor, reputation

familia, -ae, *f.*, household, family

familiāris, -e, *adj.*, of/belonging to a household; *m. and f.*, friend, servant

familiāritās, -ātis, *f.*, familiarity, friendship

fās, *n.*, *defective noun*, divine law; + **esse,** to be right, lawful, possible

fascis, -is, *m., in pl.,* fasces (bundle of rods and an axe carried before a magistrate)

fastīgium, -ī, *n.,* peak, summit, highest degree, most exalted rank

fateor, -ērī, fassus sum, to confess

fax, facis, *f.,* torch

fēlīcitās, -ātis, *f.,* luck, good fortune, happiness

fēlix, -īcis, *adj.,* happy

fēmina, -ae, *f.,* woman

fera, -ae, *f.,* wild animal

feriō, -īre, —, —, to strike, hit

feritās, -ātis, *f.,* wildness, ferocity

fermē, *adv.,* nearly, almost

ferō, ferre, tulī, lātum, to bring, bear, report, relate

ferrum, -ī, *n.,* iron, sword

ferus, -a, -um, *adj.,* wild, cruel

fessus, -a, -um, *adj.,* weary, tired, weak

festīnō (1), to hurry

festus, -a, -um, *adj.,* festive, celebrating a holiday

fidēs, -ēī, *f.,* trust, assurance, good faith

fīdūcia, -ae, *f.,* trust, reliance

fīdus, -a, -um, *adj.,* sure, trustworthy

fīgō, -ere, fixī, fixum, to affix

fīlia, -ae, *f.,* daughter

fīlius, -ī, *m.,* son, child

fingō, -ere, finxī, fictum, to fashion, represent, imagine, conceive

fīniō, -īre, -īvī, -ītum, to enclose, restrain, determine, prescribe, finish, die

flāgitiōsus, -a, -um, shameful

flāgitium, -ī, *n.,* disgrace, shameful act, crime of passion

flāmen, -inis, *m.,* flamen (priest of a particular deity)

flamma, -ae, *f.,* fire, flame

flammō (1), to inflame, burn

Flāviānus, -a, -um, *adj.,* of Flavius, Flavian

flectō, -ere, flexī, flexum, to bend, curve

flexus, -ūs, *m.,* bend

flōreō, -ēre, -uī, —, to bloom, flourish; to be prosperous

fluctus, -ūs, *m.,* wave

flumen, -inis, *n.,* river

fluō, -ere, fluxī, fluxum, to flow, overflow, pour, stream

foedē, *adv.,* cruelly, foully

foeditās, -ātis, *f.,* filthiness

foedō (1), to defile, disfigure

foedus, -a, -um, *adj.,* foul, loathsome

foedus, -eris, *n.,* treaty, compact

fore, *fut. infinitive of* **sum**

foris, -is, *f.,* door, gate

forma, -ae, *f.,* nature, form, appearance, beauty

fors, fortis, *f.,* chance, luck; *abl.,* by chance

fortis, -e, *adj.,* brave, strong

fortuītus, -a, -um, *adj.,* accidental, fortuitous

fortūna, -ae, *f.,* chance, fortune

forum, -ī, *n.,* forum, market-
place
foveō, -ēre, fōvī, fōtum, to
favor, support, keep warm
frāter, -tris, *m.,* brother
frequens, -entis, *adj.,* repeated,
frequent, assiduous
fretum, -ī, *n.,* strait, channel,
sea
frons, frontis, *f.,* forehead, front
fruor, -ī, fructus sum, + *abl.,* to
enjoy, delight in
frustrā, *adv.,* in vain
fuga, -ae, *f.,* flight
fundō, -ere, fūdī, fūsum, to
pour, scatter, lie down
furō, -ere, —, —, to rave, rage
fustis, -is, *m.,* cudgel, club

Gāius, -ī, *m.,* Gaius (a man's
name)
Galba, -ae, *m.,* Galba (a man's
name)
Gallia, -ae, *f.,* Gaul
Gallus, -ī, *m.,* Gallus (a man's
name)
Gambriviī, -ōrum, *m. pl.,* the
Gambrivii (a German tribe)
gaudium, -ī, *n.,* joy, delight,
gladness
gener, -erī, *m.,* son-in-law
generō (1), to beget, produce,
create; *pass.,* to spring/
descend from
gens, gentis, *f.,* clan, tribe,
people
genu, -ūs, *n.,* knee
genus, -eris, *n.,* origin, race,
descent; class, sort

Germanī, -ōrum, *m. pl.,* the
Germans
Germānia, -ae, *f.,* Germany
Germānicus, -ī, *m.,*
Germanicus (a man's name)
gerō, -ere, gessī, gestum, to
carry, wear, show, have,
entertain
gignō, -ere, genuī, genitum,
to beget, produce, occasion;
pass., to be born, arise
gladius, -ī, *m.,* sword
gliscō, -ere, —, —, to grow up,
blaze up, burst forth, swell
glōria, -ae, *f.,* glory, fame
gnārus, -a, -um, *adj.,* known
grandis, -e, *adj.,* great
Granius, -ī, *m.,* Granius (a
man's name)
grātēs, *f. pl., defective noun
usually only in abl. or acc.,*
thanks, gratitude
grātia, -ae, *f.,* favor
grator, -ārī, -ātus sum, to
rejoice, congratulate
gravis, -e, *adj.,* heavy, laden,
serious, dangerous,
oppressive
graviter, *adv.,* deeply, severely
gubernāculum, -ī, *n.,* helm

habeō, -ēre, -uī, -itum, to have,
hold, possess, occupy
habitus, -ūs, *m.,* condition,
appearance, comportment,
dress, attire
haereō, -ēre, haesī, haesum, to
cling
haud, *adv.,* hardly, not at all

haurio, -īre, hausī, haustus, to drain

hedera, -ae, *f.,* ivy

Helvīdius, -ī, *m.,* Helvidius (a man's name)

hercule, *interj.,* by Hercules; assuredly, indeed

Herculeius, -ī, *m.,* Herculeius (a man's name)

hērēditās, -ātis, *f.,* inheritance

Herennius, -ī, *m.,* Herennius (a man's name)

Hermionēs, -um, *m. pl.,* Hermiones (a German tribe)

hibernum, -ī, *n.,* winter; *pl.,* winter camp

hic, haec, hōc, *pron.,* this

hinc, *adv.,* from here, after this

Hirtius, -ī, *m.,* Hirtius (a man's name)

Hispānia, -ae, *f.,* Spain

Hispo, -ōnis, *m.,* Hispo (a man's name)

hodiē, *adv.,* today

hodiernus, -a, -um, *adj.,* of today, of the present

homo, -inis, *m.,* human being, man

honestus, -a, -um, *adj.,* upright, virtuous

honor, -ōris, *m.,* honor, repute, public office

honōrus, -a, -um, *adj.,* honorable

horridus, -a, -um, *adj.,* bristly, frightful, wild

hortor, -ārī, -ātus sum, to exhort

hortus, -ī, *m.,* garden

hospitium, -ī, *n.,* hospitable reception, entertainment

hostia, -ae, *f.,* sacrifice

hostis, -is, *m.,* enemy

hūc, *adv.,* to this place, hither

humanus, -a, -um, *adj.,* human

humus, -ī, *f.,* earth, ground

iacio, -ere, iēcī, iactum, to throw, hurl, let fly

iactus, -ūs, *m.,* throw, cast

iam, *adv.,* now, already

iānua, -ae, *f.,* door, entrance

ictus, -ūs, *m.,* stroke, blow

īdem, eadem, idem, *pron.,* the same one; *n. as adv.,* likewise, similarly

ideo, *adv.,* on that account, therefore

igitur, *conj.,* then, thereupon, therefore

ignārus, -a, -um, *adj.,* ignorant of

ignāvus, -a, -um, *adj.,* idle, cowardly

ignis, -is, *m.,* fire

ignōrō (1), to be unaware

ignōtus, -a, -um, *adj.,* unknown, lowborn

ille, -a, -ud, *adj. and demonstrative pron.,* that; he, she, it

illecebra, -ae, *f.,* allurement, enticement

illīc, *adv.,* there, in that place

illicio, -ere, illexī, illectum, to entice, attract, allure

illūc, *adv.,* to that place, thither

imāgō, -ginis, *f.,* likeness, statue

imbuō, -ere, -uī, -ūtum,
to imbue, give initial
instruction in

immensus, -a, -um, *adj.,*
immeasurable, boundless,
vast

immō, *adv.,* on the contrary,
rather

impediō, -īre, -īvī, -ītum, to
hamper, hinder, obstruct

impellō, -ere, -pulī, -pulsum,
to push, drive, incite

imperātor, -ōris, *m.,* emperor,
commander

imperitō (1), to command,
govern

imperium, -ī, *n.,* command,
order, empire

imperō (1), to command, order,
rule

impetus, -ūs, *m.,* attack, charge,
violent assault

imprimō, -ere, -pressī,
-pressum, to press upon

imprūdentia, -ae, *f.,*
imprudence

impudīcitia, -ae, *f.,* lewdness,
shamelessness

in, *prep.* + *abl.,* in, among; +
acc., into, to, against

inaccessus, -a, -um, *adj.,*
inaccessible

incalescō, -ere, -caluī, —, to
grow warm

incautus, -a, -um, *adj.,*
inaccessible, incautious,
careless

incēdō, -ere, -cessī, -cessum, to
go, march

incendium, -ī, *n.,* fire,
conflagration

incendō, -ere, -cendī,
-censum, to set fire to,
burn

incertus, -a, -um, *adj.,*
uncertain, doubtful

incidō, -ere, -cidī, -cāsum, to
happen, fall upon

incipiō, -ere, -cēpī, -ceptum,
to begin

incitāmentum, -ī, *n.,* incentive,
enticement

inclīnō (1), to cause to lean,
bend, incline, turn back,
yield; to grow worse

incolumis, -e, *adj.,* sound,
unharmed, safe, in good
condition

incolumitās, -ātis, *f.,* safety

increpō, -āre, -uī, -itum,
to make a noise, chide,
upbraid, reproach

incuriōsus, -a, -um, *adj.,*
indifferent

incusō (1), to accuse

inde, *adv.,* therefore, from that
time

indecōrus, -a, -um, *adj.,*
unseemly, unsightly

indicium, -ī, *n.,* indication,
sign, evidence

indigena, -ae, *m.,* a native

indō, -ere, -didī, -ditum, to put
into/in/on

indolēs, -is, *f.,* innate, inborn/
native quality, character

indomitus, -a, -um, *adj.,*
unrestrained

industria, -ae, *f.,* industry, diligence

ineō, -īre, -īvī, -itum, to enter into, undertake

inertia, -ae, *f.,* laziness, idleness

inēvītābilis, -e, *adj.,* unavoidable

infāmia, -ae, *f.,* ill fame, infamy

infantia, -ae, *f.,* infancy, early childhood

inferior, -or, -us, *adj.,* lower, farther down

infernus, -a, -um, *adj.,* associated with the underworld

inferō, -ferre, -tulī, illātum, to carry/put into, attack

infestus, -a, -um, *adj.,* dangerous, unsafe, hostile

infirmitās, -ātis, *f.,* weakness

informis, -e, *adj.,* ugly, unformed, shapeless, misshapen, deformed

infrā, *prep.* + *acc.,* below, beneath

Ingaevonēs, -um, *m.,* the Ingaevones (a Germanic tribe)

ingenium, -ī, *n.,* talent, natural character, inclination

ingens, -entis, *adj.,* immense, great

ingenuus, -a, -um, *adj.,* noble, freeborn

ingruō, -ere, -uī, —, to advance, threaten, attack

inhūmānus, -a, -um, *adj.,* inhumane, inhuman, savage

iniectus, -ūs, *m.,* throwing on/over

inimīcitia, -ae, *f.,* hostility, enmity

initium, -ī, *n.,* beginning, origin

inlecebra, -ae. See **illecebra**

inlectus, -ūs, *m.,* enticement

inliciō. See **illiciō**

inlustris, -e, *adj.,* bright, clear, distinguished, illustrious

inmensus, -a, -um, *adj.,* immense

inmineō, -ēre, —, —, to be a threat to, threaten

innitor, -ī, innisus sum, + *dat.,* to lean on; + *abl.,* to be supported by

inopia, -ae, *f.,* poverty

inpūnis, -e, *adj.,* without punishment

inquam, *defective verb,* to say

inquiēs, -ētis, *adj.,* restless, impatient

inquīsītiō, -ōnis, *m.,* investigation, inquiry

inrēpō, -ere, -rēpsī, —, to creep in

inritus, -a, -um, *adj.,* in vain

inrumpō, -ere, -rūpī, -ruptum, to break into

insāniō, -īre, -īvī, -ītum, to be insane, rave

insculpō, -ere, -ī, -tum, to engrave

insidiae, -ārum, *f. pl.,* ambush, plot, trap

insignis, -e, *adj.,* distinguished, noted

insimulō (1), to accuse

insistō, -ere, -stitī, —, to follow, pursue, press on; to step upon a place, occupy a place

instituō, -ere, -uī, -ūtum, to establish

institūta, -ōrum, *n. pl.*, manners

institutiō, -ōnis, *f.*, institution, education

instruō, -ere, -struxī, —, to set in order, draw up (troops), arrange

insuescō, -ere, -suēvī, -suētum, to become accustomed to

insula, -ae, *f.*, island

insum, -esse, -fuī, —, to be in/upon, to be contained within

insuper, *prep.* + *acc.*, besides

intectus, -a, -um, *adj.*, uncovered, unguarded

integer, -gra, -grum, *adj.*, untouched, whole, complete, unhurt, free, open

intellegō, -ere, -tellexī, -tellectum, to perceive, understand

intendō, -ere, -tendī, -tentum, to aim at, decide; + *ad*, to be attentive to, prepare for

intentō (1), to hold out, threaten, point (a weapon threateningly)

inter, *adv. and prep.* + *acc.*, between, among, in the midst of

intercidō, -ere, -cidī, —, to be killed, die

interclūdō, -ere, -ūsī, -ūsum, to shut out, shut off

intereā, *adv.*, meanwhile, in the interim

intereō, -īre, -iī, -itum, to go among, become lost, perish

interfector, -ōris, *m.*, murderer, assassin

interficiō, -ere, -fēcī, -fectum, to destroy, kill, murder

interiaceō, -ēre, -uī, -itum, + *dat.*, to lie between, intervene

interim, *adv.*, meanwhile, sometimes

interluō, -ere, —, —, to flow between

intermittō, -ere, -mīsī, -missum, to leave off, cease, interrupt

interrogō (1), to ask, question

intersum, -esse, -fuī, —, *impers.*, it concerns, it is a matter of

intestābilis, -e, *adj.*, infamous, shameful, destestable

intrepidus, -a, -um, *adj.*, unshaken, undaunted

intrō (1), to enter

intrōeō, -īre, -īvī, -itum, to go into, enter

intrōspiciō, -ere, -spexī, -spectum, to look at, observe

intueor, -ērī, -itus sum, to consider, contemplate, look at

intus, *adv.*, on the inside, within

invādō, -ere, -vāsī, -vāsum, to go/come into, enter upon, take possession of

invalidus, -a, -um, *adj.,* infirm, weak

inveniō, -īre, -vēnī, -ventum, to come/light upon, find, find out

inveterascō, -ere, -veterāvī, —, to start to grow old

invideō, -ēre, -vīdī, -vīsum, to hate

inviolātus, -a, -um, *adj.,* inviolable, unhurt

invītō (1), to summon, request, urge

invītus, -a, -um, *adj.,* unwilling

ipse, -a, -um, *pron.,* himself, herself, itself, in person, he/she/it (*emphatic*)

īra, -ae, *f.,* anger

is, ea, id, *pron.,* he, she, it; *adj.,* this, that

Istaevonēs, -um, *m. pl.,* the Istaevones (a German tribe)

ita, *adv.,* thus

Ītalia, -ae, *f.,* Italy

iter, itineris, *n.,* path, road, journey

iubeō, -ēre, iussī, iussum, to command

Iūdaea, -ae, *f.,* Judaea

iūdicium, -ī, *n.,* judgement, law court, decision, opinion, belief

iugulō (1), to butcher, cut the throat, kill, slay

iugulum, -ī, *n.,* throat

iugum, -ī, *n.,* mountain ridge, yoke

Iulia, -ae, *f.,* Julia (a woman's name)

Iulius, -a, -um, *adj.,* of the Julian clan

Iulius, -ī, *m.,* Julius (a man's name)

Iullus, -ī, *m.,* Iullus (a man's name)

iūs, iūris, *n.,* law, right

iussus, -ūs, *m.,* order, command

iustitia, -ae, *f.,* justice

Iustus, -ī, *m.,* Justus (a man's name)

iuvenīlis, -e, *adj.,* youthful

iuvenis, -is, *m.,* youth, young man

iuventa, -ae, *f.,* age of youth, youth

iuxtā, *prep + acc.,* near, next to, close by; *adv.,* near, alike, as much, almost

kalendae, -ārum, *f. pl.,* the kalends (i.e., the first day of the month, abbreviated *kal.*)

lābor, -ī, lapsus sum, to fall, slide

labor, -ōris, *m.,* toil, work, hardship

Lacedaemoniī, -ōrum, *m. pl.,* the Lacedaemonians, the Spartans

lācrima, -ae, *f.,* tear

lacus, -ūs, *m.,* lake, vat

Laecanius, -ī, *m.,* Laecanius (a man's name)

laetor, -ārī, -ātus sum, to rejoice

laetus, -a, -um, *adj.,* happy, glad, rejoicing

lāmentum, -ī, *n.,* lamentation

languescō, -ere, languī, —, to weaken

laniātus, -ūs, *m.,* a mangling, lacerating

laniō (1), to mutilate

largītiō, -ōnis, *f.,* giving, largesse; bribery

lascīvia, -ae, *f.,* playfulness, licentiousness, lasciviousness

lascīviō, -īre, -iī, -ītum, to run riot

latēbra, -ae, *f.,* hiding place, refuge

Latīnī, -ōrum, *m. pl.,* the Latins

lātus, -a, -um, *adj.,* wide, broad

latus, -eris, *n.,* side, flank

laudō (1), to praise, commend, eulogize

laus, laudis, *f.,* praise, approval

lectus, -ī, *m.,* couch, bed

legiō, -ōnis, *f.,* body of soldiers, legion

legō, -ere, lēgī, lectum, to read, gather, collect

lēnis, -e, *adj.,* easy

lentus, -a, -um, *adj.,* slow

lēnunculus, -ī, *m.,* small boat, bark, skiff

Lepida, -ae, *f.,* Lepida (a woman's name)

Lepidus, -ī, *m.,* Lepidus (a man's name)

lex, lēgis, *f.,* law

libellus, -ī, *m.,* little book, pamphlet

liber, librī, *m.,* book

līberī, -ōrum, *m. pl.,* children

lībertās, -ātis, *f.,* freedom, liberty

lībertīnus, -ī, *m.,* freedman

lībertus, -ī, *m.,* freedman

libet, -ēre, libuit, *impers.,* it is pleasing (+ *acc.* + *infinitive*)

libīdō, -inis, *f.,* pleasure, desire, passion, lust

libita, -ōrum, *n. pl.,* wishes, pleasures, will

lībrō (1), to balance, make even/ level

licens, -entis, *adj.,* free, unrestrained, licentious

licentia, -ae, *f.,* freedom, license, leave

lictor, -ōris, *m.,* lictor

līmen, -inis, *n.,* threshold

littera, -ae, *f.,* letter

lītus, -oris, *n.,* shore

Līvia, -ae *f.,* Livia (a woman's name)

locuplēs, -ētis, *adj.,* wealthy

locus, -ī, *m.,* place, spot, position

Lolliānus, -a, -um, *adj.,* of/ belonging to Lollius

longinquus, -a, -um, *adj.,* long, distant, far off

longitūdō, -inis, *f.,* length

longus, a, -um, *adj.,* long

loquor, -ī, locūtus sum, to speak, say

lūbricus, -a, -um, *adj.,* slippery, hazardous

Lūcānia, -ae, *f.*, Lucania (a region in south central Italy)

Lūcrīnus, -a, -um, *adj.*, Lucrine, of Lake Lucrinus

Lūculliānus, -a, -um, *adj.*, of Lucullus

lūdībrium, -ī, *n.*, mockery, jest

lūdicrum, -ī, *n.*, a show

lūdicrus, -a, -um, *adj.*, related to sport or the stage

lūmen, -inis, *n.*, light, lamp

Lutatius, -ī, *m.*, Lutatius (a man's name)

luxuriōsus, -a, -um, *adj.*, luxuriant, wanton, excessive

luxus, -ūs, *m.*, extravagance, luxury

māchināmentum, -ī, *n.*, machine

māchinātor, -ōris, *m.*, contriver of plots or events

Macro, -ōnis, *m.*, Macro (a man's name)

maereō, -ēre, —, —, to mourn, grieve

maestus, -a, -um, *adj.*, sad, sorrowful, mourning

magis, *adv.*, more, rather

magistrātus, -ūs, *m.*, office, magistracy

magnificus, -a, -um, *adj.*, noble, magnificent

magnus, -a, -um, *adj.*, large, great

maiestās, -ātis, *f.*, treason, dignity, grandeur

māiorēs, -um, *m. pl.*, ancestors

maleficus, -a, -um, *adj.*, wicked, harmful

malignē, *adv.*, spitefully

Mallius, -ī, *m.*, Mallius (a man's name)

malus, -a, -um, *adj.*, bad, evil; *n.*, an evil, mischief

mandō (1), to entrust

maneō, -ēre, -sī, -sum, to remain

manifestus, -a, -um, *adj.*, clearly visible, conspicuous

Mannus, -ī, *m.*, Mannus (a god of the Germans)

manus, -ūs, *f.*, hand

Marcellus, -ī, *m.*, Marcellus (a man's name)

mare, -is, *n.*, sea

marītus, -ī, *n.*, husband

Marius, -ī, *m.*, Marius (a man's name)

Marsī, -ōrum, *m. pl.*, the Marsi (a Germanic tribe)

Martius, -ī, *adj.*, of Mars

māter, -tris, *f.*, mother

Māternus, -ī, *m.*, Maternus (a man's name)

mātrimōnium, -ī, *n.*, wedlock, marriage

maximē, *adv.*, most, especially

maximus, -a, -um, *adj.*, large, great

Maximus, -ī, *m.*, Maximus (a man's name)

meātus, -ūs, *m.*, course

medicus, -ī, *m.*, physician

medius, -a, -um, *adj.*, middle

memor, -oris, *adj.*, mindful of, remembering

memoria, -ae, *f.*, memory, history

memorō (1), to remember, recount, mention

mercimōnium, -ī, *n.*, merchandise

mereō, -ēre, -uī, -itum, to earn, deserve

Messālīna, -ae, *f.*, Messalina (a woman's name)

Metellus, -ī, *m.*, Metellus (a man's name)

metuō, -ere, -uī, -ūtum, to fear

metus, -ūs, *m.*, fear

meus, -a, -um, *pron. possessive*, my, mine

mīles, mīlitis, *m.*, soldier; *pl.*, infantry, soldiery

mīlitāris, -e, *adj.*, martial

minae, -ārum, *f. pl.*, threats

minimē, *adv.*, by no means

minimus, -a, -um, *adj.*, least, smallest

ministerium, -ī, *n.*, duty

minus, *adv.*, less

mīrus, -a, -um, *adj.*, wonderful, extraordinary

misceō, -ēre, miscuī, mixtum, to mix, intermingle, blend

miser, -era, -erum, *adj.*, wretched

miserātiō, -ōnis, *f.*, pity, compassion

miseria, -ae, *f.*, affliction, distress

misericordia, -ae, *f.*, pity, compassion, mercy

mittō, -ere, mīsī, missum, to send

moderātē, *adv.*, moderately, in a controlled manner

modestia, -ae, *f.*, propriety, restraint

modestus, -a, -um, *adj.*, restrained, modest, unassuming

modicus, -a, -um, *adj.*, small, moderate

modo, *adv.*, only, just now

mollis, -e, *adj.*, soft

mons, montis, *m.*, mountain, hill

monstrō (1), to show, demonstrate, indicate, point out

monumentum, -ī, *n.*, monument

mora, -ae, *f.*, delay, hindrance

morbus, -ī, *m.*, disease

mors, mortis, *f.*, death

mortālis, -e, *adj.*, mortal

mortālitās, -ātis, *f.*, mortality, death

mōs, mōris, *m.*, custom, behavior, way, practice

mox, *adv.*, soon, afterwards

multiplex, -icis, *adj.*, manifold, various

multitūdō, -inis, *f.*, great number, crowd, throng

multus, -a, -um, *adj.*, much, many

mūnia, -ōrum, *n. pl.*, duties

mūnicipālis, -e, *adj.*, municipal, provincial

mūnīmentum, -ī, *n.*, defence, fortification

mūrus, -ī, *m.*, wall

mūtō (1), to move, alter, change

mūtuus, -a, -um, *adj.,* mutual

nam, *conj.,* for

Narbōnensis, -e, *adj.,* + **Gallia,** Gaul (the province beyond the Alps)

Narcissus, -ī, *m.,* Narcissus (a man's name)

nascor, -ī, nātus sum, to be born

nātālis, -is, *m.,* birth, origins

nato (1), to swim, float

nātūra, -ae, *f.,* nature

nāvālis, -e, *adj.,* naval

nāvigium, -ī, *n.,* ship, boat

nāvis, -is, *f.,* ship

nē, *adv. and conj.,* no, not; **ne . . . quidem,** not even

nec. *See* **neque**

necdum, *conj.,* and not yet, nor yet

necessitās, -ātis, *f.,* difficult straits; necessity, force, compulsion

necessitūdō, -inis, *f.,* necessity, obligation; close family connection, relative; friend

nēmō, -inis, *m. and f.,* no one, nobody

nepōs, -ōtis, *m.,* grandson

neque, *conj.,* and not, also not; **neque . . . neque,** neither . . . nor

nequeō, -īre, -īvī, -itum, to be unable

Nero, -ōnis, *m.,* Nero (a man's name)

Nerva, -ae, *m.,* Nerva (a man's name)

nesciō, -īre, -īvī, -ītum, to not know

nescius, -a, -um, *adj.,* ignorant, unknown

nex, necis, *f.,* death, murder

nī, *adv.,* if not, unless, that not

nihil, *n., defective noun,* nothing

nisi, *conj.,* if not, unless, except

nītor, -ī, nīxus sum, to lean, incline, rest one's weight on

nō (1), to swim, float

nōbilis, -e, *adj.,* noble

nōbilitās, -ātis, *f.,* renown; nobility

nocturnus, -a, -um, *adj.,* nocturnal

nōlō, nolle, nōluī, —, to be unwilling, to not wish to

nōmen, -inis, *n.,* name

nōn, *adv.,* not

nōnus, -a, -um, *adj.,* ninth

nōs, nostrum, *pron.,* we, us

noscō, -ere, nōvī, nōtum, to know, acknowledge

noster, -stra, -strum, *pron.,* our, ours

noverca, -ae, *f.,* stepmother

novus, -a, -um, *adj.,* new, recent

nox, noctis, *f.,* night

noxius, -a, -um, *adj.,* harmful; *n.,* injury, offense

nūbō, -ere, nupsī, nuptum, to marry

nullus, -a, -um, *adj.,* no, none

num, *adv.,* surely not

nūmen, -inis, *n.,* divine power, divinity

numerus, -ī, *m.,* rhythm, division, troop, number

numquam, *adv.,* at no time, never

nunc, *adv.,* now

nuntiō (1), to announce, report

nuntius, -ī, *m.,* messenger

nūper, *adv.,* recently

nuptiae, -ārum, *f. pl.,* marriage

nuptiālis, -e, *adj.,* of a marriage, nuptial

ob, *prep.* + *acc.,* on account of

Obaritus, -ī, *m.,* Obaritus (a man's name)

obferō, -ferre, -tulī, -lātum, to offer

obiciō, -ere, -iēcī, -iectum, to throw before, expose; to object

oblinō, -ere, -lēvī, -litum, to smear, coat, make dirty/foul

oblīviscor, -ī, oblītus sum, to forget

obnoxius, -a, -um, *adj.,* exposed, subject to injury

obscūrus, -a, -um, *adj.,* obscure, hidden

obsequium, -ī, *n.,* servility, compliance

observō (1), to observe, notice

obses, obsidis, *m. and f.,* hostage

obtegō, -ere, -texī, -tectum, to conceal, protect

obtentus, -ūs, *m.,* cover, pretext

obtineō, -ēre, -tinuī, -tentum, to take hold of, occupy

obvertō, -ere, -vertī, -versum, to turn towards/against, be inclined to, be engaged in

obviam, *adv.,* in the way, to meet

obvius, -a, -um, *adj.,* in the way, lying in the path, presenting him/her/itself

occāsiō, -ōnis, *f.,* occasion, event; opportunity

occidens, -entis, *adj.,* west

occīdō, -ere, -cīdī, -cāsum, to kill

occultus, -a, -um, *adj.,* secret

occupō (1), to take possession of, seize; to attack

occurrō, -ere, occurrī, occursum, to turn up, occur; + *dat.,* to meet

occursus, -ūs, *m.,* meeting, falling in with

Ōceanus, -ī, *m.,* ocean

Octāvia, -ae, *f.,* Octavia (a woman's name)

octāvus, -a, -um, *adj.,* eighth

oculus, -ī, *m.,* eye

odium, -ī, *n.,* hatred, grudge

offendō, -ere, -fendī, -fensum, to offend

offerō, -ferre, obtulī, oblātum, to offer

ōlim, *adv.,* once

omnīnō, *adv.,* wholly, entirely, altogether, only

omnis, -e, *adj.,* all, every

onus, -eris, *n.,* load, burden

opīnor, -ārī, -ātus sum, to suppose, imagine

opperior, -īrī, -tus sum, to wait, wait for

opprimō, -ere, -pressī, -pressum, to suppress, smother

ops, opis, *f.*, power, might, wealth, aid, support

optimus, -a, -um, *adj.*, best

opus, -eris, *n.*, work; *with* esse + *abl. and dat.*, (of person) to be necessary

ōrātiō, -ōnis, *f.*, speech

ōrātor, -ōris, *m.*, speaker, orator

orbis, -is, *m.*, orb, world

orbō (1), to deprive of

ordō, ordinis, *m.*, order

oriens, -entis, *adj.*, east

orīgō, -inis, *f.*, source, origin, lineage, ancestor

orior, -īrī, ortus sum, to rise, appear

ornātus, -ūs, *m.*, decoration, embellishment

ornō (1), to outfit, decorate

ōrō (1), to pray, beseech

ortus, -ūs, *m.*, birth, rising

ōs, ōris, *m.*, mouth

ostentō (1), to offer, promise

Ostia, -ae, *f.*, Ostia

Ostiensis, -e, *adj.*, of Ostia, Ostian

Otho, -ōnis, *m.*, Otho (a man's name)

ōtium, -ī, *n.*, leisure

Pacorus, -ī, *m.*, Pacorus (a man's name)

paelex, -icis, *f.*, mistress, concubine

paenitentia, -ae, *f.*, repentance

paenitet, -ēre, -uīt, —, *impers.*, to repent, be sorry, grieve

Paetus, -ī, *m.*, Paetus (a man's name)

palam, *adv.*, openly

Palātīnus, -a, -um, *adj.*, of/ relating to the Palatine, Palatine

palūs, -ūdis, *f.*, marsh

Pannonia, -ae, *f.*, Pannonia (a Roman province)

Pansa, -ae, *m.*, Pansa (a man's name)

Papīrius, -ī, *m.*, Papirius (a man's name)

pār, paris, *adj.*, equal

parātus, -ūs, *m.*, provision, ornament

parcus, -a, -um, *adj.*, sparing

parens, -entis, *m. and f.*, parent, ancestor

pariēs, -etis, *m.*, wall

pariō, -ere, peperī, partum, to bring forth, bear, produce, create

pariter, *adv.*, equally, alike

parō (1), to make ready, prepare, contrive

parricīdium, -ī, *n.*, murder of a parent, parricide

pars, partis, *f.*, part, faction

Parthī, -ōrum, *m. pl.*, the Parthians

partus, -ūs, *m.*, birth, delivery, offspring

passim, *adv.*, everywhere, far and wide, in every direction

pateō, -ēre, -uī, —, to lie open

pater, -tris, *m.*, father, forefather; + conscriptus, senator

paternus, -a, -um, *adj.*, fatherly, paternal

patiens, -entis, *adj.*, patient, suffering, supporting

patientia, -ae, *f.*, endurance, suffering, submission

pātria, -ae, *f.*, homeland, country

pātricius, -a, -um, *adj.*, patrician, noble

patrō (1), to carry through, accomplish

patrōnus, -ī, *m.*, patron, advocate

paucus, -a, -um, *adj.*, few, little

paulātim, *adv.*, little by little, gradually

pauper, pauperis, *adj.*, poor

paveō, -ēre, pāvī, —, to be struck with fear, tremble

pavor, -ōris, *m.*, terror

pax, pācis, *f.*, peace

pectus, -oris, *n.*, chest, breast

pecunia, -ae, *f.*, money

pelliciō, -ere, -lexī, -lectum, to entice, coax

pellis, -is, *f.*, skin

pellō, -ere, pepulī, pulsum, to beat, strike, push, drive out/back, hurl

penātēs, -ium, *m. pl.*, household gods, home, hearth, family

penes, *prep. + acc.*, at the house of, with, belonging to

penetrāle, -is, *n.*, innermost part

penitus, *adv.*, thoroughly

per, *prep. + acc.*, throughout, through, by means of, on account of

percellō, -ere, -culī, -culsum, to strike down

percontātiō, -ōnis, *f.*, questioning, inquiry

percussor, -ōris, *m.*, murderer, assassin

perdō, -ere, -didī, -ditum, to lose, destroy

pereō, -īre, -īvī, -itum, to pass away, perish

perficiō, -ere, -fēcī, -fectum, to finish, complete

perfugiō, -ere, -fūgī, —, to flee, take refuge

pergō, -ere, perrexī, perrectum, to go on, proceed

perīculum, -ī, *n.*, danger

permisceō, -ēre, -miscuī, -mixtum, to mix together, intermingle

perniciēs, -ēī, *f.*, destruction, death

perpellō, -ere, -pulī, -pulsum, to compel, prevail upon

persequor, -ī, -secūtus sum, to follow up, accomplish

persuāsiō, -ōnis, *f.*, a conviction

pertractō (1), to work on, handle

pertrahō, -ere, -traxī, -tractum, to conduct by force; to entice, allure

pervagor, -ārī, -ātus sum, to range through, spread out, be widely spread

pēs, pedis, *m.*, foot

pessum, *adv.*, to the ground, to the bottom, down; + **dare,** to destroy, ruin

petō, -ere, -īvī, -ītum, to fall upon, attack, aim at, seek

pietās, -ātis, *f.*, responsibility, duty

Pīlātus, -ī, *m.*, Pilate (a man's name)

Pisō, -ōnis, *m.*, Piso (a man's name)

plācāmentum, -ī, *n.*, means of pacifying/appeasing

placidus, -a, -um, *adj.*, calm

plānus, -a, -um, *adj.*, flat; *n.*, level ground, plain

plausus, -ūs, *m.*, clapping, applause

Plautius, -ī, *m.*, Plautius (a man's name)

plēbēius, -a, -um, *adj.*, plebeian, common

plebs, plebis, *f.*, people, multitude

plērus, -a, -um, *adj.*, most, the majority

plumbeus, -a, -um, *adj.*, lead, made of lead

plumbum, -ī, *n.*, lead

plūs, plūris, *adj.*, more

pōculum, -ī, *n.*, cup, goblet

poena, -ae, *f.*, penalty, punishment

Poenus, -ī, *m.*, a Cathaginian

polleō, -ēre, —, —, to be strong, prevail

Polliō, -ōnis, *m.*, Pollio (a man's name)

polluō, -ere, -uī, -ūtum, to pollute, violate

Pompēiānus, -a, -um, *adj.*, of/belonging to the Pompeian *gens*

Pompēius, -ī, *m.*, Pompeius (Pompey; a man's name)

pondus, -eris, *n.*, weight, load, burden

pontifex, -ficis, *m.*, high priest, pontiff

Pontius, -ī, *m.*, Pontius (a man's name)

popīna, -ae, *f.*, cook-shop, eating-house

populor, -ārī, -ātus sum, to ravage, devastate

populus, -ī, *m.*, people, populace

Porcius, -ī, *m.*, Procius (a man's name; the clan name)

porrō, *adv.*, forward, moreover

poscō, -ere, poposcī, —, to demand, request

possum, posse, potuī, to be able

post, *adv. and prep.* + *acc.*, after, afterwards

posteā, *adv.*, afterwards

posterus, -a, -um, *adj.*, following, next; *m. pl.*, descendants

postpōnō, -ere, -posuī, -positum, to put after, postpone, esteem less

postquam, *adv. and conj.*, after

postrēmō, *adv.*, at last, finally

postrēmum, *adv.*, finally

postulō (1), to ask, demand, claim

potens, -entis, *adj.*, powerful

potentia, -ae, *f.,* power, political power

potestās, -ātis, *f.,* power

potior, -īrī, -ītus sum, to take possession of, get, obtain; *often + gen. or abl.*

potissimum, *adv.,* especially, chiefly

potius, *adv.,* rather, more preferably, more

praealtus, -a, -um, *adj.,* very high

praebeō, -ēre, -uī, -itum, to furnish, show, exhibit

praecellō, -ere, to surpass, excel

praeceps, -cipitis, *adj.,* steep, headlong

praecipuus, -a, -um, *adj.,* especial, distinguished, important

praeclārus, -a, -um, *adj.,* splendid, famous

praeda, -ae, *f.,* spoil, plunder

praefectūra, -ae, *f.,* office of commander or governor, prefecture

praeficiō, -ere, -fēcī, -fectum, to set over, appoint as commander of (takes *acc.* of person + *dat.*)

praegredior, -ī, -gressus sum, to precede

praelegō, -ere, -lēgī, -lectum, to sail along

praepōnō, -ere, -posuī, -positum, to place before or first, prefer; to set over as commander

praesāgium, -ī, *n.,* presentiment, foreboding

praesens, -entis, *adj.,* present; *n.,* present time

praestans, -antis, *adj.,* excellent, outstanding

praetendō, -ere, -tendī, -tentum, to hold out as a pretext, allege

praeter, *prep. + acc.,* past, before, besides, except

praetereō, -īre, -īvī, -itum, to pass by

praetor, -ōris, *m.,* praetor

praetōrius, -a, -um, *adj.,* of/ belonging to the Praetorian Guard

praevaleō, -ēre, -uī, —, to carry more weight

prēlum, -ī, *n.,* press, winepress

premō, -ere, pressī, pressum, to press, weigh down, crush, conceal

pressus, -a, -um, *adj.,* deliberate, subdued, plain

prex, precis, *f.,* prayer, entreaty

prīdem, *adv.,* long ago, long since

primō, *adv.,* at first

prīmordium, -ī, *n.,* commencement, beginning of a new reign

prīmus, -a, -um, *adj.,* first, foremost; *n. as adv.,* first, firstly

princeps, -cipis, *adj.,* first, chief; *m.,* the ruler, emperor

principātus, -ūs, *m.,* the principate, empire, sovereignty

principium, -ī, *n.,* beginning;
  pl., general's quarters
prior, -ōris, *adj.,* prior, former
Priscus, -ī, *m.,* Priscus (a man's
  name)
prīvātus, -a, -um, *adj.,* private,
  personal; *m.,* private citizen
prīvignus, -ī, *m.,* stepson
prō, *prep.* + *abl.,* for, on behalf
  of, instead of
probābilis, -e, *adj.,*
  commendable, likely,
  probable
probrum, -ī, *n.,* disgrace,
  shameful act, insult
procax, -ācis, *adj.,* shameless,
  wanton
procul, *adv.,* at a distance, far
prōcūrātor, -ōris, *m.,*
  administrator, governor
prōdigus, -a, -um, *adj.,* prodigal
prōdo, -ere, -didī, -ditum, to
  relate, report
proelium, -ī, *n.,* battle, combat
profectō, *adv.,* surely, certainly
proferō, -ferre, -tulī, -lātum, to
  bring forward
professor, -ōris, *m.,*
  philosopher
prōfluō, -ere, -fluxī, -fluctum,
  to drift, flow forth or along
prōgredior, -ī, -gressus sum, to
  go forward, advance
prohibeō, -ēre, -uī, -itum, to
  hold back, prohibit
proiciō, -ere, -iecī, -iectum, to
  throw out
proindē, *adv.,* just so, in the
  same manner

prōlātō (1), to prolong
prōloquor, -ī, -locūtus sum, to
  speak out, foretell
prōmissum, -ī, *n.,* promise
prōmōveō, -ēre, -mōvī,
  -mōtum, to advance
promptus, -a, -um, *adj.,*
  resolute, visible, public,
  ready
prōnus, -a, -um, inclined,
  favorable
prope, *adv.,* near, nearly
properō (1), to hasten, prepare
properus, -a, -um, *adj.,* quick,
  speedy, hastening
propinquus, -a, -um, *adj.,*
  at hand; *n.,* vicinity; *m.,*
  relation, relative, kinsman
prorsus, *adv.,* straight forward,
  right onwards, direct
prōrumpō, -ere, -rūpī,
  -ruptum, to break forth,
  rush forth
proscrībō, -ere, -scripsī,
  -scriptum, to proscribe,
  outlaw
proscriptiō, -ōnis, *f.,*
  proscription, confiscation
prōsequor, -ī, -secūtus sum,
  to follow after, accompany,
  attend
prosperus, -a, -um, *or* **prosper,**
  -era, -erum, *adj.,* favorable,
  fortunate, prosperous
prōtegō, -ere, -texī, -tectum, to
  protect
prōtendō, -ere, -dī, -sum,
  to stretch forth, extend,
  prolong

prōturbō (1), to drive off

prōvincia, -ae, *f.*, province

prōvinciālis, -is, *m.*, provincial, inhabitant of a province

prōvolvō, -ere, -volvī, -volūtum, to roll forward, bowl over, fall down, prostrate one's self

proximus, -a, -um, *adj.*, nearest, nearby, next

prūdens, -entis, *adj.*, foreseeing, knowing, sensible, aware

pūbēs, -is, *f.*, youth, puberty

pūblicus, -a, -um, *adj.*, of/ belonging to the people, state, public, common

pudendus, -a, -um, *adj.*, shameful, disgraceful

pudīcitia, -ae, *f.*, modesty, chastity, virtue

pudor, -ōris, *m.*, shame, modesty

pueritia, -ae, *f.*, childhood, youth

pugna, -ae, *f.*, fight, battle

pugnō (1), to fight, combat, contend, struggle

pulchritūdō, -inis, *f.*, beauty

purgāmenta, -ōrum, *n. pl.*, sweepings, dirt

pūrus, -a, -um, *adj.*, pure

quā, *adv.*, on which side, where

quadrāgēsimus, -a, -um, *adj.*, fortieth

quaerō, -ere, quaesīvī, quaesītum, to look for, seek, inquire

quaesītus, -a, -um, *adj.*, extraordinary, far-fetched

quaestiō, -ōnis, *f.*, questioning, inquiry

quaestor, -ōris, *m.*, quaestor

quālis, -e, *adj.*, of what sort/ kind

quam, *adv.*, in what manner, how; + *compar. adj.*, as, than

quamquam, *conj.*, though, although, however, nevertheless

quamvīs, *adv. and conj.*, although, albeit, however much

quantus, -a, -um, *adj.*, how great, how much, how many

quasi, *adv. and conj.*, as if, just as; about, nearly, partly

quatiō, -ere, —, quassum, to shake

-que, *conj.*, and

questus, -ūs, *m.*, complaint

quī, quae, quod, *pron.*, who, which, that

quia, *conj.*, because, wherefore

quīdam, quaedam, quoddam, *pron.*, a certain, somebody, something

quidem, *adv.*, indeed

quidvīs, *pron.*, whatever, whatever you want/please

quiēs, -ētis, *f.*, peace, quiet, tranquility, neutrality

quiescō, -ere, -evī, -ētum, to rest, keep quiet

quīn, *conj.*, wherefore not

quindecim, *cardinal number*, fifteen

quinque, *cardinal number,* five
quintus, -a, -um, *adj.,* fifth
quippe, *adv.,* of course, naturally
quis, quid, *pron.,* someone, something; who, what
quisquam, quaequam, quidquam, *pron.,* anyone, anything
quisque, quaeque, quodque, *pron.,* whoever, whatever, each, every
quisquis, quidquid, *pron.,* whoever, whatever, whichever
quō, *adv.,* where
quoad, *adv.,* as long as
quod, *conj.,* because, the fact that
quōdam, *adv.,* in a certain manner
quōniam, *adv.,* since, because
quoque, *conj.,* also, too
quotiēns, *adv.,* how often, how many times, as often as

Raetia, -ae, *f.,* Raetia (a Roman province)
rapiō, -ere, -uī, -tum, to seize
raptim, *adv.,* hastily, suddenly
raptor, -ōris, *m.,* plunderer
raptus, -ūs, *m.,* abduction, rape, plundering
rārus, -a, -um, *adj.,* thin, rare
ratiō, -ōnis, *f.,* reckoning, method, rule
recens, -entis, *adj.,* recent
recenseō, -ēre, -censuī, -censum, to reckon, review

recessus, -ūs, *m.,* refuge
reciperō (1), to recover, regain back
recipiō, -ere, -cēpī, -ceptum, to admit, receive, accept
recitō (1), to recite
rēclīnis, -e, *adj.,* reclining
recordātiō, -ōnis, *f.,* recollection
recreō (1), restore, revive
rector, -ōris, *m.,* guide, leader, ruler
reddō, -ere, reddidī, redditum, to give back, reproduce, reflect
redeō, -īre, -īvī, -itum, to return
refoveō, -ēre, -fōvī, -fōtum, to restore, revive
rēfringō, -ere, -frēgī, -fractum, to break open
rēgius, -a, -um, *adj.,* royal
regnō (1), to rule, reign
regnum, -ī, *n.,* sovereignty, rule, royal power
regō, -ere, rexī, rectum, to lead, govern, rule
regredior, -ī, -gressus sum, to turn back, return
relinquō, -ere, -līquī, -lictum, to leave behind
reliquiae, -ārum, *f. pl.,* remains
remedium, -ī, *n.,* cure, remedy, aid
remeō (1), to return
rēmex, -igis, *m.,* oarsman
remittō, -ere, -mīsī, -missum, to send back, return
removeō, -ēre, -mōvī, -mōtum, to remove

rēmus, -ī, *m.*, oar
repens, -entis, *adj.*, sudden, hasty, fresh, new, recent
repentīnus, -a, -um, *adj.*, sudden, hasty
reperiō, -īre, -ī, -tum, to find, discover
repetō, -ere, -īvī, -ītum, to repeat, return
reposcō, -ere, —, —, to demand back
reprehensiō, -ōnis, *f.*, blame, criticism
reprimō, -ere, -pressī, -pressum, to press back, check, repress
reputō (1), to think over
requīrō, -ere, -quīsīvī, -quīsītum, to ask of
rēs, reī, *f.*, thing, affair, event, circumstance, operation, state, government; + **pūblica,** republic
respectō (1), to look back, regard
rēspiciō, -ere, -spexī, -spectum, to look back at, consider
rēspondeō, -ēre, -dī, -sum, to answer, reply
rēstinguō, -ere, -stinxī, -stinctum, to put out, extinguish
retineō, -ēre, -tinuī, -tentum, to hold back, retain
reus, -ī, *m.*, the accused, defendant
revocō (1), to call back, recall, recover

rex, rēgis, *m.*, king
Rhēnus, -ī, *m.*, the Rhine
Rhodos, -ī, *f.*, Rhodes
rīmor, -ārī, -ātus sum, to pry into
rīte, *adv.*, duly, legally, solemnly
rōbur, -oris, *n.*, strength, vigor
Rōmānus, -a, -um, *adj.*, Roman
Rōmulus, -ī, *m.*, Romulus (Rome's first king)
rudis, -e, *adj.*, unpolished, uncultivated, of tender years
rūmor, -ōris, *m.*, rumor
rumpō, -ere, rūpī, ruptum, to break, tear
ruō, -ere, -ī, -tum, to rush down, fall down, charge, hurry, hasten
rursus *or* **rursum,** *adv.*, backwards, back, again, in turn, on the contrary
Rusticus, -ī, *m.*, Rusticus (a man's name)

Sabīnus, -a, -um, *adj.*, of the Sabines, Sabine
sacerdōs, -ōtis, *m.*, priest
sacrificālis, -e, *adj.*, sacrificial
sacrificō (1), to sacrifice
sacrō (1), to dedicate
saeculum, -ī, *n.*, period, age
saepe, *adv.*, often
saepiō, -īre, -psī, -ptum, to surround, fence in, enclose
saepius, *adv.*, more often
saeviō, -īre, -iī, -ītum, to rage, be angry

saevitia, -ae, *f.*, cruelty

saevus, -a, -um, *adj.*, fierce,
cruel, harsh

Samnīs, -ītis, *m.*, a Samnite

sānē, *adv.*, by all means, truly

sanguis, -inis, *m.*, blood

sapientia, -ae, *f.*, wisdom

Sarmata, -ae, *m.*, a Sarmatian

satiō (1), to satiate

satis, *adv.*, enough

saxum, -ī, *n.*, rock, stone

Scaurus, -ī, *m.*, Scaurus (a
man's name)

scelus, -eris, *n.*, wickedness,
evil deed, crime

scīlicet, *adv.*, of course,
evidently

scortum, -ī, *n.*, prostitute

Scriboniānus, -ī, *m.*,
Scribonianus (a man's name)

scriptor, -ōris, *m.*, writer

scrūtor, -ārī, -ātus sum,
to search or examine
thoroughly

sēcrētum, -ī, *n.*, secret, secret
interview

sector, -ārī, -ātus sum, to
follow continually/eagerly

Secundus, -ī, *m.*, Secundus (a
man's name)

sēcūritās, -ātis, *f.*, safety,
security

sēcūrus, -a, -um, *adj.*, secure,
safe

sed *or* set, *conj.*, but

sēdēs, -is, *f.*, home, settlement

segniter, *adv.*, sluggishly; +
haud, none the slower,
quickly

segnitia, -ae, *f.*, weakness,
inertia

Sēiānus, -ī, *m.*, Sejanus (a man's
name)

Sēius, -ī, *m.*, Seius (a man's
name)

Seleucia, -ae, *f.*, Seleucia (a city
in Asia Minor)

sella, -ae, *f.*, chair

sellārius, -ī, *m.*, courtesan

semel, *adv.*, once

sēmōtus, -a, -um, *adj.*, separate,
distant, remote

sēmustus, -a, -um, *adj.*, half-
burnt

senātōrius, -a, -um, *adj.*,
senatorial

senātus, -ūs, *m.*, senate

Seneciō, -ōnis, *m.*, Senecio (a
man's name)

senectūs, -ūtis, *f.*, old age

senescō, -ere, -uī, —, to grow
old

senex, -is, *m.*, old man

senior, -ius, *compar. adj.*, older

Senonēs, -um, *m. pl.*, Senones
(a Gallic tribe)

sententia, -ae, *f.*, opinion,
feeling

sēparō (1), to separate

septentriōnālis, -e, *adj.*,
northern

septimus, -a, -um, *adj.*, seventh

septuāgēsimus, -a, -um, *adj.*,
seventieth

septuāgintā, *cardinal number*,
seventy

sequor, -ī, secūtus sum, to
follow

sērius, -a, -um, *adj.,* grave, serious

sermō, -ōnis, *m.,* speech, rhetorical style, conversation, common talk

servīlis, -e, *adj.,* slavish, servile

Servilius, -ī, *m.,* Servilius (a man's name)

serviō, -īre, -īvī, -ītum, + *dat.,* to be a slave to

servitium, -ī, *n.,* slavery; *pl.,* slaves

servitūs, -ūtis, *f.,* servitude, slavery

Servius, -ī, *m.,* Servius (a man's name)

servō (1), to guard, preserve

servus, -ī, *m. and f.,* slave, servant

sescentēsimus, -a, -um, *adj.,* six hundredth

seu, *conj.,* or if; **seu . . . seu,** whether if . . . or if

sevērus, -a, -um, serious, strict, severe

sex, *cardinal number,* six

sī, *conj.,* if, since

sīc, *adv.,* so, thus, in this manner

sīcut, *conj.,* as, just as

sīdus, -eris, *n.,* constellation, star

signum, -ī, *n.,* sign

silentium, -ī, *n.,* silence

sileō, -ēre, -uī, —, to be silent/ still, rest

Silius, -ī, *m.,* Silius (a man's name)

similis, -e, *adj.,* similar

simul, *adv.,* at the same time, together, as soon as

simulācrum, -ī, *n.,* likeness, appearance

simulātiō, -ōnis, *f.,* pretence

simulō (1), to pretend, feign

sīn, *conj.,* but if

sine, *prep.* + *abl.,* without

singulus, -a, -um, *adj.,* each

sinister, -ra, -um, *adj.,* adverse, left

sinō, -ere, sīvī, situm, to let, permit

sinus, -ūs, *m.,* heart, bay, lap

sitis, -is, *f.,* thirst

situs, -a, -um, situated (on), positioned, established

sīve. *See* **seu**

socer, -erī, *m.,* father-in-law

socius, -a, -um, *adj.,* confederate, allied; *m.,* ally

sōcordia, -ae, *f.,* sluggishness, inaction

solidus, -a, -um, *adj.,* thorough, solid, whole

sōlitūdō, -inis, *f.,* wilderness, desert, solitude

solitus, -a, -um, *adj.,* usual, customary; *n.,* the customary way

sollertia, -ae, *f.,* skill, shrewdness, ingenuity

solum, -ī, *n.,* ground, floor

sōlus, -a, -um, *adj.,* alone, only, single

solvō, -ere, soluī, solūtum, to release, unbridle; to pay as due

sons, sontis, *adj.,* guilty

soror, -ōris, *f.,* sister

spatium, -ī, *n.,* space, length

speciēs, -ēī, *f.,* appearance, shape, pretense

spectāculum, -ī, *n.,* show, spectacle

spectātor, -ōris, *m.,* observer, spectator

spēs, speī, *f.,* hope

spintria, -ae, *m.,* male prostitute

spolium, -ī, *n.,* spoils

stadium, -ī, *n.,* stadium, race course, furlong

statim, *adv.,* immediately

statiō, -ōnis, *f.,* station, posting

statua, -ae, *f.,* statue

statuō, -ere, -uī, -ūtum, to set up, establish, decide

sternō, -ere, strāvī, strātum, to spread, scatter

stō, stāre, stetī, statum, to stand, remain

Strabō, -ōnis, *m.,* Strabo (a man's name)

strepitus, -ūs, *m.,* noise, din

strepō, -ere, -uī, -itum, to shout, make noise

struēs, -is, *f.,* heap, pile

studiōsē, *adv.,* eagerly

studium, -ī, *n.,* study, pursuit, inclination

stūprum, -ī, *n.,* defilement, disgrace, lewdness

suādeō, -ēre, suāsī, suāsum, to urge, exhort

sub, *prep.* + *abl.,* below, beneath, under

subdō, -ere, -didī, -ditum, to put under, substitute falsely, supply

subdolus, -a, -um, *adj.,* cunning, deceptive

subeō, -īre, -īvī, -itum, to go under, submit, take upon oneself; enter stealthily

subitus, -a, -um, *adj.,* sudden; *n. as adv.,* suddenly

submergō, -ere, -mersī, -mersum, to sink, submerge

subolēs, -is, *f.,* sprout, offshoot, offspring

subscrībō, -ere, -scrīpsī, -scrīptum, to write below; to assist a prosecution

subsidium, -ī, *n.,* help, relief, reserve troops

subtīliter, *adv.,* accurately, subtly, minutely, precisely

subveniō, -īre, -vēnī, -ventum, to come to one's assistance, help

successor, -ōris, *m.,* follower, successor

Suēbī, -ōrum, *m. pl.,* the Suebi (a northeastern Germanic tribe)

Sulla, -ae, *m.,* Sulla (a man's name)

Sulpicius, -ī, *m.,* Sulpicius (a man's name)

sum, esse, fuī, —, to be

summus, -a, -um, *adj.,* uppermost, highest

sūmō, -ere, sumpsī, sumptum, to take, take up, assume

super, *adv.,* over, above, moreover, besides; *prep.* + *abl. or acc.,* over, above, on on top of

superbia, -ae, *f.,* arrogance, haughtiness

superstes, -itis, *adj.,* survivor

superstitiō, -ōnis, *f.,* unreasonable religious belief, superstition

supersum, -esse, -fuī, —, to be left, remain, survive

superus, -a, -um, *adj.,* upper, higher

suppliciter, *adv.,* in supplication

supplicium, -ī, *n.,* punishment, penalty; + **adficior,** to be put to death

sūprā, *adv.,* above, over, formerly

Surrentum, -ī, *n.,* Surrentum (a city of Campania)

suus, -a, -um, *pron.,* his, her, hers, their, theirs; himself, herself, itself, themselves

Syria, -ae, *f.,* Syria (a Roman province)

taberna, -ae, *f.,* shop, inn

tabula, -ae, *f.,* tablet, written record

tābum, -ī, *f.,* foul matter

taceō, -ēre, -uī, -itum, to be silent

tam, *adv.,* so, so much, as; **tam . . . quam,** as/so much . . . as/than

tamen, *adv.,* nevertheless

tamquam, just as, just as if

tantus, -a, -um, *adj.,* so great, so much, so many, of such size; *n. as adv.,* only

tardus, -a, -um, *adj.,* slow

Tarentīnus, -a, -um, *adj.,* of Tarentum

tectum, -ī, *n.,* covering, shelter

tegō, -ere, texī, tectum, to cover

tēlum, -ī, *n.,* projectile

tempestās, -ātis, *f.,* storm

tempestīvus, -a, -um, *adj.,* timely

templum, -ī, *n.,* sanctuary, shrine, temple

temptō (1), to try, test, handle, touch

tempus, -oris, *n.,* time, condition, phase

teneō, -ēre, -uī, -tum, to hold, keep

Terentius, -ī, *m.,* Terentius (a man's name)

tergum, -ī, *n.,* back, skin, hide

terminus, -ī, *m.,* end

terra, -ae, *f.,* land

terrestris, -e, *adj.,* terrestrial

terror, -ōris, *m.,* dread, terror

theātrum, -ī, *n.,* theater

Thrasea, -ae, *m.,* Thrasea (a man's name)

thyrsus, -ī, *m.,* thyrsus (a staff twined with ivy and vine-shoots carried by Bacchants)

Tiberis, -is/-idis, *m.,* the Tiber

Tiberius, -ī, *m.,* Tiberius (a man's name)

timeō, -ēre, -uī, —, to fear, dread

tolerō (1), to bear, tolerate

tot, *indecl. adj.,* so many

totiens, *adv.,* so/as often, so/as many times

tōtus, -a, -um, *adj.*, all, the whole of, entire

tractō (1), to drag, handle, manage

trādō, -ere, -idī, -itum, to hand down

tragoedia, -ae, *f.*, tragedy

trahō, -ere, traxī, tractum, to draw out, drag, carry

Trāiānus, -ī, *m.*, Trajan (a man's name)

trāmittō. *See* **trānsmittō**

transeō, -īre, -īvī, -itum, to go/ pass over

transferō, -ferre, -tulī, -lātum, to bring over

transigō, -ere, -ēgī, -actum, to stab through

trānsmittō, -ere, -mīsī, -missum, to cross, send across

Transpadānī, -ōrum, *m.*, the nations beyond the Po

trepidātiō, -ōnis, *f.*, fear, nervousness

trēs, tria, *cardinal number*, three

tribūnīcius, -a, -um, *adj.*, of a tribune, tribunitial

tribūnus, -ī, *m.*, tribune

triērarchus, -ī, *m.*, captain of a trireme, trierarch

trīs. *See* **trēs**

tristis, -e, *adj.*, sad, gloomy, stern, harsh

tristitia, -ae, *f.*, sadness, sorrow

triumphō (1), to triumph over, celebrate a triumph

triumvir, -irī, *m.*, a commission of three men

trucidō (1), to slaughter

truncō (1), to maim

truncus, -a, -um, *adj.*, maimed, mutilated, dismembered

tū, *pron.*, *gen.* **tuī,** you (sing.)

tueor, -ērī, tuitus sum, to watch, uphold, preserve

Tuistō, -ōnis, *m.*, Tuisto (progenitor of the Germans honored as a god)

tum, *adv.*, then, next, at that time

tunc, *adv.*, then, at that point

turbō (1), to disturb, agitate, throw into disorder

Tuscī, -ōrum, *m. pl.*, the Etruscans

Tusculum, -ī, *n.*, Tusculum (a town in Latium)

tūtus, -a, -um, *adj.*, safe

tuus, -a, -um, *pron. possessive*, your, yours

ubī, *adv.*, where, when

ulciscor, -ī, ultus sum, to avenge, punish

ullus, -a, -um, *adj.*, any, other

ultimus, -a, -um, *adj.*, extreme, far

ultiō, -ōnis, *f.*, revenge

ultrā, *adv.*, beyond

ultrō, *adv.*, voluntarily

umerus, -ī, *m.*, upper arm, shoulder

unde, *adv.*, from where, from which, whence

undique, *adv.*, from every quarter, from all directions

ūniversus, -a, -um, *adj.*, all together

ūnus, -a, -um, *adj.*, one, single

urbs, urbis, *f.*, city

urgeō, -ēre, ursī, —, to press

ūrō, -ere, ussī, ustum, to burn

usquam, *adv.*, anywhere

usque, *adv.*, as far as, right until, up to the point of

ūsus, -ūs, *m.*, use

ut, *conj.*, + *indicative*, as, when; + *subjunctive*, that, so that, with the result that

uterque, utraque, utrumque, *pron.*, each one (of two), both

uterus, -ī, *m.*, belly, womb

ūtilitās, -ātis, *f.*, use, utility, service, benefit

ūtor, -ī, ūsus sum, + *abl.*, to use, exercise, indulge

utque, *conj.*, as, like, and as

ūtrimque, *adv.*, from/on both sides

uxor, -ōris, *f.*, wife

uxōrius, -a, -um, *adj.*, of/ belonging to a wife

vacuus, -a, -um, *adj.*, empty, vacant

Valens, -tis, *m.*, Valens (a man's name)

valeō, -ēre, -uī, -itum, to prevail

validus, -a, -um, *adj.*, strong, powerful

valītūdō, -inis, *f.*, health, illness

vallum, -ī, *n.*, the palisaded earthworks around a camp

Vandaliī, -ōrum, *m. pl.*, the Vandals (a north German tribe)

Vārianus, -a, -um, *adj.*, of/ belonging to Varus

variē, *adv.*, differently, diversely

varius, -a, -um, *adj.*, different, various

Varrō, -ōnis, *m.*, Varro (a man's name)

Vārus, -ī, *m.*, Varus (a man's name)

vastō (1), lay waste

-ve, *conj.*, or

Vēdius, -ī, *m.*, Vedius (a man's name)

vehiculum, -ī, *n.*, conveyance, vehicle

vehō, -ere, vexī, vectum, to carry, convey

vel, *conj.*, or, and even, and indeed

vēlōcitās, -ātis, *f.*, speed, velocity

velut *or* **velutī**, *adj.*, even as, just as

venditātor, -ōris, *m.*, braggart

venēnum, -ī, *n.*, poison

venia, -ae, *f.*, indulgence, favor, pardon

veniō, -īre, vēnī, ventum, to come

venter, -tris, *m.*, belly, womb

Ventidius, -ī, *m.*, Ventidius (a man's name)

ventus, -ī, *m.*, wind

vēnum, -ī, *n.*, that which is for sale; **veno dare,** to give for sale

verbum, -ī, *n.*, word

Vergiliō, -ōnis, *m.*, Vergilio (a man's name)

vertex, -icis, *m.*, peak

vertō, -ere, vertī, versum, to turn, divert, cause to turn

vērum, *conj.*, but; *adv.*, truly

vērus, -a, -um, *adj.*, true, real

Vestālis, -is, *f.*, a priestess of Vesta

vestis, -is, *f.*, clothing, garments

veterānus, -ī, *m.*, veteran

Vettius, -ī, *m.*, Vettius (a man's name)

vetus, -eris, *adj.*, old, former

vetustās, -ātis, *f.*, old age, age, antiquity, long duration

vexillārius, -ī, *m.*, standard-bearer

via, -ae, *f.*, road, highway

Vibidia, -ae, *f.*, Vibidia (a woman's name)

vicem, adv., + *in*, in turn, in succession

victor, -ōris, *m.*, victor

victōria, -ae, *f.*, victory

victus, -ūs, *m.*, sustenance, nourishment

vīcus, -ī, *m.*, block of houses, group of streets

videō, -ēre, vīdī, vīsum, to see

vigeō, -ēre, -uī, —, to live, thrive

vigescō, -ere, viguī, —, to flourish

vigilantia, -ae, *f.*, vigilance

vīgintī, *cardinal number,* twenty

villa, -ae, *f.*, country house, villa

vinciō, -īre, vinxī, vinctum, to bind, surround

vinclum. *See* **vinculum**

vinculum, -ī, *n.*, bond, fetter

vincō, -ere, vīcī, victum, to conquer

vindēmia, -ae, *f.*, grape-gathering, vintage

vīnum, -ī, *n.*, wine

violentia, -ae, *f.*, violence

vir, virī, *m.*, man

virgō, -inis, *f.*, virgin, girl

virītim, *adv.*, man by man, individually

virtūs, -ūtis, *f.*, courage, manliness, virtue

vīs, vis, *f.*, force, power, strength

vīsō, -ere, -ī, -um, to visit, go and see

vīsus, -ūs, *m.*, sight, vision

vīta, -ae, *f.*, life

Vitelliānus, -a, -um, *adj.*, of the emperor Vitellius

vitium, -ī, *n.*, vice

vītō (1), to avoid, escape

vix, *adv.*, scarcely

vocābulum, -ī, *n.*, designation, name

vōciferor, -ārī, -ātus sum, to cry out, scream

vocō (1), to call, summon, invoke

volō, velle, voluī, —, to want/wish

voluptās, -ātis, *f.*, enjoyment, pleasure

vōs, vestrum, *pron.*, you

vōtum, -ī, *n.*, prayer, wish, vow, pledge

vox, vōcis, *f.*, voice, utterance

vulgus, -ī, *n.*, mass, multitude, throng, people

vulnus, -eris, *n.*, wound

Vulscī, -ōrum, *m. pl.*, the Volscians (an Italic tribe)

Vulsiniī, -ōrum, *m. pl.*, Vulsinii (an Etruscan city)

ℬℭ **LATIN** Readers

Series Editor: RONNIE ANCONA, HUNTER COLLEGE
AND CUNY GRADUATE CENTER

Other Readers Also Now Available

An Apuleius Reader
*Selections from the
METAMORPHOSES*
ELLEN D. FINKELPEARL
(2012) ISBN 978-0-86516-714-8

A Caesar Reader
*Selections from BELLUM
GALLICUM and BELLUM
CIVILE, and from Caesar's
Letters, Speeches, and Poetry*
W. JEFFREY TATUM
(2012) ISBN 978-0-86515-696-7

A Cicero Reader
*Selections from Five Essays
and Four Speeches,
with Five Letters*
JAMES M. MAY
(2012) ISBN 978-0-86515-713-1

A Latin Epic Reader
Selections from Ten Epics
ALISON KEITH
(2012) ISBN 978-0-86515-686-8

A Livy Reader
*Selections from
AB URBE CONDITA*
MARY JAEGER
(2011) ISBN 978-0-86515-680-6

A Lucan Reader
Selections from CIVIL WAR
SUSANNA BRAUND
(2009) ISBN 978-0-86516-661-5

A Martial Reader
Selections from Epigrams
CRAIG WILLIAMS
(2011) ISBN 978-0-86516-704-9

A Plautus Reader
Selections from Eleven Plays
JOHN HENDERSON
(2009) ISBN 978-0-86516-694-3

A Roman Army Reader
*Selections from Literary,
Epigraphic, and Other
Documents*
DEXTER HOYOS
(2013) ISBN 978-0-86515-715-5

A Roman Verse Satire Reader
*Selections from Lucilius,
Horace, Persius,
and Juvenal*
CATHERINE C. KEANE
(2010) ISBN 978-0-86515-685-1

A Sallust Reader
*Selections from
BELLUM CATILINAE,
BELLUM IUGURTHINUM,
and HISTORIAE*
VICTORIA E. PAGÁN
(2009) ISBN 978-0-86515-687-5

A Seneca Reader
*Selections from
Prose and Tragedy*
JAMES KER
(2011) ISBN 978-0-86515-758-2

A Suetonius Reader
*Selections from the
LIVES OF THE CAESARS
and the LIFE OF HORACE*
JOSIAH OSGOOD
(2011) ISBN 978-0-86515-716-2

A Terence Reader
*Selections from
Six Plays*
WILLIAM S. ANDERSON
(2009) ISBN 978-0-86515-678-3

A Tibullus Reader
Seven Selected Elegies
PAUL ALLEN MILLER
(2013) ISBN 978-0-86515-724-7

Forthcoming in 2013 and Beyond

An Ovid Reader
CAROLE E. NEWLANDS
ISBN 978-0-86515-722-3

A Propertius Reader
P. LOWELL BOWDITCH
ISBN 978-0-86515-723-0

A Roman Women Reader
SHEILA K. DICKISON
and JUDITH P. HALLETT
ISBN 978-0-86515-662-2

**VISIT THE SERIES WEBSITE FOR UPDATES
ON AVAILABLE VOLUMES:**
www.bolchazy.com/BCLatinReaders.aspx